Language Teacher Identities

NEW PERSPECTIVES ON LANGUAGE AND EDUCATION
Series Editor: Professor Viv Edwards, *University of Reading, Reading, Great Britain*
Series Advisor: Professor Allan Luke, *Queensland University of Technology, Brisbane, Australia*

Two decades of research and development in language and literacy education have yielded a broad, multidisciplinary focus. Yet education systems face constant economic and technological change, with attendant issues of identity and power, community and culture. This series will feature critical and interpretive, disciplinary and multidisciplinary perspectives on teaching and learning, language and literacy in new times.

Recent Books in the Series
Distance Education and Languages: Evolution and Change
  Börje Holmberg, Monica Shelley and Cynthia White (eds)
Ebonics: The Urban Education Debate (2nd edn)
  J.D. Ramirez, T.G. Wiley, G. de Klerk, E. Lee and W.E. Wright (eds)
Decolonisation, Globalisation: Language-in-Education Policy and Practice
  Angel M. Y. Lin and Peter W. Martin (eds)
Travel Notes from the New Literacy Studies: Instances of Practice
  Kate Pahl and Jennifer Rowsell (eds)
Social Context and Fluency in L2 Learners: The Case of Wales
  Lynda Pritchard Newcombe
Social Actions for Classroom Language Learning
  John Hellermann
Teaching English as an International Language: Identity, Resistance and Negotiation
  Phan Le Ha

Other Books of Interest
Cross-linguistic Similarity in Foreign Language Learning
  Håkan Ringbom
Developing Minority Language Resources
  Guadalupe Valdés, Joshua A. Fishman, Rebecca Chávez and William Pérez
Deep Culture: The Hidden Challenges of Global Living
  Joseph Shaules
Education for Intercultural Citizenship: Concepts and Comparisons
  Geof Alred, Mike Byram and Mike Fleming (eds)
From Foreign Language Education to Education for Intercultural Citizenship
  Michael Byram
Language and Identity in a Dual Immersion School
  Kim Potowski
Language Learning and Teacher Education: A Sociocultural Approach
  Margaret R. Hawkins (ed.)
Language, Space and Power: A Critical Look at Bilingual Education
  Samina Hadi-Tabassum
Online Intercultural Exchange: An Introduction for Foreign Language Teachers
  Robert O'Dowd (ed.)
Understanding Deaf Culture: In Search of Deafhood
  Paddy Ladd

For more details of these or any other of our publications, please contact:
**Multilingual Matters, Frankfurt Lodge, Clevedon Hall,
Victoria Road, Clevedon, BS21 7HH, England
http://www.multilingual-matters.com**

NEW PERSPECTIVES ON LANGUAGE AND EDUCATION
Series Editor: Viv Edwards

Language Teacher Identities
Co-constructing Discourse and Community

Matthew Clarke

MULTILINGUAL MATTERS
Clevedon • Buffalo • Toronto

Library of Congress Cataloging in Publication Data
Clarke, Matthew
Language Teacher Identities: Co-constructing Discourse and Community/Matthew Clarke.
New Perspectives on Language and education
Includes bibliographical references and index.
1. English language–Study and teaching–United Arab Emirates 2. English language–Study and teaching–Arabic speakers. 3. English teachers–Training of–United Arab Emirates 4. English language–United Arab Emirates 5. Women–Education–United Arab Emirates 6. Second language acquisition. I. Title.
PE1068.T84C53 2008
428.007105357–dc22   2008000303

British Library Cataloguing in Publication Data
A catalogue entry for this book is available from the British Library.

ISBN-13: 978-1-84769-082-1 (hbk)
ISBN-13: 978-1-84769-081-4 (pbk)

Multilingual Matters
UK: Frankfurt Lodge, Clevedon Hall, Victoria Road, Clevedon BS21 7HH.
USA: UTP, 2250 Military Road, Tonawanda, NY 14150, USA.
Canada: UTP, 5201 Dufferin Street, North York, Ontario M3H 5T8, Canada.

Copyright © 2008 Matthew Clarke.

All rights reserved. No part of this work may be reproduced in any form or by any means without permission in writing from the publisher.

The policy of Multilingual Matters/Channel View Publications is to use papers that are natural, renewable and recyclable products, made from wood grown in sustainable forests. In the manufacturing process of our books, and to further support our policy, preference is given to printers that have FSC and PEFC Chain of Custody certification. The FSC and/or PEFC logos will appear on those books where full certification has been granted to the printer concerned.

Typeset by Saxon Graphics Ltd.
Printed and bound in Great Britain by the Cromwell Press Ltd.

Contents

Acknowledgements ix

Foreword by Donald Freeman xi

Introduction 1
    Learning to Teach within an Evolving Community of
    Practice 1
    Learning to Teach: A Brief Review 3
    Learning to Teach and Identity 8

1   Discourse, Identity and Community 15
    Exploring Discourse 15
    Exploring Identity 20
       Culturalism and cultural identities 20
       Discourse and positional identities 23
       Figured worlds and figurative identities 25
       Improvisation and authored identities 26
       Agency within structure 28
    Exploring Communities of Practice 29
       Dimensions of a community of practice 30
       Locality 33
       Boundaries and border practices 34
    Dimensions of Identity and Modes of Belonging 35
    Co-constructing Identity, Discourse and Community 37
    Conclusion 39

2   The Discursive Context 41
    Discourse and the Formation of the UAE 41
       The Islamic period 42
       The transformational period 43
       The colonial period 43
       The contemporary period 44
    Discourses of Contemporary Collective Identity in the UAE ... 47
    Discourses of UAE Education 48

Discourses of globalization and nationalism in
 UAE education 50
Discourses of gender in UAE education 51
Discourse and Teacher Education 53
Student Teachers as Agents of Change 54
 A change in pedagogy 55
 A change in the nature of the content and focus
  of English lessons 55
 A change in the breadth of teacher knowledge 56
 A change in mode of learning 56
Foundational-Overarching Principles: Vygotsky,
 Dewey and Bakhtin in UAE Teacher Education 57
 Assisted performance 57
 Situated learning 58
 Social thinking 58
 Reflective dialogue 59
Researching Language Teacher Identities 60
 Research participants 60
 Reflexivity 61
 Epistemology 61
Data Collection 62
 Focus groups 63
 Online discussions 63
Discourse and Material Practice 65
Data Analysis 66
 Critique of discourse analysis 67
 Discourse analysis and social practice 68
 Discourse analysis and textualization 69
Conclusion 70

3 The Formation of a Community of Practice 75
Choosing Teaching as an Act of Belonging 76
 Family connections 76
 Discourses of gender 78
 Teachers as role models 80
 Surpassing past teachers 81
 Choosing English 83
Belonging and Engagement 85
 Evolving forms of mutual engagement 85
 Developing a common understanding of the
  joint enterprise 88

Developing a shared discourse repertoire 90
Belonging and Alignment 92
Locality 92
Boundaries and border practices 94
Belonging and Imagination 98
Self-consciousness and reflection 98
Creation 101
Conclusion 103

4 The Discursive Construction of Systems of Knowledge
  and Belief 105
  Constructing the 'New' Teachers of the Present/Future
  Against the 'Traditional' Teachers of the Past 105
  'Sensitivity' versus 'insensitivity' 111
  Learners as homogenous 'empty vessels' versus
  heterogeneous 'geniuses' 113
  'Student-centred' versus 'teacher-centred' teaching 117
  'Passive' versus 'active' learning 119
  'Low' motivation and self-esteem versus 'high'
  motivation and self-esteem 120
  'Hierarchy' versus 'equality' 122
  Teacher as 'transmitter' versus 'facilitator' 123
  Teaching as 'easy' versus 'complex' 124
  Discourses of Language and Culture in the Classroom 127
  Discourses of Gender in Education 131
  Conclusion 133

5 The Discursive Construction of Interpersonal Relations 136
  Interpersonal Address 136
  Maintaining and Monitoring the Community Beliefs 140
  Legitimation 141
  Embracing a struggling soul 146
  Setting the Agenda for the Future 149
  Tempering the Mission 153
  Conclusion 156

6 The Discursive Construction of Intrapersonal Identity 157
  Commitments to Truth: What I Believe 159
  Belief and modality 159
  Belief and evaluation 164
  Commitments to Necessity: What Has to Be Done 167

Moral Commitments: What Is Right 169
  'Rights' and 'wrongs' in the classroom 169
  'Rights' and 'wrongs' in the school system 172
Summing Up and Looking Ahead 177
Conclusion 180

7 Summary of Findings and Future Directions 182
  Revisiting the Research Issues 182
  Discourse and Differentiation 185
  Interpreting the Research Findings 187
  Looking to the Future 192
    Discursive hegemony and antagonism 193
    From antagonism to agonism 194
    Future directions 196
  Conclusion 198

References 200

Index 212

Acknowledgements

Thanks to the many people whose support, encouragement, generosity, time and ideas have contributed in various ways to this book. In particular, I want to thank my parents, Ted and Mary, for their unwavering belief over many years, and Liz, my first reader, for her patience and interest in my writing. I also want to give special thanks to Ray Misson and Kristina Love for being truly exceptional mentors, guides and friends. Their inclusive collegiality and intellectual curiosity has been a source of inspiration. Many thanks too to Chris Davison and Donald Freeman for their encouragement and to Hinemoa Xhori, Leo Hoye and Issa Danjun Ying for patiently critiquing earlier drafts and suggesting improvements. Lastly, thanks to series editor Viv Edwards for her support in this project, to Marjukka Grover and Ken Hall at Multilingual Matters for making the publication process so smooth. And last but not least, I would like to convey my sincere appreciation to all the students at the Higher Colleges of Technology in the United Arab Emirates who generously participated in the research that led to this book.

Foreword

Matthew Clarke has written a book that is at once as familiar as it is surprising, one that is filled with echoes of the known and with explorations of the new. The theme – that education is a means of both individual and social transformation – is a familiar one; as is the underlying pull in that transformation between the values and perceptions of the present and future on the one hand and those of the past on the other. And in terms of learning processes, tracing the development of new teachers' practices and identities through their preparation and onwards into schools is a recognizable trajectory in the search to understand how professional learning takes place and how contexts of place shape the exercise of that learning. Further, within that trajectory, the demands that preparation in curriculum and in classroom pedagogy must induct these new teachers into different ways of thinking and teaching than their predecessors is also usually a given.

Amongst these many markers of familiarity however, Clarke's argument and design stand out as different and distinctive. What makes them new is the degree to which he is able to expose what is often invisible in the processes of individual and social learning, and the resources that seem to shape these processes. The context of his work brings together a unique constellation of gender and professional identity with the learning and exercise of pedagogy and subject matter, all within a newly transforming society.

In an almost eerie way, the voices of these Emirati women who are becoming new teachers at the beginning of the 21st century in a country recently united from separate states, or emirates, echo those of their sisters of another time and place. Two centuries earlier, in the first half of the 1800s, as the colonial United States was expanding westward, public education took on a central role in promoting social cohesion. The one-room schoolhouse, presided over by the 'school marm', had its central mission to develop children's skills in literacy and numeracy, which in turn would support male suffrage and extend the new economy westward. Gender played a central role in this social calculus. Reformers of the period – Emma Willard, Catherine Beecher, and others – argued that women were best suited to providing this education that could create and support the social integration of these new communities into a new nation and thus to create a vision and discourse of social cohesion. In her 1846 treatise titled, *The evils suffered by American women and American children: The causes and remedies*, which gives a flavour of that time, social and educational reformer Catherine

Beecher cited both data and ideology to support this movement, when she wrote:

> Wherever education is most prosperous, there woman is employed more than man. In Massachusetts, where education is highest, five out of seven of the teachers are women; while in Kentucky, where education is so much lower, five out of six of the teachers are men. ... The educating of children, that is the true and noble profession of a woman – that is worthy the noblest powers and affections of the noblest minds. ...

Beecher continues, arguing that while women are uniquely matched to teaching, there must be appropriate preparation.

> As it is, the employment of teaching children is regarded as the most wearing drudgery, and few resort to it except from necessity; and one very reasonable cause of this aversion is the utter neglect of any arrangements for preparing teachers from this arduous and difficult profession.[1]

Thus it seems that gender and teaching have often coalesced in the knitting of nationhood, whether in the United States of the early 1800s or the United Arab Emirates of the 2000s. And just as often, the forces that create conditions and propel this work are overlooked or under-studied. The work of building social coherence through classroom teaching is invisible work, both because of who has done it and the fact that we have generally been poorly equipped to follow the strands of public reasoning and discourse into the individual worlds of teaching. These social forces, whether in early 19th century America or the early 21st century in the UAE, are powerful and largely invisible to the conventional lens. They can be found in language, in the social and political discourses that offer sources of reasoning for action.

Clarke's careful analysis brings this politics of invisibility closer to the surface. In showing how these women weave together reasoning drawn from the rhetoric and framing of national debates, and the social history of teaching in the Emirati context, along with the ideology of 'modern' language pedagogy, Clarke lays out their work of becoming new teachers. And then into all this complex mix comes the English language, as a subject matter and as a means of social and global access. Its global, lingua franca dimension is fundamental, not just to what these new teachers teach but just as much to how they learn to be the teachers they are and hope to be. In fact, to continue the parallel, the literacy of the American one-room schoolhouse, though originally conceived as pluralizing access to the Bible as a religious text, quickly took on a wider role in social access and participation. So too one could argue, the English which is a subject matter in these Emirati classrooms is a ramp to a different world. Participating in the language changes it; teaching it as a young woman to a new generation of Emirati students will likely alter the language as it changes them. And in any case, like the dancer and the dance, the two processes cannot be separated, which is at the heart of the identity dilemmas that Clarke frames.

So this is a principal contribution of Matthew Clarke's work, I would argue, namely that to study this politics of invisibility, one has to situate one's examination. And that situating is not simply a research process; it is centrally about the phenomenon of identity in practice. Language is key to the situating, both as a methodology for making more evident how the politics of invisibility operate through discourses, ideas, and notions of what is 'modern' and 'right' and also as the object being studied. It is rare to find work on teacher identity that brings together these two dimensions with as much rigour, care, and attention to both the specifics of participants' words and to the wider frames of discourse.

In her poem of the same title, Alice Luterman writes about the constant challenge of the daily, which she calls 'the invisible work that stitches up the world day and night'. In a very real sense, teaching can also be invisible work. The important dimensions are not, as one Emirati teacher notes in a series of rhetorical questions, the public and visible aspects of the job; they are, as Catherine Beecher would have agreed, the underlying values work:

> I also always asked myself questions: Is education only a page to be taught in a book? Does education mean using a stick to deal with inappropriate behavior? Does education mean to show your power over students?... What values are fostered in the teaching and learning of young learners? (Chapter 6, p. 000)

Matthew Clarke's book helps to make the mechanisms of new teachers learning to do this 'values' work visible. It is, arguably, work that has been done for centuries – mainly by young women – in many diverse societies on the cusp of social transformation; it is certainly work that deserves the more careful thought and consideration brought to it by this study.

Donald Freeman
School of Education
University of Michigan
and
the School for International Training
Ann Arbor, Michigan

Note

1. Hoffman, N. (ed.). 2003. *Women's 'True' Profession: Voices from the History of Teaching* (2n ed) (pp.74–75). Cambridge, MA: Harvard University Press.

Introduction

Learning to Teach within an Evolving Community of Practice

> There is more than a verbal tie between the words common, community, and communication ... The communication which insures participation in a common understanding is one which secures similar emotional and intellectual dispositions.
> Dewey, 1963 [1916]: 4–5

> The individual consciousness not only cannot be used to explain anything, but on the contrary is itself in need of explanation from the vantage point of the social ideological medium.
> Volosinov, 1973 [1929]: 12

This book explores the development of the first cohort of students to complete a new teacher education degree in the United Arab Emirates (UAE). As part of this exploration, it offers a way of thinking about teacher formation as a dynamic process of identity development within an evolving community of practice. It draws on insights from recent work in discourse theory to account for the co-construction of knowledge, identity and community, and to recognize the inescapably political nature of the meanings through which identity and community are constructed. In addition, the book offers insights into the ongoing processes of educational, social and cultural development, in a country located in a part of the world that is of immense geopolitical significance, yet at the same time is both under-researched and often subject to stereotyping and caricature. Finally, the book suggests some possible directions for future research to provide greater understanding of language teacher education that may have resonance for teacher education more widely.

Within the context of increasing globalization, the Middle East is critical to any understanding of our contemporary world. Home of much of the world's oil reserves, and hence central to global energy issues, as well as unwitting host to the conflicts that have in many ways become the litmus test of East–West relations, including the Israeli–Palestinian struggle and more recently the invasion, and subsequent fracturing, of Iraq, the region assumes a significance that far outweighs its geographical size or population. The Middle East is also a region that has gone through – and continues to experience – startling change, progress and development in many sectors, wrought by industrialization, urbanization and modernization. In coming decades, the impact of these changes, the continuation or resolution of the above regional conflicts, along with the challenges of implementing human development policies and political revitalization, all comprise the complex array of factors that will be key to the region's long-term development and hence to world economic and political security. Within this dynamic and volatile context, language teacher education takes on particular significance and import.

The UAE, which celebrated independence in 1971, is a rapidly changing environment where aspects of traditional Bedouin culture coexist with the immense changes resulting from the forces of globalization and the wealth brought about by the development of the oil industry. Yet while economic development continues at an ever-increasing rate, the federal government's allocation of resources to K–12 education and the effectiveness of the school system continue to lag behind. As with other sectors in a country where UAE nationals are a minority, comprising approximately 20% of the population, schools rely on foreign workers and the majority of school teachers are currently expatriates drawn from other Arabic-speaking countries, such as Egypt, Jordan and Syria. These teachers, who have varying levels of education and whose tenure is vulnerable to the UAE's Emiratization, or nationalization of the workforce programme, are the same teachers that supervise the student teachers – all UAE female nationals – during their teaching practice placements.

The Higher Colleges of Technology's (HCT) Bachelor of Education (B. Ed.) degree in Teaching English to Young Learners is a four-year programme that prepares the Emirati women who enter it for English teaching positions in government primary schools, as part of the UAE's Emiratization process. Although currently offered only at each of the six women's colleges within the HCT, the intention and hope is to eventually attract male Emirati students to undertake the degree and enter the teaching profession. Like all the HCT's programmes the Bachelor of Education in Teaching English to Young Learners is delivered in English. The first cohort that forms the basis of this study began their teacher education degree in September 2000 and completed the degree in June 2004.

Any researcher's perspective is inevitably both situated and partial; mine is so in particular ways. I initially came to the UAE as a consultant from the University of Melbourne, and later led the HCT's Education division, working in the central Abu Dhabi curriculum leadership office. In both these roles, I was involved in all aspects of development of the HCT B.Ed. degree. Although, I was not the 'teacher' of the students in this study, I worked with student teachers across the six HCT women's colleges, in addition to my main administrative duties, providing guest lectures and classes. This involvement clearly makes me an 'interested' observer. Nevertheless, in this study I have striven to adhere to Freebody's (2003: 70) call to educational researchers to be both 'respectful of and intrigued by the objects of their study' in ways that are explained more fully in Chapter 2.

Learning to Teach: A Brief Review

One of the major challenges – though also a source of opportunity – in developing the new B.Ed. (Teaching English to Young Learners) degree at the HCTs in the UAE was the lack of any model or precedent in the local educational environment. The closest thing to a model was the B.Ed. degree offered at the University of the United Arab Emirates. This programme however had major drawbacks. One visiting academic, who worked in the mid-1990s as a consultant and advisor to the university's faculty of education, noted how the faculty 'has structured its student teaching programme so that students are in schools only one weekend [sic] day per week for one semester, a situation affording few opportunities for a vital, invigorating introduction to teaching' (W. Gardner, 1995: 295). It was also criticized for devoting the majority of its curriculum to linguistics rather than education (Loughrey *et al.*, 1999).

Moreover, many of the expatriate teachers in UAE schools, who still comprise the majority of the teaching force, have little specific educational training, reflecting the priorities of a system that values academic over specifically Education qualifications. This lack of any model to build on led to an extensive review of the literature on the process of learning to teach. From this review, the following foundational principles in terms of what a degree of this nature should be were formulated:

The HCT's Education programs aim to produce teachers for UAE schools who are recognized for their commitment to excellence and innovation and who are able to provide an environment in which learners, however diverse their background, engage collaboratively in productive, purposeful learning. This is reflected in and facilitated through the following basic principles:

Program development will be driven by the question of what students need to learn to become effective teachers in UAE schools who are able to contribute to the development of education and the teaching profession.

All elements of the program will be integrated with each other to create a coherent whole rather than a collection of related subjects. Cross-course projects will reflect this holistic emphasis.

The provision of opportunities for practical experience in schools is the central feature of the program: what students learn at HCT will be actualized in the practicum, and experience in schools will subsequently inform and test what is taught in classes at HCT.

The program models as well as teaches internationally recognized best practice in pedagogy, emphasizing active and collaborative engagement on the part of the students and providing them with multiple opportunities to master both the global and the local cultures' tools and technologies through purposeful use.

The program develops intellectual independence in students, preparing them with strategies for and a commitment to life-long learning, as well as challenging them to develop their interests and abilities.

The program is informed by the latest research in teacher education as well as by the latest research in the effective teaching of English to young learners

The first of these foundational principles highlights an obvious question that teacher educators, particularly those developing a new B.Ed. programme, inevitably have to confront at some point: what do student teachers need to know? Yet prior to this question is perhaps the even more fundamental question of *how* teachers learn to teach; this question is inextricably entwined with questions as to the nature (as opposed to just the content) of teachers' knowledge. This may seem an obvious point but, historically, Western teacher-education programmes have not been congruent with a clear conception of what it means to be a teacher (Beattie, 1997). Nor have they operated with a clear conception of how teachers make the transition from being students of teaching to becoming competent teachers (Korthagen, 2001: 32–33) or how students are to integrate theory and practice (Cochran-Smith, 2000; Furlong & Maynard, 1995; Korthagen, 2001; Loughran & Russell, 1997; Roberts, 1998). These issues are addressed by Furlong and Maynard (1995), who outline the various changing models of teacher education in the UK during the post-war period. A similar overview of UK teacher education is provided by Calderhead and Shorrock (1997), though they also refer to differences in thinking about teaching and the role of teachers across different international contexts and make the point that different conceptualizations of what it means to be a teacher will inevitably lead to differences in thinking about teacher education. Meanwhile, Roberts (1998) and Crandall (2000) trace a similar progression within language teacher education.

A summary of these various successive models of learning to teach, based largely on the work of Furlong and Maynard (1995) and Roberts (1998), is briefly outlined in the following section. Although this outline is based on programmes in Western societies, the transplanting of Western educational models to non-Western societies (Willinsky, 1998) means that the patterns described here are likely to have resonance in other contexts.

During the 1950s what has become known as the 'craft' approach dominated teacher education, where an expert tutor acted as moral and professional guide to the student teacher. Practice was privileged over theory within this model. However, this approach, as is implied by the term 'craft', came to be viewed as too 'cosy' and lacking in academic rigour. Fuelled by the increasing strength and prestige of the social sciences, this growing criticism led to the craft approach being replaced during the 1960s by applied science models. Whereas practical experience had previously been paramount, in the new approach 'practice' was demoted to a lesser role in relation to 'theory'. Indeed, overall, teacher education programmes became less integrated and more fragmented as students were exposed to a range of different expertise and left to integrate the resulting knowledge themselves. This problem has been a persistent weakness of teacher education programmes (Korthagen, 2001) and is echoed in Freeman's comment, in the context of American teacher education programmes, that 'teacher education is predicated on the assumption that knowing something in one context will convert into doing it in another' (Freeman, 1994: 1, cited in Johnson, 1999: 9). According to this scheme of things, 'theories are generated exclusively in universities and research and development centers and...only practice exists in schools' (Zeichner & Liston, 1996: 14).

Mounting criticism of the divorce of theory from practice was reinforced by the increasingly conservative political climate that has gained ascendancy since the 1980s, where '"living in the real world" serves as an epistemological bludgeon' (Richards, 1999: 21). As a result, and further justified by charges of 'producer capture' on the part of teacher education institutions, the late 1980s and 1990s saw various neo-liberal and neo-conservative governments entering the field and offering a restricted core definition of teacher professionalism (Furlong *et al.*, 2000) that once again valorized practice over theory, rather than seeing the two as inseparable. It could be argued in turn that the language of 'producer capture', couched in the discourse of economics, is symptomatic of the capture of the political agenda by an economic rationalist ideology that prioritizes economic values over any others, and has a tendency to translate all aspects of life into purely economic terms (Corson, 2001; Gee et al. 1996; Gray, 1997; Marginson, 1997). Regardless of the precise reasons, however, in an attempt to wrest control of teacher education away from universities, governments have laid down specific standards and competencies that prospective teachers must meet in order to achieve qualified teacher status.

These competency models fall into two broad types (Furlong & Maynard, 1995). The first are the performance models that specify what it is that beginner teachers should be able to actually do in the form of skill-based competencies. The second type of competency model attempts to move beyond this limitation by incorporating cognitive and moral competencies in addition to skill competencies. Yet by listing knowledge competencies alongside skill competencies, even with the inclusion of overarching professional characteristics and values, the more comprehensive competency model still reflects an atomistic approach and thus fails to overcome the theory–practice split that has been something of an endemic Achilles heel in teacher education. Indeed, whatever the inadequacies of the 'applied science' models of teacher education arising from the 1960s, producing as it did people who knew about teaching but not how to teach, the performance-based competency model is also inadequate 'because it produces people who are able to teach but do not understand what they are doing' (Furlong & Maynard, 1995: 32).

Characteristic of both the competency and the applied science models of teacher education is that they see knowledge as something external to the teacher, reflecting what Marion Williams refers to as a 'parcel' view of knowledge (M. Williams, 1999). By contrast, the approaches discussed below have focused on notions of 'personal practical knowledge' (Connelly & Clandinin, 1989) or 'practical professional knowledge' (Furlong & Maynard, 1995) and have sought to overcome dichotomies such as *theory–practice*, *teaching–research*, *teacher educator–teacher* and *theorist–practitioner* (Kumaravadivelu, 1999; Kuzmic, 2002). In a similar vein, Eraut (1994) argues that student teachers need to be able to make dialogic connections between personal theories, public theories and their own experience, rather than being in thrall to any one of these. Marion Williams makes the same point:

> What is important in teacher education is to develop the ability to relate theory to practice in different ways, to use personal theories in practice, to infer personal theories from practice, to use and reconstruct public

theories, to generate personal theories from public ones, and to generate public theories from personal ones. (M. Williams, 1999: 15)

These emphases find echoes in sociocultural theory, which emphasizes 'knowing-in-action', as part of 'situated activity' (Lave & Wenger, 1991; Wells, 1999; Wenger, 1998). Researchers such as Furlong and Maynard argue that rather than residing in books and courses, waiting to be transferred to teachers' heads, practical professional knowledge is literally embodied in teachers' practices. Such notions draw on Schön's (1983, 1987) concept of 'knowledge-in-action'. According to Schön, the work of competent professionals in a range of fields involves the deployment of intelligent action in dialogue with a given situation. Such knowledge, grounded in experience, is an integral part of fluent performance and is embedded in skilful action. Johnson makes the point thus: 'Ultimately, teachers' knowledge is tacitly embodied in their practices since it functions as the foundation for reasoning teaching' (1999: 25).

This emphasis on teachers' practical professional knowledge provides a theoretical underpinning for viewing experience in real classrooms and real teaching situations as the vital foundation of competent teachers' knowledge. The clear implication for teacher education programmes is that student teachers need exposure to real classrooms and real teaching situations early in their professional development and that they need continued exposure to a wide range of teaching experiences in order to provide adequate time for the development of practical professional knowledge. They also need opportunities for engaging in classroom research, so as to enable them to become 'teacher-scholars' (Kumaravadivelu, 1999: 42), which in turn 'serves to validate one's role as a teacher and one's teaching' (Kuzmic, 2002: 227).

Indicative of these concerns, a number of new approaches gained prominence, both within pre-service and in-service teacher education, during the course of the 1990s. These approaches emerged partly as an attempt to embody the ideal of practical professional knowledge by elevating the pivotal role of experience; partly building on the move towards the transcendence of dichotomies such as theory–practice, fact–imagination, cognition–feeling, and instead recognizing the whole person in teaching, something which was implicit but not fully realized in the second type of competency model above; and partly in opposition to the 'technologies of control' inherent in performance, skill-based competency models of learning to teach (Furlong et al., 2000: 176). Among the new approaches were the reflective practice (J. Richards & Lockhart, 1996; Schön, 1983, 1987; Zeichner & Liston, 1996) and the classroom action research movements

(Burns, 1999; Kemmis & McTaggart, 1988, 2000; the latter work uses the term *participatory* action research in recognition of the convergence of theory and practice in the teacher), as well as the self-study movement (Loughran & Russell, 2002; Samaras, 2003).

In the specific field of language teaching, the 1990s witnessed a burgeoning of research into teacher knowledge and teacher beliefs. Much of this work is summarized in Borg's comprehensive review of research into language teacher cognition (2003). However, as reflected in the term 'cognition', this work is often underpinned by a psychological approach, with a focus on individual minds, in contrast to the socio-discursive and socio-cultural approaches drawn on in the research underpinning this book.

Learning to Teach and Identity

Building on developments in social and cultural theory, a number of theorists have framed teacher education in terms of the development of a teacher identity, where identity references individuals' knowledge and naming of themselves, as well as others' recognition of them as a particular sort of person. The emphasis in work that conceptualizes learning to teach as the development of a teacher identity, rather than on the acquisition of a set of skills and techniques, is an ongoing process of 'becoming':

> Learning to teach can be learning the skills and knowledge to perform the functions of a teacher or it can be developing a sense of oneself as teacher. In the former, one is 'being the teacher', whereas in the latter, one is 'becoming a teacher'. As has been shown, allowing an emphasis on 'being the teacher' (i.e. the functions of the teaching role) can result in knowledge of content and strategies becoming goals in their own rights. Preservice teacher education becomes irrelevant and survival becomes a goal in its own right. These distinctions have significant implications for the design and conduct of teacher education programs. (Mayer, 1999: 5)

This line of thinking draws on the work of Britzman, who argues against teaching as competence in a range of skills and techniques, arguing that 'Learning to teach – like teaching itself – is always the process of becoming: a time of formation and transformation, of scrutiny into what one is doing, and who one can become' (1991: 8). She argues elsewhere that 'role speaks to function whereas identity voices investments and commitments' (1992: 29). Similarly, Danielewicz (2001: 4) writes, 'I regard "becoming a teacher" as an identity forming process whereby individuals define themselves and are viewed by others as teachers'. Writing specifically in the context of language teaching, Varghese *et al.* argue that 'In order to understand language teaching and learning we need to understand teachers: the professional, cultural, political and individual identities which they claim or which are assigned to them' (2005: 22). Moreover, processes of identity formation are intimately related to the discourses and the communities that we work within. Miller Marsh puts it thus:

> In other words, we are continually in the process of fashioning and refashioning our identities by patching together fragments of the discourses to which we are exposed ... understanding how teachers fashion their identities is especially important, since much of the work that is done in the classrooms by teachers and their students involves the crafting of identities with and for one another. (Miller Marsh, 2003: 8–9)

This shift is reflected in the growing use of identity as an 'analytic lens' in educational research (Gee, 2000). Within teacher education such research has included studies of teachers' personal and professional lives (Day *et al.*, 2006; Goodson & Sikes, 2001; MacLure, 1993; Mitchell & Weber, 1999; Reid & Santoro, 2006), as well as the formation of teachers' emotions (Evans, 2002; Zembylas, 2003a, 2003b) and thinking (Britzman, 1991; Danielewicz, 2001; Miller Marsh, 2003). This trend has been paralleled by an increasing acceptance of interpretive and discourse-based approaches in researching education (Freebody, 2003; MacLure, 2003) and language teaching and learning generally (Kamberelis & Dimitriadis, 2005; K. Richards, 2003), and teacher identities in particular (Alsup, 2006; Britzman, 1994; Brown & McNamara, 2005; Phillips, 2002; Santoro, 1997; Søreide, 2006). It has also been paralleled by an emphasis on identity and community in education generally, not just within teacher education:

> Education in its deepest sense and at whatever age it takes place, concerns the opening up of identities – exploring new ways of being that lie beyond our current state ... Education is not merely formative – it is transformative. ... issues of education should be addressed first and foremost in terms of identities and modes of belonging and only secondarily in terms of skills and information. (Wenger, 1998: 263)

Wortham (2003: 283) similarly notes how 'Social identification, power relations and interpersonal struggles routinely overlap with subject matter, argument, evidence and academic learning', though he points out that formal education is not always an empowering experience with students (and teachers) sometimes being caught in the tensions between opposing roles, for example between 'good' student and 'cool' peer-group member.

Notions of education as identity transforming resonated with me personally in relation to my own experience and professionally in the context of my work in teacher education in the UAE. Indeed, over the four years during which this first cohort of HCT teacher education students has been completing their degree, a number of related factors struck me as having particular significance and requiring further exploration. First was the degree to which the student teachers were exemplifying teacher education as the taking on of a new identity. Second was the strength of the community the student teachers were creating. And third was the passion and commitment with which the students embraced and took up particular discourses of education that they encountered in their degree.

Taken together these three factors led to the development of the research issue that underpinned and drove this study; namely, in what ways are the social and educational discourses that have shaped the contemporary UAE context and the HCT's teacher education programme taken up by the students as they construct their identities as teachers within an evolving community of practice? In addressing this issue and examining the developing teacher identities of students in the B.Ed. degree at the HCT, I explore 'the ways in which teacher thought is socially constructed yet individually enacted' (Miller Marsh, 2003: 10). This book therefore contributes to and complements recent developments in teacher education and educational theory in a number of ways. The first relates to recent theorizations of teacher education as a process of identity formation, as briefly outlined above. The second relates to communities of practice as a productive construct in thinking about teacher education (Kornerup, 2001; Porter, 2003; Walker, 2003). The third relates to research into the role of discourse in identity construction and group formation (Benwell & Stokoe, 2006; Burr, 1995; De Fina *et al.*, 2006; Edwards & Potter, 1992; Laclau & Mouffe, 1985; Mansfield, 2000; Torfing, 1999; Weedon, 1987), as well as the ways second language learners take up discourses as part of the process of constructing a new identity in their additional language (Cummins *et al.*, 2005; Norton, 2000; Pavlenko & Blackledge, 2004b).

Critically, this book is 'constitutive', rather than 'empirical', by which I mean that it is concerned with describing and interpreting socially produced meanings, rather than providing a causal explanation for them (Howarth, 2000: 130). But to the extent that the book 'uncovers' how the UAE B.Ed. programme contributes to the shaping of the new professional identities of its participants, it inevitably offers an evaluative perspective. In particular, the book is about the power of discourse and community in shaping identities; it is about the ways in which a particular cohort of English language student teachers uses available discourses to construct powerfully 'oppositional' identities; and it is about the dangers inherent in – and the consequent need to problematize – the reductiveness of dichotomous frameworks, be these based on notions of 'native–non-native' speakers, 'EFL–ESL' contexts, 'global–local' cultures or, to foreshadow later chapters of this book, 'traditional–progressive' pedagogies. The book's analysis of the playing out of dichotomous models of curriculum and pedagogy, learners and learning, teachers and teaching, as part of the co-construction of discourse, community and identity, provides the basis for the recommendations for language teacher education practice and programme redesign that are discussed in the final chapter.

In broad outline then, the book involves an attempt to provide an initial understanding of the phenomena of the study by outlining the theoretical and empirical context, prior to a discursive analytic inquiry that attempts to supplement these initial understandings with fuller and deeper insights as a basis for tentative interpretations and recommendations. The detailed outline of the book is as follows.

Chapter 1 looks at the key notions of discourse, identity and communities of practice, examining the complementary congruencies and articulations among these constructs. The notions of discourse, identity and communities of practice provide an integrated conceptual framework throughout this study at the levels of theoretical principles, methodology, analysis and interpretation. These theoretical concepts are introduced for their productive capacity, for as Phillips and Jorgensen (2002: 21) note, 'It is by seeing the world through a particular theory that we can distance ourselves from our taken for granted understandings and subject our material to other questions than we would be able to do from an everyday perspective.' It is critical therefore to examine each of these concepts in some depth, to illustrate their appropriateness for researching teacher education and to highlight their complementary contributions in addressing the questions motivating this book.

Chapter 2 uses the notion of discourse to provide insights into the development of the student teachers' evolving community of practice by examining some of the contextual factors that have shaped that development. This is carried out on two levels: first, by providing an overview of the historical development of the contemporary UAE from a socio-discursive perspective (Davidson, 2005; Kazim, 2000); and second, by examining the content and structure of the HCT B.Ed. degree from a perspective on teaching as an 'amalgam' of discourses (Coldron & Smith, 1995). This chapter also provides a brief outline of the methodology, describing how the research data were derived from focus groups and online discussions over the final two years of the students' degree and explaining how these data were analysed in terms of three levels of discursive construction: systems of knowledge and beliefs, interpersonal relations and intrapersonal identity.

Chapter 3 analyses the data to support the perspective on the student teachers in the B.Ed. degree as what I have called an evolving community of practice. It explores why the students chose teaching, and English teaching in particular, as a career and examines the formation of an evolving community of practice in terms of the three modes of belonging, drawn from Wenger's (1998) model of communities of practice: *engagement, alignment* and *imagination*. In terms of belonging and engagement, this chapter examines developing forms of 'mutual engagement', developing understandings of the enterprise at hand, i.e. learning to teach English, and developing repertoires of styles and language. In terms of belonging and alignment, the chapter looks at the evolving community of practice's relation to other communities in their 'constellation', such as the currently practising teachers in the school system, as well as exploring boundary issues and border practices. In terms of belonging and imagination, the chapter looks at self-consciousness, reflection and creation as means through which community members continually reinvent their community of practice.

Chapter 4 examines the discursive construction of the student teachers' evolving community of practice in terms of the first of the three constitutive effects of discourse noted above: the construction of reality as reflected in systems of knowledge and belief, locating these within wider social structures and practices, as reflected in the relevant social, historical, cultural and political discourses outlined in Chapter 2. We see how the student teachers construct their community in terms of its system of knowledge and beliefs through a powerful series of binary oppositions, organized around a basic division between the 'traditional' teachers of the past – 'them', and the 'new' teachers of the future – 'us'. Fleshing out the details of this overarching opposition we have see a series of further oppositions, such as that between sensitivity and insensitivity in the classroom, and between a vision of learners as homogenous versus viewing learners as heterogeneous. We see a critical distinction drawn between 'teacher-centred' teaching as opposed to 'learner/student/child-centred' teaching, with an emphasis on active learning, high motivation and self-esteem, as opposed to passive learning, low motivation and low self-esteem, which are constructed as characteristics of the former, 'teacher-centred' classrooms. These dichotomies, which provide much of the material for the evolving community's discursive self construction, are characterized by a startling degree of consensus. This consensus is supported and reinforced

Introduction

by the shared linguistic repertoire of the community that we examined in Chapter 3, which reifies particular ways of understanding teaching while at the same time excluding others. Thus emerges a major theme of the book in terms of the effect of these patterns in a discourse characterized by a powerful differentiation between 'us' – the members of the community and 'them' – the government school teachers, that at times takes the form of outright antagonism and hostility and that informs Chapter 7's recommendations for a move from 'antagonism' to 'agonism' in thinking about pedagogy and curriculum.

Chapter 4 also explores an aspect of the community's discursive self construction, where beliefs were more divided among the members, which relates to issues of language and culture. Here we see some members advocating practices reflecting a 'conservative', 'traditional' discourse of protecting and preserving Arab-Islamic cultural values in the face of outside influence while other members advocate the value of practices reflecting a 'progressive' discourse of, if not embracing then at least pragmatically utilizing, the potential benefits offered by external cultural influences. These two lines of argument reflect wider discursive 'conversations' in the UAE community, as explained in Chapter 2.

Chapter 5 explores the discursive construction of interpersonal relations among the members of the community. As Dewey (1963) recognized, the very act of participating in the community entails a certain degree of alignment in terms of communication, including thoughts, ideas, values and beliefs. Thus the ongoing self-definition of the student teachers' community requires considerable coherence and cohesion within the community in terms of their common purpose, beliefs and values. In this chapter I explore some of the ways in which this work unfolds: through the use of particular forms of interpersonal address; through statements that serve to monitor and maintain the community's beliefs and coherence; and through statements that serve to set the agenda for the community's future mission. As we have seen in previous chapters, however, the need for a 'constitutive outside' leads to the community's 'us' being defined in opposition to the 'them' of 'traditional' teachers and teaching, which the student teachers construct as characterizing UAE government schools. This chapter also provides some examples where the evangelical sense of mission and the consequent antagonism towards the school teachers that is emerging, is tempered in the reflections of a small minority of student teachers, who demonstrate some awareness of the contingency and constructedness of the community and its beliefs.

Chapter 6 looks at the development of the evolving community of practice through the lens of intrapersonal identity. By necessity, focusing on intrapersonal identity requires a focus on the individual and so this chapter will concentrate on the identity of one student teacher. By focusing in some depth on the intrapersonal construction of one student teacher's ('Manal') identity, as constituted through the comments that are discursive-performatives of her attitudes, values and beliefs, we are able to get a sense of the meaning of the community and its enterprise, as literally embodied in 'real people'. This chapter thus provides a complement to the more thematic focus that emerged when looking at the discursive construction of the community's systems of knowledge and belief. In this chapter we see how, as was the case with the construction of the community's system of knowledge and beliefs, to a large extent Manal's self-constitution is through what I term, following Danielewicz (2001), an 'oppositional affiliation' in relation to the practising (and mostly Arab-expatriate) teachers in the UAE school system.

Chapter 7, the final chapter, examines the implications of the study in relation to the complexity of the factors operating in the contemporary HCT and UAE context and to the findings to other regional studies of Middle East teacher education (e.g. Eilam, 2002, 2003). Drawing on Laclau and Mouffe's (1985; Mouffe, 2000, 2005) work on discourse theory and the 'logic of eqiuvalence', as well as Zizek's (2003) writing on the dangers of zealotry, the discussion reveals different angles and perspectives and hence new shades of meaning in the overall findings of the study and makes a plea for language teacher educators and student teachers to resist thinking within dichotomous frameworks, as part of what can be described as a positioned opening for discussion (Phillips & Jorgensen, 2002). This final chapter also considers possible ways forward, such as the exploration of notions of 'nomadic' identities, both in relation to the immediate context of the study and in terms of potential directions for future research in language teacher education

Chapter 1
Discourse, Identity and Community

This chapter outlines the theoretical framework underpinning the book and my reasons for adopting it. In the process, I hope to make the nature of my engagement with the issues implicit in the book explicit, as well as to provide an opening for further debate and discussion (Holliday, 2002; Kamberelis & Dimitriadis, 2005; Phillips & Jorgensen, 2002).

The notions of discourse, identity and communities of practice provide an integrated and aligned conceptual framework throughout this study at the levels of epistemology, theoretical principles, methodology, analysis and interpretation (Kamberelis & Dimitriadis, 2005: 15). These theoretical concepts are introduced for their productive capacity, for as Phillips and Jorgensen (2002: 21) note, in the quote cited in the Introduction, 'It is by seeing the world through a particular theory that we can distance ourselves from our taken for granted understandings and subject our material to other questions than we would be able to do from an everyday perspective.' It is critical therefore to examine each of these concepts in some depth, to illustrate their appropriateness for researching teacher formation and to highlight their complementary contributions in addressing the questions motivating this study. I begin by examining discourse since in many ways it forms a bridge between the social worlds of communities of practice and identities.

Exploring Discourse

In the introductory chapter I noted the passion with which the student teachers were embracing the discourses of education as one of the sources of impetus for this study. Indeed, among other things, this study is crucially concerned with the power of discourse. However, in order to fully appreciate this productive power, we need to unpack the complex meanings carried by this term.

Discourse, like culture, is one of the most widely used terms in social and educational discussions, and like culture, it is also a term that is often used in different ways though often left undefined (Mills, 2004). These uses include reference to extended stretches of language beyond the sentence level, as well as to linguistically embodied systems of meaning, knowledge and belief, akin to notions referenced by the term ideology[1]. These different senses are of course related, in that systems of belief will be evident in language-in-use. Discourse in the broader 'systems of meaning' sense is also used in different ways. We can refer to 'discourse' as an abstract noun, meaning something along the lines of language as social practice, or as a countable noun, when speaking of particular discourses (Fairclough, 1992). Within this latter use, at times we refer to the discourse of a field, such as the discourse of law, or teaching, while at other times we refer to the discourse of a social community, such as Emirati women, urban educated youths, upper-class Brits, etc. So discourse references both knowledge and communities. But discourses should not be thought of as separate, self-contained silos of meaning; rather, there will be polyvalent relationships between and among them involving differing degrees and combinations of articulation and overlap, complementariness and contradiction, similarity and difference, as a result of which discourses may produce, transmit and reinforce, but also contest and undermine, social meanings and social relations (Bove, 1995; Foucault, 1978, p. 100–102).

Overall, the most fruitful approach with discourse is to maintain a degree of openness and flexibility in relation to its meaning since the value of the term is as a heuristic tool, similar again to culture, and that value is likely to be lost if we try to pin the meaning of the term down too precisely (Phillips & Jorgensen, 2002). Working definitions of the term *discourse*, consonant with this study include the fairly loose: 'a relational ensemble of signifying sequences' (Torfing, 1999: 91), as well as the more detailed: 'a pattern of thinking, speaking, behaving, and interacting that is socially, culturally, and historically constructed and sanctioned by a specific group or groups of people' (Miller Marsh, 2003: 9).

Related to the wide usage of the term, are four common misunderstandings about discourse-based theories (Torfing, 1999: 94–96). These include:

(1) The view that discourse theory involves a belief that there is no external world – rather, discourse theory asserts that it is only through discourse that we can talk meaningfully about the external world.
(2) The view that discourse refers to the merely linguistic within the wider social world – rather, discourse theory views the linguistic and the social as coextensive in that 'All actions have meaning and to produce or disseminate meaning is to act' (Torfing, 1999: 94).
(3) The view that relations and identities within discourse are entirely arbitrary, stemming from Saussure's arguments about the arbitrary relationship between the signifier and signified within the sign – rather, discourse theory views the relationship between the whole and the

parts, as well as between the parts, within discourse as one of reciprocal and mutual conditioning.
(4) The view that discourse theory entails a chaotic flux of meaning – rather, meaning within discourse is constrained by what Torfing (1999: 96), drawing on Derrida, refers to as a 'determinate openness', in that the fixation of meaning within discourse is always only temporary and partial.

Of the above misconceptions, the first is perhaps the most prevalent and one to which Laclau and Mouffe provide a robust response:

> The fact that every object is constituted as an object of discourse has *nothing to do* with whether there is a world external to thought, or with the realism/idealism opposition. An earthquake or the falling of a brick is an event that certainly exists, in the sense that it occurs here and now, independently of my will. But whether their specificity as objects is constructed in terms of 'natural phenomena' or 'expressions of the wrath of God', depends on the structuring of a discursive field. What is denied is not that such objects exist externally to thought, but the rather different assertion that they could constitute themselves as objects outside any discursive conditions of emergence. (Laclau & Mouffe, 1985: 108)

Torfing's work is primarily concerned with the discourse theory of Laclau and Mouffe (1985). In this book, I draw on Laclau and Mouffe's view of discourse as a series of temporary, unstable and ambiguous closures of meaning and their post-structuralist insights into the way that the positive content of any discourse relies on the strategy of positing of an 'other' or 'constitutive outside', against which the terms of a particular discourse are negatively defined. But there are many other possible approaches and I draw on Laclau and Mouffe's discourse theory as one of a number of related approaches, all of which reject notions of totalizing and universalizing knowledge, beliefs or identities emanating from an ultimate centre. The positive value of such principled eclecticism as part of a 'multiperspectival' approach is recognized by Phillips and Jorgensen, who note how 'many discourse analysts work across disciplinary borders, and there are many theoretical points and methodological tools that cannot be assigned to one particular approach' (Phillips & Jorgensen, 2002: 3). Indeed, while on the one hand Laclau and Mouffe's discourse theory is a particularly broad-ranging social theory and offers valuable theoretical insights, on the other hand, it offers little in the way of detailed method for discourse analysis. Its reach can be extended by supplementing it, as in this study, with an approach that has developed a detailed set of tools, such as Fairclough's critical discourse analysis (Fairclough, 1992, 2003).

Despite this eclecticism, however, it is important to realize that discourse theory is a 'complete package' in the sense that it is not valid to use its tools and methods unless one embraces its philosophical tenets and principles. 'In discourse analysis, *theory* and *method* are intertwined and researchers must accept the basic philosophical premises in order to use discourse analysis as their method of empirical study' (Phillips & Jorgensen, 2002: 4). Indeed, alongside their various differences, all discourse analytical approaches agree on the following points (Phillips & Jorgensen, 2002: 12) with regard to the word/world relationship. First, language is not a reflection of a pre-existent reality, in the sense that thought and language only become meaningful in discourse, as well as in that language use patterned as discourse both produces and reflects particular ways of understanding or talking about the world. Second, discourse is not 'context-free' in the historical sense that it changes over time and in the sense that at any given time, discourse is coextensive with social relations of position and power. Third, discourses are maintained or transformed in discursive practices which involve a constant negotiation and renegotiation of meaning. Fourth, the maintenance or transformation of these patterns can be explored through the specific contexts in which language is used in action, as part of a process of discourse analysis.

Thus discourse implies a mode of acting upon the world as well as a means of expression or form of representation. It also implies a mutually constitutive relationship between language and society, between the word and the world at multiple levels: at the level of systems of knowledge and belief; at the level of social relationships and groupings, such as gender, class or institutions; and at the level of effects such as social identities (Fairclough, 1992). It is through discourse that the social production of meaning takes place, through discourse that social relations are created and maintained and through discourse that social identities are produced.

At the level of systems of knowledge and belief, 'Discourse is a practice not just of representing the world, but of signifying the world, constituting and constructing the world in meaning' (Fairclough, 1992: 64). In constituting 'reality' discourses determine what can and cannot be said; as Foucault's rarefied definition has it, discourses 'are practices that systematically form the objects of which they speak' (1972: 49). (It is worth noting Sim's (1998: 245) comment that whenever 'discourse' is mentioned 'we find Foucault's ghostly presence'.) An example of this constitutive capacity from education is the distinction between 'traditional' and 'new' methods of teaching in progressive educational discourse that we will encounter in Chapter 4. Thus the development of new ways of talking about teaching and learning in the wake of the Piagetian and Vygotskian 'revolutions' from the 1960s onwards led to the creation of the 'traditional' and the 'progressive' teacher as distinct categories, as well as to other distinctions such as that between 'teacher centred' and 'student centred' classrooms or between 'active' and 'passive' learning.

At the level of interpersonal relations, the regulatory and productive capacity of discourse constitutes certain social relationships and social groupings at the same time as it constitutes meanings. Thus discourses of advertising and consumption simultaneously constitute a consumerist understanding of the world and a community of consumers characterized by this understanding (Fairclough, 1992: 134). Of course, just as people adhere to multiple systems of knowledge and belief in different aspects of their lives, so they are members of multiple discourse communities that may overlap or be quite discrete, cohere or conflict.

At the level of intrapersonal identities, discourse is constitutive of who we are and how we are perceived by others. Thus within schools, colleges and universities, educational and pedagogical discourses and their associated practices construct certain people as teachers and others as students. However, as noted above, this is not a matter of straightforward or predictable determination; discourses and discursive practices are myriad and the individual is formed in the interface between these multiple and often competing discourses and practices. As Holland *et al.* note,

> the idea of plural, even competing sites of self, is now common to a variety of disciplines ... the demise of the privileged concept of bounded, discrete coherent cultures has made room for the recognition that people are exposed to competing and differentially powerful and authoritative discourses and practices of the self. (Holland *et al.*, 1998: 29)

In similar fashion, and writing specifically in the context of the power of discourse in shaping teacher identities, Britzman (1994: 56) explains how 'In this way, language – or more specifically discourse – becomes the site of the struggle, a place where the real is constructed, truth is produced and power is effectuated'.

Overall, discourse is central to this book. In Chapter 2, discourse is used to explore UAE history and society before going on specifically to look at discourses in relation to education and teacher education. I also use discourse as the basis for analysing the data gathered as part of this study, as also outlined in Chapter 2, in order to explore the discursive construction of the student teachers' community of practice and the constitution of their teacher identities. Indeed, discourse can be viewed as forming a bridge between communities of practice and identity, inasmuch as it is through discourse that the social is reflected in the individual and it is through discourse that the individual engages with the social. In this sense discourse links individual and social identities. It is to the question of identity that I turn next.

Exploring Identity

Like the construct discourse, the notion of *identity* was also implicated in the impetus for the study on which this book is based, insofar as I was intrigued by the student teachers' embodiment of learning to teach as the taking on of a new identity. By this I mean that the students seemed to exude a whole new sense of self as they reconceived themselves as 'teachers'.

Identity has long been one of the key issues in social and cultural theory with questions posed in terms of how it is that we endure as the same person over time. The concept of identity has also fascinated and preoccupied poets, playwrights and novelists. For example, in Pirandello's novella, *The Late Mattia Pascal* (1964 [1904]), a man fakes his own death in order to recast his life as a different person, only to discover that the psychological and social ties to his old 'self' constrain the possibilities for the new 'self' to the point of almost inhuman two-dimensionality. A similar exploration was carried out more recently in Hanif Kureishi's short story, *The Body* (2003). These stories raise many of the questions that philosophers have grappled with over time. Does the self reside in individual consciousness – in memories, thoughts and emotions – or is the individual created by the consistent reactions and responses of others that call forth each person as a separate and continuous individual? These questions are related to the timeless philosophical debate between structure and agency, between determination and freedom (Archer, 2000, 2003). One of these potentially determining forces, which featured prominently in a recent discussion about teacher education in the UAE, is culture. The following section explores the relationship between culture and identity in the context of this discussion.

Culturalism and cultural identities

Culture, like identity, has been one of the utilized and useful constructs in 20th century social theory and has been thoroughly incorporated into educational literature. Yet as Raymond Williams and others have pointed out, 'culture' is one of the most complex words in the English language in terms of its history and etymology, so it is not surprising to find it used in a range of disparate senses (Eagleton, 2000; R. Williams, 1983). Over 50 years ago, Kroeber and Kluckhohn (1952, cited in Seel, 2000) reviewed different meanings of culture and identified 156 different definitions. It is certainly a word that is loaded with issues and ambivalences. 'Within this single term, questions of freedom and determinism, agency and endurance, change and identity, the given and the created come dimly into focus' (Eagleton, 2000: 2).

Reflecting the prevalent use of culture as a concept in education, an article in an educational development journal stated as its main purpose 'to compare key assumptions of reflective practice with the major cultural values about education in the United Arab Emirates' (Richardson, 2004: 429). Relying on an interpretation of culture as 'the collective programming of the mind which distinguishes the members of one group or category of people from another' (Hofstede, 1994: 4, cited in Richardson, 2004: 431), Richardson characterizes Emirati students as programmed by Arab-Islamic culture and thus circumscribed in a number of specific ways. These posited cultural limitations include the following: 'resistance to making the change and taking more responsibility for their own learning' (2004: 432); difficulty in forming 'a comfortable relationship with her college supervisor, given ... the expectations of high power distance between her and her supervisor' (2004: 434); and 'aversion to risk and uncertainty ... [and] thus may rely on outdated professional practices to use as models' (2004: 434). The problem with these views is that they rely on an essentialized notion of culture that is potentially reductive and is unable to do justice to the complexity of history and society in the UAE. Moreover, they ignore past and present contestations over the meaning of the 'values' that are cited as the underlying reason for the posited cultural characteristics. To understand why Richardson feels able to make these claims, we need to explore further the notion of culture underpinning her work.

In common usage, culture is variously defined as a way of life, a network of meanings, a system of values and beliefs. The problem with these attempts at defining culture is that they convey the impression that culture is a static, synoptic thing. Such a conceptualization of culture lends itself to a compartmentalized world view where different cultures are each self-contained and separate. Within this model individuals are seen as belonging to *a* particular culture. From here it is a small step to see culture as the main exegetic tool in understanding individuals as well as comprehending all social, educational and political issues (Holliday, 1997). Such utilization of culture as a universal key has been variously termed cultural essentialism (Gandhi, 1998) and culturalism (McConaghy, 2000).

For McConaghy, 'Culturalism is the perception of subjectivity as primarily "cultural" ... it privileges "culture" as an explanatory tool for knowing matters of social difference; and it uses 'culture' indiscriminately to explain issues in colonial contexts' (2000: 43). Holliday (1997) draws attention to 'culturalism' as a particular understanding of culture that has become dominant in, though not restricted to, applied linguistics and hence operates in contexts like the UAE where the teaching of English as a foreign language is a major educational industry. Holliday describes how culturalism in such contexts draws parallels between conceptions of culture and of language.

> The notion of culture is thus modeled on the notion of language and tries to fix culture into families and regional or ethnic identities, in the way that language has been fixed. Thus, *a* culture has an objective identity, based on the physical and conceptual nature of its artifacts, in the same way as *a* language has an objective identity based on the physical and conceptual nature of its grammar, vocabulary and sound system. (Holliday, 1997: 212)

The consequences of such reductionism is the sort of formulaic stereotyping and overgeneralizing reflected in certain comments of Richardson's, for example, 'Arab students prefer prescriptive learning environments where they are told exactly what to do and directed along a single path' (Richardson, 2004: 432). As Holliday goes on to point out, criticism based on such a dichotomous framework works towards 'an other-isation or tribalisation of the victim "cultures" by reducing them to peripheral, non-thinking automata' (1997: 214).

That 'culture' came to occupy such an important role in education and the social sciences generally was an understandable reaction to universalist thinking and tendencies, whereby concepts and paradigms that predominated in the 'western' academy were surreptitiously – or more generously, unwittingly – inserted into a role as representatives of 'human nature'. The difficulty is that both universalist and culturalist positions tend towards a static, timeless conceptualization of both the individual and society.

What is needed are constructs that move beyond this framework and allow for a more dynamic, developmental view of both individuals and society and encourage a more differentiated and dialogic relationship between the two. While we need to recognize that individual lives take shape and have meaning within cultural worlds, we need to resist seeing any single construct such as 'culture', as all-determining. This call has been answered by post-structuralist approaches, which emphasize how cultures and identities are constructed through the articulation of multiple factors; this in turn has been facilitated through the adoption in the recent decades of discourse, which we discussed in the previous section Exploring Discourse, as a theorization through which to better understand the dynamic, contested and contingent aspects of notions of culture and identity. The relationship between discourse and identity is explored below.

Discourse and positional identities

Over the course of the 20th century, writers and researchers in the social sciences been increasingly questioned the notion of what C. Taylor (1989) calls 'the disengaged self', rejecting the notion of a core, stable, atomized individual identity:

> All human identities are in some sense – and usually in a stronger rather than a weaker sense – *social* identities. It cannot be otherwise, if only because identities are about meaning, and meaning is not an essential property of words and things. Meanings are always the outcome of agreement or disagreement, always a matter of convention and innovation, always to some extent shared, always to some extent negotiable. (Jenkins, 1996: 3, emphasis in original)

Likewise, in his overview of 20th century theories of subjectivity, Mansfield (2000) identifies a fundamental division between approaches, typically found in psychoanalytic theories, which view the self as a 'thing', and approaches in social and cultural theory that view the self as a 'construct' (see also du Gay et al., 2000). Within the latter approach, with which this study is in broad alignment, the rise of post-structuralist theories of language and meaning in recent decades has involved the utilization of the notion of 'discourse' to shift away from notions of a core, ineffable, essentialist identity towards notions of contingent, multiple and discursively constructed identit*ies*.

In the previous section I offered the following as a working definition: 'A discourse can be described as 'a pattern of thinking, speaking, behaving, and interacting that is socially, culturally, and historically constructed and sanctioned by a specific group or groups of people' Miller Marsh (2003: 9). The notion of discourse is linked to a radical rethinking of identity over the past three decades, challenging ideas of the self as homogenous, self-contained and self-sufficient subject. 'When the 'I' seeks to give an account of itself, it can start with itself, but it will find that this self is already implicated in a social temporality that exceeds its own capacities for narration' (Butler, 2005: 7). Specifically, post-structuralist perspectives on identity have pointed out that individuals do not autonomously construct their identities in a social, cultural and political vacuum; rather, sociocultural and sociopolitical discourses will determine what resources are available for use in the ongoing project of identity construction, just as the outcomes of this process, in terms of identities, will in turn shape the discursive patterns at work in different contexts (Burr, 1995; Butler, 2005; Hall & du Gay, 1997; Jenkins, 1996; Weedon, 1987):

> Discourse practices form a bridge between the micro- and macro-contexts in that discourse depends upon the prior existence of culturally and institutionally specific forms of communication and upon the creative use of those forms by people in their interactions with each other. (Forman & McCormick, 1995: 151)

However, it is important to bear in mind that the meanings reflected in discursive practices are relational in that they establish what something is in terms of what it is not. Discursive meanings are dependent on connections of equivalence and relations of difference. This emphasis on connections and relations is resonant with Bakhtinian dialogic thought as we can see from Holquist's comment that

> Dialogism argues that all meaning is relative in the sense that it comes about only as a result of the relation between two bodies occupying *simultaneous but different* space, where bodies may be thought of as ranging from the immediacy of our physical bodies to political bodies and to bodies of ideas in general (ideologies). (Holquist, 1990: 20-21, emphasis in original)

Dialogism is both a theory of language and a theory of 'self' as Holquist points out: 'there is an intimate connection between the project of language and the project of self-hood' since in both, difference is the basis of simultaneity in the sense that meaning is created where two or more different voices come into contact (1990: 23).

The discursively constructed self is useful in the context of this study, in that it enables us to view student teachers' identities as always becoming: as constructed through discursive interaction, as the result of discussion and argument, agreement and disagreement, similarity and difference, interaction and negotiation. It reminds us, that, as Jenkins comments, 'Identity is not "just there", it must always be established' (Jenkins, 1996: 4), through a process MacLure (1993) describes as arguing for your self. In this sense, discursively constructed selves potentially enable us to move towards a model of the 'individual in society'/'society in the individual' that allows for the constrained, but not completely determined, nature of social existence, involving both the locating and the transgressing of boundaries. Inasmuch as discourses are socially valued ways of talking, thinking and acting, they reference what we can call 'positional' identities in that they relate to our alignment vis-à-vis social relations of power, of entitlement and deference. But just as we saw with the 'culturalist' position, it is possible to go to an extreme 'constructivist' position where the individual is merely a blank sheet to be written upon, or 'positioned', by the discursive practices of society. We still need further constructs to free ourselves from the potential prison of determinism. Imagination is one of the key constructs in accomplishing this project.

Figured worlds and figurative identities

The imaginative capacity was highlighted in human development by Vygotsky, who drew theoretical insights from our tendency as children to suspend everyday reality and engage in make-believe play, so that a stick becomes a horse or a sister picks up a stick, taps it on the wall and becomes a teacher. Such symbolic objects act as 'mediating devices', enabling some degree of control over the environment. Language is perhaps the most significant semiotic mediating device in gaining increasing control over social situations. In later childhood games the rules may become more explicit but children must still suspend their everyday sense of who they are and submit to the game's premises, treating the world of the game as the real world.

In similar fashion, throughout our lives we all participate in socially meaningful activity by 'casting' ourselves and others into socially constructed roles. Together these activities and roles make up what Holland *et al.* refer to as 'figured worlds', which 'rest upon people's abilities to form and be formed in collectively realized "as if" realms' (Holland *et al.*, 1998: 49). This competence can be seen in cultural and institutional life where people appropriate particular discourses and particular ways of being as they take on roles as parents, managers, doctors or teachers as part of their figured worlds:

> Under the rubric of culturally figured worlds or figured worlds we include all those cultural realms peopled by characters from collective imaginings: academia, the factory, crime, romance, environmental activism, games of Dungeons and Dragons ... A figured world is peopled by the figures, characters, and types who carry out its tasks and who have styles of interacting within, distinguishable perspectives on, and orientations toward it. (Holland *et al.*, 1998: 51)

However, although they draw and build on the key human capacity for imagination as identified by Vygotsky, these figured worlds do not arise from nothing. They are not the result of unconstrained free will, of untrammelled individual fantasy divorced from sociocultural resources and limitations. Rather, they entail a social process of learning through the appropriation of, and engagement with, the meanings embodied in social narratives and practices. In this sense, figured worlds form the second social or collective aspect of identity, in addition to the 'positional' aspects of identity. But whereas the latter relate to one's sense of place in society vis-à-vis others, figured worlds provide the basis for narrative- and practice-focused, 'figurative' identities.

In moving from culturalism to discourse and figured worlds we have moved from an essentialized conception of identity as the imprint of a monolithic culture embodied in the individual, to one that incorporates positional dimensions of identity, vis-à-vis alignment with discursive practices and social relations, and figurative dimensions, vis-à-vis engagement in narrative- and practice-focused, figured worlds. Such identities are already complex and multidimensional, constructed across innumerable sites and situations and within a range of contexts by individuals, utilizing the resources of imagination, as they negotiate and make sense of multiple, often competing discourses and populate particular figured worlds. As such, any resulting identities are likely to be only a temporary and localized stability. However, although we have introduced notions of imagination in relation to figured worlds, we can explore possibilities for agency within social structures further by considering the role of multiple discourses and varied voices, or 'heteroglossia', in creating 'spaces for authoring'.

Improvisation and authored identities

In Laclau and Mouffe's discourse theory, discursive determination is never complete because in the absence of a fixed centre or foundation (God, Reason, Nature), the field of discursivity (the theoretical horizon of possibilities for the construction of discursive meaning) always exceeds the partial fixation of meaning instantiated in any concrete discourse(s) (Laclau & Mouffe, 1985; Torfing, 1999). The idea is that the meaning of an event or thing will always exceed our knowledge of it and our capacity to 'capture' it in representational systems such as language. In terms of identity this leads to the idea that 'There is more in my life than any official definition of identity can express. I am not exhausted by my identity. I am not entirely captured by it, even though it is stamped upon me – and even though it enables me' (Connolly, 2002: 120). This is also related to the 'unfinalizability' of identity, to the idea that identity somehow constantly integrates remembered pasts, imagined futures and present selves, and thus to the notion that 'Identity is always deferred and in the process of becoming – never really, never yet, never absolutely "there"' (MacLure, 2003: 131).

Similarly, in Bakhtin's theory of dialogism, individuals are confronted with a situation of 'heteroglossia', that is, with a cacophony of disparate voices, an inchoate riot of languages, world views and discourses each making overlapping and often conflicting claims. In response to these claims, individuals have no option but to become 'a space of dialogue' (Dimitriadis & Kamberelis, 2006: 51) and to author themselves and the world, since the world must be answered (Holquist, 1990). This implies that rather than being totally determined by social structures and discourses, 'individuals are agentive beings who are constantly in search of new social and linguistic resources which allow them to resist identities that position them in undesirable ways' (Pavlenko & Blackledge, 2004a: 27); although it is important to acknowledge creative possibilities for agency and identity formation that are not tied to resistance (Mahmood, 2005). This involves developing an 'authorial stance' through what Archer (2000; 2003) refers to as the 'internal conversation', as part of a process of agentive improvisation, in the sense of going beyond the limitations of, or transforming into enablements, the constraints of the currently available social and cultural resources.

The development of an authorial stance entails the development and utilization of an 'internally persuasive discourse [which] mediates the reorganization and extension of social speech into new forms of inner speaking. It changes the nature of subjectification' (Holland et al., 1998: 182). As we will see in the discussion of this study's research methods in Chapter 2, the development of this internally persuasive discourse can be facilitated through public discussions, especially through written formats which provide space and time for imagination, consideration and reflection. We can see clear similarities here to Vygotsky's notion of the social origins of individual cognition where development occurs in two planes, the first social and external, prior to internalization at the individual level. Indeed, the complementarity between appropriation of social speech and the negotiation of an authorial stance forms a developmental, dialogic cycle as the social and inner voices continually interanimate each other on an ongoing basis. And just as in using language we shape our utterances in relation to the perceived conceptual world of our interlocutor, so too with respect to identity, we represent ourselves to ourselves from the perceived perspective of others. As Holland *et al.* put it:

Identity, as the expressible relationship to others, is dialogical at both moments of expression, listening and speaking ... the self is a position from which meaning is made, a position which is 'addressed' by and 'answers' others and the 'world' (the physical and cultural environment. In answering (which is the stuff of existence), the self 'authors' the world – including itself and others. (Holland et al., 1998: 172–173)

The notion of 'spaces of authoring' forms the third context of 'authored' identities. However, the authored response may be orchestrated more or less freely depending on the specific configurations of culturally figured worlds and social discourses within which individuals are situated at any given time and place. The emphasis on the cultural and social dimension of these resources means that the notion of spaces of authoring can be related to Vygotsky's notion of mediation through cultural resources. As in Vygotskian approaches to learning and development, the emphasis here in terms of identities is on becoming rather than being.

Agency within structure

Taken together, the concepts of discourse, figured worlds and spaces for authoring offer a set of possibilities for recognizing the complex historical and social worlds within which individuals are required to make meaning from their experiences, but also for recognizing and incorporating an element of scope for agency within socially determining structures, for acknowledging affordances and enablements as well as constraints. In the context of teacher education, they allow us to posit a model of teacher formation where particular social conversations are appropriated and reconstructed within the ongoing and never-completed work of self-fashioning. As Miller Marsh notes, 'From this perspective, teacher thinking is a mélange of past, present, and future meanings that are continually being renegotiated through social interaction' (Miller Marsh, 2003: 6).

If we think about this in relation to learning to teach, we can see that each student teacher is faced with the challenge of, in a sense, 'authoring' a teaching identity for themselves in their current spatial and temporal context. But in working on this project of creating a teaching self they are not creating something out of nothing; they are not able to forge a new, local (in the sense of this place and time) meaning of 'teacher' and 'teaching' that bears no relation to meanings of teacher and teaching in the wider social and historical context – in existing 'figured worlds' and social discourses. Rather, they have to draw on pre-existing, discursive practices and meanings relating these to their own 'local' experiences and context.

In sum, we have seen how the culturalist position reflects an essentialist notion that undervalues the power of the social; whereas the extreme constructivist stance takes the social to the point of denying – or at least leaving no meaningful space for – the agency of the individual. To overcome this dichotomy we have followed Holland *et al.* in drawing on the insights of Bakhtin and Vygotsky. In particular we have identified 'imagination', and discursive non-closure or (more positively) heteroglossia, as providing 'spaces' for authoring and improvisation that allow for some element of agency within socially persuasive structures. Such a view enables us to acknowledge the 'unfinalizabilty of consciousness' (Clark & Holquist, 1984: 247) and to account for new, unanticipated situations where actions are contested and where individuals must improvise new, unrehearsed responses.

In the discussion so far the implicit emphasis has been on individuals acting within socially and culturally constrained situations. However, this underplays the collective, collaborative dimensions of the student teachers' enterprise of learning to teach. The new world is actually being *co-constructed*. These collective aspects can generate particular and powerful synergies when people are mutually engaged in a common enterprise, drawing on the same repertoire of social and cultural tools as part of what we can call an evolving 'community of practice' (Lave & Wenger, 1991; Wenger, 1998). This is the focus of the next section.

Exploring Communities of Practice

The third impetus for the UAE study was my fascination with the strength of the community the student teachers were creating and the powerful synergies that were operating among them as they learned to teach within the B.Ed. programme. A fruitful framework for thinking about the sort of synergies that working together and being part of a group can engender is offered by the concept of a 'community of practice' (Lave & Wenger, 1991; Wenger, 1998). The notion of 'communities of practice' has received considerable acceptance and recognition from the education and social science community, particularly following the publication of Wenger's book of the same title (Barton & Tusting, 2005b; Boud & Middleton, 2003; Buysse *et al.*, 2003; Fetterman, 2002; Graham *et al.*, 1998; Hung & Nichani, 2002; Lee & Valdarrama, 2003; Moreno, 2001; Porter, 2003; Rover, 2003; Wesley & Buysse, 2001). In terms of the preceding discussion of identities and identity development, the communities of practice framework draws on much of the same foundational literature, particularly the sociocultural theories of Vygotsky, though it also draws on ideas from anthropology and social theory (Barton & Tusting, 2005a). As we will see, there is a considerable and significant degree of affinity between the three dimensions of identity described above and the three modes of belonging to a community of practice that are described below. Since 'communities of practice' is a theory of learning, a theory of identity, a theory of meaning, a theory of community and a theory of practice, it offers considerable potential for thinking about a community of students whose common enterprise is to learn the practices of teaching. Discourse is central here too, since as discussed in the section, Exploring Discourse, discourse produces and reflects both the subject matter of knowledge and learning, and the community of users of that knowledge. Within the communities of a practice model, learning is both the 'engine of practice' and a 'source of social structure' (Wenger, 1998: 96). The notion of a community of practice as embodying a shared history of learning is thus a useful model for describing and capturing the emergent, nascent features of a group whose very raison d'être as a group is centred around learning. But what do we mean by a 'community of practice'?

Dimensions of a community of practice

A community of practice is a group whose coherence as a community is defined (Wenger, 1998) as comprising three dimensions: *mutual engagement, joint enterprise* and *shared repertoire*

Mutual engagement refers to participation in an endeavour or practice whose meanings are negotiated among participants. We can distinguish here between sustained, continuously reproducing communities, whose members' engagement in practice is part of some enterprise that matters, and the looser affiliation and more transient existence of, say, a working party or a professional association (Barab & Duffy, 2000). In the context of this study, learning to teach is an enterprise that matters in the former sense and one that clearly engages those included in it. Inclusion in and engagement with the relevant practice are two sides of a coin here: 'Being included in what matters is a requirement for being engaged in a community's practice, just as engagement is what defines belonging' (Wenger, 1998: 74). Indeed, the significance of mutual engagement is such that it has the capacity to overcome difference and diversity. However, this does not imply homogeneity within the community. Aside from the differences individuals bring with them, members of a community may have distinct roles and make complementary contributions to the enterprise in question. At times, as Creese (2005) points out, Wenger tends to emphasize the communal rather than the conflictual aspects of communities of practice, with newcomers inducted into the meanings and practices established by old-timers, but at other times the possibility of tension and conflict are acknowledged:

> In real life, mutual relations among participants are complex mixtures of power and dependence, pleasure and pain, expertise and helplessness, success and failure, achievement and deprivation, alliance and competition, ease and struggle, authority and collegiality, anger and tenderness, attraction and repugnance, fun and boredom, trust and suspicion, friendship and hatred. (Wenger, 1998: 77)

This prompts the question, raised by Gee (2005: 214), as to whether membership is a helpful notion when 'there are so many different ways and degrees of being a member in some communities'. In the context of the UAE study, however, membership remains a fruitful concept, given the relative homogeneity of the community, as we shall see in later chapters.

Joint enterprise refers to the focus of activity that links members of a community of practice. In the context of the UAE study, the joint enterprise was learning to teach which, as argued in the section, Exploring Identity, entails the formation of a teacher identity. In practice, neither the choice of this enterprise, nor its conditions, need – and most likely will not – have been created or be controlled by the members. In the context of the HCT B.Ed. degree, the student teachers did not get together as a group and decide to learn to become teachers, establishing the structures to facilitate this activity. Nevertheless, through their ongoing negotiation of their response to the conditions of this activity, it can be said to 'belong[s] to them in a profound sense, in spite of all the forces and influences that are beyond their control' (Wenger, 1998: 77). This is not to say that their responses to the conditions constraining them will be identical. On the other hand, their community is created by and reflected in the common focus of their differing responses.

Shared repertoire refers to the common resources for creating meaning that result from engagement in joint enterprise. In the world of teachers for example, timetables, tests, lessons, projects, photocopiers, assemblies and staff meetings are all given meaning and coherence within the joint enterprise of teaching. Within this coherence, the elements of a shared repertoire will be quite disparate and may include 'routines, words, tools, ways of doing things, stories, gestures, symbols, genres, actions or concepts that the community has produced or adopted in the course of its existence, and which have become part of its practice' (Wenger, 1998: 83).

A community's set of shared resources has both a synoptic or 'reificatory' dimension and a dynamic 'participatory' dimension. These dimensions are related in that temporarily reified historical meanings have to be continually renegotiated within the context of participation in ongoing practice. Historical meanings thus both constrain new meanings while at the same time providing a foundation for, and enabling the development of, new meanings. Indeed, Wenger specifically links his notion of a shared repertoire of meanings that are continually renegotiated in practice, to discourse (see Note 12 in Wenger, 1998: 289), in the sense of a resource for constructing statements about the world and coordinating engagement in practice, as defined by Foucault (1972) and Gee (1996); nonetheless, a number of commentators have critiqued the lack of a fully developed theory of 'language in use' in Wenger's communities of practice model (Barton & Tusting, 2005a; Creese, 2005; Tusting, 2005), a point which is addressed in this book by utilizing linguistic tools of discourse analysis.

The dual aspects of meaning, 'reification' and 'participation' are part of Wenger's overall model linking the ongoing (re)creation of a community with the negotiations of meaning entailed by the evolution of its practices, necessitating ongoing learning and resulting in identity (trans)formation. However, it is worth noting that the identity-transforming implications of learning by engaging in the practices of a community are not necessarily positive and may entail a loss of familiarity that can be challenging, even threatening (Harris & Shelswell, 2005) and that, given the multiple nature of identities, can also lead to conflict between the demands of different dimensions of identity (Wortham, 2003).

First though, it is worth noting that the features of mutual engagement, joint enterprise and shared repertoire do not need to be consciously and explicitly articulated – or reified – as such for a community of practice to exist. On the other hand, the experience of meaningfulness that a community of practice engenders may be all the harder to move beyond or to modify and adapt when circumstances change, if meanings are not consciously and explicitly articulated. In either case, the sense of meaningful coherence engendered by a community of practice can be both liberating and constraining, both a strength and a weakness. This has relevance for the HCT student teachers given the temporal limits – at least for each cohort of students – of the situation that engendered the community, though we need to bear in mind changes of membership are part and parcel of any community of practice.

As was discussed in relation to discourse, the most useful concepts are often ones that are best defined at what might be called a mid-range level of precision. In this spirit, we do not want to label any group or community a community of practice, but neither do we want exact parameters defining a community of practice ('more than six but less than twenty five members, with regular weekly interaction'). What is essential is that the characteristics of mutual engagement, joint enterprise and shared discourse repertoire are present to a substantial and meaningful degree. This does, however, raise the question of how to account for groups that may be outside, but nevertheless impinge upon, a given community of practice. This question is addressed by the notion of locality.

Locality

To account for the possibility that groups and their activities may be related without them forming a community of practice we can talk of 'locality', including proximity of practices, which may involve but is not limited to geographical proximity, institutional affiliation and frequency of interaction. We can talk in terms of 'constellations' of practices on the basis of any of the following: shared history; related enterprises; institutional membership; similar challenges or conditions; common members; common artefacts; relations of proximity or interaction; common or overlapping practices, styles or representational repertoire; and being in competition for common resources (Wenger, 1998: 127). However, 'the relations that constitute practice are *primarily* defined by learning' (Wenger, 1998: 131, emphasis added); hence, there are valid reasons for not considering just any related configurations of individuals and activities a 'community of practice'.

For example, the students in a given institution like the HCT, enrolled in different disciplines, are not engaged in the same enterprise; some are learning to be computer software designers, others to be business managers, while the B.Ed. students are learning to teach. Similarly, although the teacher education students at the HCT, Zayed University and the University of the United Arab Emirates are all learning to teach, they have all developed different repertoires and routines according to the parameters set by their institutions and programmes. Nor do the groups from various institutions interact with each other except at special, occasional events such as conferences. For different reasons, the friendship groups within the B.Ed. students are not a community of practice in that they are not defined by significant enterprises that are different from the wider group of B.Ed. students.

In particular, it is worth examining how, despite the fact that the mainly Western expatriate HCT college teachers and the mainly Arab expatriate school teachers are integrally related to the HCT student teachers and their activities, the latter comprise a distinct community of practice. For although there is a degree of common discourse and practice, as well as some relations of mutuality, between the student teachers, the college teachers and the school teachers, there are also significant distinctions that make for a complex set of interrelations. The student teachers share Arabic as a common first language with the government school teachers, but the professional discourse the students subscribe to is shared with the college teachers, while at the same time being used by the student teachers to dissociate themselves from the government school teachers, despite the fact that the students' future lies within the government school teachers' community. Contributing to this dissociation is the fact that the government school teachers are not trained as mentors and hence, are positioned as merely representative of the government school system, rather than as an integral partner in the professional learning process. Yet unlike the pre-service student teachers, the college and school teachers are both communities of established professionals and they also share an evaluative relation vis-à-vis the student teachers, although there are significant constructed differences in that the status of the college teachers is significantly 'higher' as reflected in the far greater weight the college teachers' evaluations carry in percentage terms and in the eyes of the students, compared to the school teachers' evaluations. In relation to the practices of teacher education, these different communities are linked in differing degrees by shared discourse features, and by mutual engagement in a common enterprise, without these features coming together in such a way as to comprise a single community of practice.

Another aspect of locality is the distinction between the global and the local. The teaching profession is practised across the world, while the language the students are learning to teach is increasingly global. Yet the students are forging identities as teachers of English in the specific local context of the UAE; and within the UAE in diverse settings including dynamic international cities, like Dubai, as well as more rural and relatively quiet towns, like Ras Al Khaimah. Thus the student teachers' identities are being constructed in a context that draws on both local and global discursive resources for making meanings.

Boundaries and border practices

Inevitably, since we have been talking about communities, constellations of communities, proximity and locality, we need to consider the issue of boundaries and borders. Just as in considering identities we are defined as much by who we are not, so communities of practice have explicit and implicit markers of inclusion and exclusion, be these reified objects, symbols or instruments, or be they practices, such as acting and interacting in certain ways rather than others. Whichever aspect we are viewing, object or practice, it is the particular configuration, rather than the individual practices and objects that distinguishes a community.

The shared objects and practices that provide connections across communities can be thought of as boundary objects and border practices and they are often the means by which we connect with and influence each other. In the educational context, the portfolio is a good example of such a shared object which, with its associated practices, can introduce elements from one community into another. Portfolios were originally the favoured method of assessment in art and architecture programmes but have now become common in a range of different educational areas. Within teacher education, portfolios cross-pollinate ideas, practices and experiences as they travel between schools and universities.

As well as objects and practices, members may also cross boundaries by being members of multiple communities with the potential to be a source of continuity and/or discontinuity across different communities and practices. Overall, we need to note that boundaries and boundary practices can be both a source of transformative connections as well as a source of risk, insomuch as they have the potential to become barriers and lead to conflicts that stifle those same transformations (Harris & Shelswell, 2005: 170–172).

In the Introduction I argued that learning to teach could usefully be considered a process of identity formation. The discussion in this section has provided a brief introduction to the conceptual framework of communities of practice and enabled us to explore some of the ways in which this framework captures and establishes a basis for discussing the shared social meanings, processes and practices of learning to teach. Indeed, the communities of practice model is part of a social theory of learning in which identity, practice, community, learning and meaning are all interconnected. Together, these elements of learning, practice, meaning and community will both shape and constitute an evolving – in the sense that it is never complete – identity. But to capture the role of community, meaning, practice and learning in processes of formation of identities it is necessary to consider different ways or 'modes' of belonging to a community of practice, including engagement, imagination and alignment (Wenger, 1998).

Dimensions of Identity and Modes of Belonging

In order to make sense of the formation of identities in their full social, cultural and historical context we need to look beyond day-to-day engagement with practice (Wenger, 1998: 173). As Porter comments in the context of her work in teacher education, student teachers 'need to find learning environments that challenge them to contribute as whole persons, to *imagine* themselves as valued professionals whose work truly matters, and to *align* their vocation with their values' (Porter, 2003: 51, emphasis added). Wenger's three modes of belonging enable us to give due consideration to all these dimensions of teacher formation. The three modes of belonging are:

- Engagement: the active involvement in mutual processes of establishing and maintaining joint enterprises and the meanings of – and means of discussing – these.
- Imagination: creating and sharing images of world and seeing and making connections across time and space by extrapolating beyond our own experience.
- Alignment: coordinating our activities within broader structures and enterprises.

Earlier in this chapter we developed three dimensions of identities: positional identities referencing our relations to others in terms of social positioning and power; figurative identities describing our taking on of narrative-focused roles within meaningful social activity; and authored identities providing scope and space for agency through internal conversations and improvisation. Without mapping exactly onto the modes of belonging – for example both figurative and authored identities entail imagination – there is nevertheless a strong degree of congruence and affinity between the dimensions of identity as described earlier and the modes of belonging which are explained in more detail below.

Engagement is an essential starting point for achieving purposeful ends. It enables us to jointly establish, define the meaning of and sustain our activities. It provides a space in which to create a shared reality, within which we can act and construct our identities. In a sense it is a vital starting point. But for a community of practice to have an impact beyond its own boundaries it needs more as Wenger explains:

> Engagement, however, can also be narrow. The understanding inherent in shared practice is not necessarily one that gives members broad access to the histories or relations with other practices that shape their own practice. Through engagement, competence can become so transparent, locally ingrained, and socially efficacious that it becomes insular; nothing else, no other viewpoint can even register, let alone create a disturbance or a discontinuity that would spur the history of the practice onward. In this way a community of practice can become an obstacle to learning by entrapping us in its very power to sustain our identity. (Wenger, 1998: 175)

Engagement is one way of creating the space within which to construct a reality and an identity.

Imagination offers another way of doing this at either an individual or a communal level. Wenger refers here to Benedict Anderson's (1983) conception of nations and nationalism as being a form of 'imagined communities'. Indeed, at both the individual and the communal levels, imagination is rooted in shared experiences and interactions however far it moves beyond these. This also involves the notion of trajectories as a part of our identities, involving recollections of the past and anticipations of the future integrated into the ongoing present. Like engagement, however, imagination carries a risk; whereas engagement can find us locked into present realities, imagination can find us removed from them, 'losing touch with the sense of social efficacy by which our experience of the world can be interpreted as competence' (Wenger, 1998: 175).

Whereas imagination entails transcending our current realities in time and space, alignment entails connecting ours to other realities, other enterprises, other communities of practice. In this sense it has a distinctly instrumental, even political, orientation. Alignment does not have to entail copying or being subsumed within the practices of others, but at least some degree of coordination is implicit here. However, this coordination between different perspectives brings with it different possibilities for negotiability from different positions of power.

The three modes of belonging provide a dialogic framework for understanding how communities of practice are constituted and operate as well as understanding how identities are constituted within communities of practice. 'Most of what we do involves a combination of engagement, imagination and alignment, though more emphasis on one or the other gives a distinct quality to our actions and their meanings' (Wenger, 1998: 183). However, we need to bear in mind that the modes of belonging, like the dimensions of identity discussed previously, are in 'reality' interrelated and intertwined. It is also the case that 'identity work' in one mode will influence the other modes of identity and that, to be effective, each mode needs to converge and be brought to bear with the others on a given enterprise.

Co-constructing Identity, Discourse and Community

In the Introduction I mentioned that the UAE study was motivated by three interrelated factors: the student teachers' exemplification of becoming a teacher as the development of a teacher identity, the strength of the community that the student teachers created and the passion and commitment of the students to educational discourses. The three constructs of discourse, identity and community are integrally related, as will become increasingly clear as the discursive construction of identity and community in the UAE study unfolds over the course of this book. Here I will briefly explore these interrelations in theoretical terms.

In theorizing as a way of trying to understand these interrelated factors of identity, community and discourse, this book draws on a number of 'genetic' (Vygotsky's term), 'dialogic' (Bakhtin's term) or 'contextualized' models, i.e. dynamic models that inquire into origins and see any factor as interpretable only in relation to other factors, as opposed to models that operate at the level of discrete, synoptic descriptions. Such a contextual approach is common to the Hallidayan and Vygotskian theories that have provided the underpinning of the HCT B.Ed. programme, as well as to discourse theory, dialogism and the communities of practice model that are drawn on in this book.

Central to both Vygotsky's and Halliday's work is a belief in the mutually constitutive nature of culture and language, as they both shape and, in turn, are shaped by individuals, communities and their practices, and an emphasis on the dynamic and active aspect of language in use (Wells, 1999). The community of practice model similarly sees identities as co-constructed along with the learning and the meaning-making that are part of the practices of a community. Meanwhile, discourse theory (for the moment glossing over specific differences of emphasis between the discourse models discussed earlier in this chapter) likewise sees language as discourse as constitutive of 'reality' at multiple levels including systems of knowledge and belief, interpersonal social relations and intrapersonal identities (Fairclough, 1992) and, like dialogism, recognizes how individual utterances are saturated with social and ideological factors.

Thus, despite differences of emphasis,[1] there are essential complementarities here, in terms of recognition of the mutually constitutive nature of the social and the individual, yet each theoretical model offers different insights into the processes at work. Vygotskian theory allows us to conceptualize how the students' ongoing development as individuals occurs within the affordances mediated by the social practices and discourses of the student teachers' community. The communities of practice model enables us to see how the student teachers' co-construct both identities and community through their mutual engagement in the joint enterprise of learning to teach, their alignment with a shared discourse and their imaginative integration of past and future in the present. Discourse theory illuminates how the co-construction of the student teachers' identities and their community unfolds via the articulation of a partial, contingent and differential (in the sense of operating through systems of equivalence and difference) fixation of meaning, and hence allows us to explore power-related issues of inclusion and exclusion. Halliday's theory of language as social semiotic offers the sort of detailed linguistic framework that is lacking in both Vygotsky's theories and the communities of practice framework, and allows us to supplement discourse theory with detailed linguistic tools, so as to identify and explore detailed instances of the students' utterances and interactions discursively construing the ideational content of their systems of knowledge and belief, the interpersonal relations of their community and their intrapersonal identities. Dialogism helps us recognize the essential intertextuality and heterogeneity of discourse, while also emphasizing the work of authorship involved as the student teachers answer the multiple-voiced discourses addressing them.

Thinking of identity, discourse and communities of practice, we see a continual interplay between representation, in terms of categories and labels, and lived practice, as the former shape, but are also continually reshaped, renegotiated and reworked within the practices of day-to-day life. This tension between fixation–reification and negotiation–participation is common to social practices and discourses as each shapes and, in turn, is shaped by identities and communities.

Thus, as a function of the multiple and dynamic social worlds and social conversations that we participate in over time and space, each of us has a configuration of multiple identities forged in the dynamic interplay between discourse and practice, reification and participation, individual reflection and social recognition; indeed, identity arises out of this perpetual tension (Woodward, 2002: 100). This interplay resonates with that between positional, figurative and authored identities. These identities are constructed as we position ourselves, and are positioned by others, within discourse; as we learn through participation in meaningful activities that comprise the figured worlds (including their associated representational-symbolic frameworks) that have value within particular communities; and as we self-author ourselves in the interstices, silences, tensions and contradictions that constantly emerge within and between discursive and social practices. This ongoing process of becoming involves trajectories and connections across time and space, linking past, present and future, global and local; it is in this complex sense that identity arises from the co-construction of discourse and community.

Conclusion

This chapter has provided an overview of a theory of discourse. I have argued that it is through discourse that the social production of meaning occurs. This entails a view of discourse as constitutive of, rather than merely reflective of 'reality'; of discourse as structured patterns of language; of discursive practices as maintaining or transforming existing social relations; and of discourse analysis as exploring these patterns in specific contexts. I have argued that discourse is foundational to a 'whole package' that includes theoretical framework and methodology as well as analysis and interpretation. I have argued for a 'multiperspectival' approach to discourse that draws on the insights of a number of theoretical elaborations but is, at the same time, principled in selecting and combining their insights.

I have outlined a theory of identity involving: positional identities concerned with relations of power and position with regard to others; figurative identities concerned with envisioning the self in relation to social narratives and situations; and authored identities concerned with agency derived from inner conversations and practices of improvisation. This model allows us to account for both the constraints of social conditions and the potential for individuality within these constraints.

I have also outlined key features of a communities of practice model, which allows us to consider identity development as part of a broader theory of learning, meaning, practice and community, and theorized the HCT B.Ed. students as an evolving community of practice characterized by mutual engagement in a joint enterprise involving a shared repertoire of discourse. Within this model I have described the three key modes of belonging to a community of practice: engagement, alignment and imagination. I described how these modes are congruent and have affinity with figurative, positional and authored identities, respectively.

Finally, I examined the congruence of discourse and practice when thinking about identities, while recognizing the tensions, for example, between participation and reification, the individual and the social, that are inevitable in thinking about identity, before briefly exploring some of the ways we can productively think in terms of the co-construction of identity, discourse and community.

The following chapter employs the notion of discourse as a means to understand the UAE context which forms the historical, cultural and social setting, and outlines the approach to discourse analysis underpinning the research on which this book is based.

Notes

1. It should be noted that there are significant differences between discourse and ideology, the most significant of which is probably the latter's implied contrast to some 'true', non-ideological alternative; see Foucault, 1980, p. 118 on this point.
2. Vygotsky's and Wenger's work foreground practice, whereas discourse is central in the work of Laclau and Mouffe, Foucault, Bakhtin and Volosinov. Nevertheless, the work of each of these theorists is multidimensional and, as

Chapter 2
The Discursive Context

In this chapter we examine some of the contextual factors that have shaped the development of the student teachers' evolving community of practice. This is carried out on two levels: first, by providing an overview of the historical development of the contemporary UAE from a socio-discursive perspective and second, by examining the content and structure of the HCT B.Ed. degree from a perspective of teaching as an 'amalgam' of discourses (Coldron & Smith, 1995). Finally, the research processes underpinning the book are briefly outlined.

Discourse and the Formation of the UAE

> Cities with skyscrapers ... a sophisticated network of highways crisscrossing the country, cars zooming about ... tree lined boulevards ... magnificent shopping malls ... fun parks ... a communications network that can be the envy of the world ... all lie side by side with the silent desert, wind tunnels and camels ... much has changed within so short a time ... if ever there was an ode to progress the United Arab Emirates would be it.

The above passage from the website of the UAE Tourism Bureau (http://www.uae.org.ae/general/contents.htm) reflects many of the discursive threads that are key to any understanding of the contemporary United Arab Emirates, including reference, through terms like 'network' and 'communications', to the discourse of globalization, to which the unchanging local world is presented as a calm backdrop offering peace and relaxation. The word 'silent' reinforces the notion that prior to oil-driven, modern development, the geographic area now the UAE was an 'empty quarter' without a significant voice or presence in regional social or economic affairs, even though it has since become an 'ode to progress', a phrase which positions the UAE as striving to catch up with ideas of modernity issuing from elsewhere. Any text is also interesting for its omissions, as much as for what is explicitly fore-grounded; in this context it is interesting to note the absence of either 'Arab/ic/ian' or 'Islam', perhaps a concession to contemporary discourses of a 'clash of civilizations' between Islam and the West.

At one level this rhetorical extolling of the harmonious multidimensional nature of the UAE is merely part of the myth-making process that inevitably accompanies nation formation – and Findlow (2000: 44) describes the UAE as a prime example of the 'invented' or 'willed' nation – but it is hard not to notice the employment of a Hegelian dialectic between the march of progress towards civilization and the West, represented by the 'cities with skyscrapers', the 'sophisticated network of highways' and 'the communications network that can be [sic] the envy of the world'; versus the timelessness of the East represented by the 'silent desert, wind tunnels and camels.' Indeed, Findlow (2005: 287) refers to the UAE as schizophrenic with its 'acute juxtaposition of the global and the local, indigenous and imported, traditional and modern, idealistic and pragmatic'.

In this context Willinsky's (1998: 1) description of the ways 'we are schooled in differences great and small, in borderlines and boundaries, in historical struggles and exotic practices, all of which extend the meaning of difference…so we can appreciate the differences between civilized and primitive, West and East, first and third worlds' has prescient relevance. Willinsky urges us to appreciate how these differences have been *constructed*. Following Foucault, he reminds us how knowledge involves an essentialized naming of a known object or 'other' by a knowing subject so they can be learned and relearned to the advantage of some and the disadvantage of others, and how any instance of knowledge is only one way of knowing the world. Willinsky captures the assumptions entailed by this knower/known, subject/object dichotomy and the 'bringing into being' that naming involves in his question, 'Where is here?' This disarmingly simple question is worth asking in any context but it seems a particularly appropriate place to begin a consideration of the contemporary UAE.

Kazim (2000) presents a reading of UAE history and society in which successive 'socio-discursive formations' have involved both continuities and discontinuities with the preceding formation(s) as society in each period strives to reproduce itself. He identifies four major socio-discursive formations over the past 1500 years: the *Islamic, transformational, colonial* and *contemporary* periods. Below, in a reading heavily indebted to Kazim's work, I briefly summarize this history, noting how traces of each period's discursive patterns can still be seen in contemporary UAE society.

The Islamic period

The Islamic period (AD 600–1500) saw the spread of Islam across the Arabian peninsula and the incorporation of the local population into the *Umma* or body of the faithful. This was accompanied by the enhanced importance of Arabic as a language in the region, the conduct of trade according to Islamic principles, and the increased prestige of the mercantile strata through discourses that emphasized their importance as agents of international Islamization and as possessors of increased wealth. These discourses exacerbated differences between the urban and rural populations, differences which were further highlighted by the growth of Islamic arts and the construction of mosques in the cities.

Among the non-urban social and economic groups, further differentiations were constructed between the settled agricultural dwellers and the nomadic, tribal dwellers, who provided protection and guidance to cross-peninsula traders. The tribal groups constructed themselves as superior through the discourse of *Nisab*, or worthy ancestry, while the agricultural groups constructed their own superiority through discourses of productivity linked to land ownership and cultivation.

The transformational period

The transformational period (1500–1820) saw the penetration of not just the Arabian peninsula and the Gulf but the wider Indian ocean region by European trade and colonial activity. This was also the period that saw the expulsion of the Arabic and Islamic population from the Iberian peninsula at its commencement and included Portuguese attempts to supplant Islam with Christianity in south Asia. The transformational period was marked by the increasing militarization of the region, still evident in the prevalence of historic forts, which now form tourist attractions. The period was also marked by the reduction of the wealth and prestige of the mercantile strata, as they were reduced to a subordinate role within regional trade, control of which was taken, first by the Portuguese and later by the Dutch, French, and finally by the British. This colonial takeover of Gulf trade and its incorporation into wider, foreign-controlled trade networks had a number of consequences, including the decline in terms of wealth and power of many of the region's cities, such as Khor Fakkan and Hormuz, at a time when European cities like Amsterdam and London were on the ascendant, the increasing significance of the pearling industry as a source of income for coastal dwelling populations, and the emergence of counter-discourses of resistance to European penetration and control.

The colonial period

The colonial period (1820–1971) commenced with the establishment of British dominance in the Arabian peninsula and closed with the emergence of the modern United Arab Emirates from what had been known as Trucial Oman (as distinct from the wider region of historic Oman). The term 'trucial' is a reference to the truces or treaties imposed on the region by the British, who seized economic and political control, justifying the practice of restricting and impounding local shipping through discourses such as fighting 'piracy' and safeguarding 'free trade', and championing 'anti-slavery' (at a time when the British were freely conducting trade with the slave-reliant Brazilian and American economies). This period saw Trucial Oman divided into seven emirates, each with its own police force, passports, postage stamps and, perhaps most significantly, its own ruling sheikh. The latter years of this period witnessed the relinking of the region to global trade networks though the discovery and development of oil and natural gas resources. British withdrawal took place against a backdrop of anti-colonial resistance movements in other parts of the world; and though their withdrawal was heralded by the British as peaceful, this was in part so as not to engender the armed resistance encountered elsewhere, for example, in Aden. The increasing role of international bodies at this time can be seen in the fact that the UAE became the one hundred and thirty second member of the United Nations and the eighteenth member of the Arab League. The increasingly prominent discourse of Arab nationalism that the League reflected was another reason behind the unification in 1971 of the seven Trucial sheikhdoms into the United Arab Emirates.

The contemporary period

The contemporary period was accompanied by the meteoric rise of income from oil revenues, particularly after the 1973 'OPEC crisis'. The central federal government's control over these revenues was an instrument for penetrating and integrating civil society through welfarism (UAE nationals are entitled to free health care and free education at all stages as well as subsidized housing and utilities and payments to assist with the costs of marriage and child raising as means of encouraging population growth), education and infrastructure. In particular, the poorer emirates are linked to Abu Dhabi through federal government expenditure on 'nation building' projects which, like UAE 'citizenship', have ensured further integration and cohesion. In a similar fashion, government accommodation of Islam through the funding of mosque construction, the payment of the salaries of imams (who are on the payroll of the Ministry of Islamic Affairs), funding of Islamic associations, the inclusion of Shari'a law within the legal code and the inclusion of Islamic studies in the school curriculum, have all meant that Islamic identity has been incorporated into UAE identity rather than becoming a locus of political discontent. Meanwhile, the continued significance of the discourse of worthy ancestry or *nisab* has facilitated social reproduction and ensured the continued power of certain groups.

The contemporary period has seen elements of earlier periods continue into the present but in altered form. Examples of such continuities are the political structures of hereditary rule, the economic structures of agriculturalism, mercantilism and industrialism, and the sociocultural structures of language, art, food, dress and religious beliefs. Other aspects of earlier periods are reconstructed within the contemporary formation to facilitate its reproduction, for example, camel racing (government sponsored along with boat racing and Arabian horse racing; for a discussion of the reconstruction of the 'tradition' of camel racing see Khalaf (2000); see Hobsbawm and Ranger (1992) for a wider discussion of 'invented traditions'), urban sculptures of coffee pots, pearl shells and sailing dhows, and traditional Bedouin 'tents' located in the marbled atria of hotels and shopping malls. At the same time, the contemporary period has its own constructions in each of these areas, for example: a UAE federal government, which develops foreign policy and issues passports in the political sphere; sophisticated oil, tourism and banking industries linked to globalization in the economic sphere; and the development of multiculturalism and consumerism in the sociocultural sphere.

The thrusts of these continuities, changing patterns and new constructions, can be seen in three key discourses structuring the contemporary UAE: the 'conservative' discourse, seeking to preserve past patterns; the 'progressive' embracing liberalization and globalization; and 'moderate' discourse, seeking a balance between the first two. All three discourses are accommodated by UAE policy makers, as each contributes in different ways to the socio-discursive reproduction of the contemporary UAE social formation (Kazim, 2000: 452-456).

As noted above, the contemporary period has been characterized by phenomenal oil-derived wealth which, along with the rapid social and economic development it has enabled, has led to dramatic growth of the expatriate population to meet the labour needs of the exponentially expanding (in the sense that new workers generate new economic demands which require new workers to meet them etc.) economic activity, to the point where Emiratis now make up only 20% of the population. The expanding economy has been given a further boost by the related discourses of consumerism and new globalism that have accompanied the increasing penetration of the economy by multinational companies and by the growth of tourism. The stratification and segmentation of the UAE workforce (by nationality, ethnicity, gender, educational level, emirate of residence and nisab) has also been facilitated by globalization, which has ensured the availability of a cheap and relatively easy to exploit labour force, and also enables expatriate populations to maintain contact with the home country through newspapers, magazines, satellite television, short wave radio, the Internet, computerized banking and films.

Yet the phenomenal wealth that has enabled this highly effective and rapid nation building has also engendered a number of problems:

> In addition to the negative and all pervading effects of rentierism on the national population and the kind of subsidy-based nonproductive culture it has promoted across the state, the development of the UAE's modernizing monarchies and their politics have suffered from a number of other significant internal pathologies. (Davidson, 2005: 238)

These 'pathologies' include the political acquiescence of the population in return for cradle to grave welfare, the extensive patrimonial and rentier networks, self-interested bureaucracies, disparities in terms of goals and objectives between elites and their clients leading to the frequent subversion of policy implementation processes, disparities between the high salaries and low skill requirements in the public sector, an enduring economic over-reliance on foreign technologies and skills, and a lack of free civic space (Davidson, 2005; Muysken & Nour, 2006). The situation is not assisted by the complete overlap between the all-powerful executive and members of the ruling families, whose power is unchecked by a non-elected legislative chamber of appointed 'representatives' that is incapable, for the most part, of critiquing or challenging the executive (Davidson, 2005).

This description of history and society in the United Arab Emirates acknowledges both change and continuity and offers a far more complex and nuanced picture than that offered by a 'culturalist' framework, reflected in Richardson's (2004) discussion of the contemporary UAE. Richardson employs expressions like 'Arab-Islamic values' and defines the country as a 'stronghold' of such values. The term 'stronghold' implies a refuge or fort, both of which carry overtones of being under siege or in a state of combat. Moreover, while religious awareness implicitly underpins all aspects of social policy in the UAE, to talk about 'Arab-Islamic values' as if these can be taken as given, ignores the fact that the relationship between Islamic and Arab identities is 'associative' and not 'intrinsic' (Findlow, 2000; Halliday, 2003). This formulation in no way does justice to the complexity of history and society in the UAE that we have glimpsed above. It also ignores past and present contestations over the meaning of these 'values' (see, for example, Halliday, 2003; Safi, 2003 for deconstructions of the constructs 'Arab' and 'Islamic'), ignoring 'the wide diversity of identity constructs in the Muslim world and within the Arab-Muslim world' (Findlow, 2000: 1).

Overall, the above reading of UAE history and society is congruent with the model of discourse and society underpinning this book, where particular social conversations, particular ways of creating meaning and of understanding the world – in other words, discourses – are appropriated, refashioned and reconstructed as part of the ongoing and never-completed work of society's self-reproduction. In the following section I look in particular at discourses of collective identity in the UAE.

Discourses of Contemporary Collective Identity in the UAE

During the postcolonial era, many nationalisms were constructed in opposition to the former colonial presence (Gandhi, 1998). In this context, Kazim (2000) argues that the UAE's collective identity has been formed, to some degree, in relation to both the internal presence of a large expatriate population and in relation to the external forces of globalization. Indeed, a key feature of the politico-economic scene in the UAE is ongoing disputes between those wary of globalization, wishing to preserve the sociocultural status quo based on an oil economy, and those arguing for pro-globalization policies, who seek to liberalize and diversify the economy. Related to these issues is a desire for economic self-sufficiency as a reaction to the dependence on foreign, imported labour that finds expression in the discourse of Emiratization or nationalization of the workforce. This is reflected in the establishment of Emiratization quotas for private employers and increasing requirements for public institutions to consider UAE nationals alongside expatriates for any vacancies.

But despite ongoing concerns about 'cultural contamination' (Davidson, 2005: 262), particularly from the West, it is a mistake to see UAE collective identity as constructed purely in reaction to perceived external threats. To the extent that the UAE is a 'willed nation' (Findlow, 2000) or an 'imagined community' (Anderson, 1983), the basis for UAE collective identity lies partly in shared social norms and partly in the common partaking in shared economic success, as well as the shared social infrastructure that, as we have seen above, this success has enabled UAE policy makers to put in place. As Findlow notes, 'the UAE government actively encourages active participation in building the country' (2000: 43) reflected in cultural narratives of a 'rags to riches' transition whereby a nation has been built out of nothing. The resulting collective identity, reinforced through the media and the education system, becomes self-reaffirming through repeated performance.

But beyond national development, there is also a desire to be at the cutting edge of modernity in terms of technological sophistication and information-communication capacity, as part of positioning the UAE as a regional business leader and a global tourist attraction. However, it is worth noting that 'the UNDP (2001) technology achievement index (TAI) classification of world countries shows that none of the Gulf countries are classified as leaders, potential leaders or dynamic adopters of technologies in the world' (Muysken & Nour, 2006: 975). Moreover, between 1996 and 2000 the UAE spent 0.02% of gross domestic product on research and development, as compared to 0.14 and 2.7% respectively, for Saudi Arabia and Korea, while the percentage of the labour force with secondary or tertiary qualifications is comparable to countries like Brazil and Mexico and lags far behind countries like Singapore and Korea (Muysken & Nour, 2006). This brings us to the development of the education sector in the UAE, which is the focus of the next section.

Discourses of UAE Education

To support the UAE's rapid economic and social development since 1971, the education system has gone from 74 schools in that year to over 600 in 2004. In terms of indicators of education levels, for example literacy rates, remarkable progress has been made; less than 20% of the population was literate prior to independence in 1971 (Kazim, 2000) in contrast to rates of 75% by 2001, according to the United Nations Development Programme (Ahsan, 2004). However, despite these successes, and despite a prevailing discourse celebrating 'education for all' (Ahsan, 2004: 186), the UAE's education system has come in for some rather severe criticisms from both internal and external sources (Gaad et al., 2006; Loughrey et al., 1999; Mograby, 1999; Muysken & Nour, 2006; Taha-Thomure, 2003). Dr Abdullah Mograby, head of the Labour and Population Studies Department at the Emirates Centre for Strategic Studies and Research, has listed unclear or conflicting missions and goals, inappropriate methods of teaching and learning, and inflexible curricula and programmes leading to high dropout rates and long duration of study (Mograby, 1999). External critics have highlighted poor alignment between educational goals, implementation and evaluation (Gaad et al., 2006), low quality teachers, poor integration between different levels and low 'school life expectancy' (Muysken & Nour, 2006), and a growing problem of graduate and school leaver unemployment, particularly among women (Lefrere, 2007), in part reflecting 'serious disincentives to hire native workers in the private sector due to lack of educational qualifications and provision of high salary and subsidy in the public sector' (Muysken & Nour, 2006: 965). Indeed, the very strength and frequency of the calls for change highlight the gap between idealized and existing levels of schooling, which is at one and the same time both a spur and an obstacle to change. Thus, although the UAE promotes itself as a society that prioritizes education, the figures present 'a discouraging picture' with the UAE's public expenditure on education, as a percentage of gross national product, at only 1.7%, compared with 3.2 and 2.7% respectively, for low income countries like Nepal and Pakistan and 7.6, 5.0 and 3.4% respectively, for the similarly high incomes countries, Israel, Spain and Qatar (Ahsan, 2004: 190). Moreover, only 1% of education spending goes into research and development, compared with between 7 and 8% in Singapore (Mograby, 1999). The challenge is to increase alignment between educational goals and the policies and practices that might support these goals (Gaad et al., 2006).

Given this picture, it is not surprising that quality professional development for teachers is rare, while the lack of career structure for teachers does little to encourage independent professional development. To this end, the increase in numbers of national teachers as a result of initiatives like the HCT B.Ed. programme, whose voices are more likely to be heard than expatriate voices, may assist. Yet again, what on the one hand prompts calls for change is at the same time an inhibiting factor: the poor training of most teachers in UAE schools, highlighted by Loughrey et al. (1999) and Mograby (1999), makes the challenge of improving teaching quality in these same schools all the harder. The situation has not been assisted by the prevailing bureaucratic discourses in UAE educational culture, reflecting 'a system that believes in delivering the content, and automatically assumes that the goals of education will be satisfied if the content is delivered' (Gaad et al., 2006: 302).

In addition, the lack of a fully developed culture of teacher education and the inexperience of most teachers in supervising student teachers means that a new teacher education programme cannot expect the levels of expert support from cooperating school teachers that would be taken for granted elsewhere. Indeed the pre-service trainees are undergoing an education that is substantially different to that of the teachers they are working with who, for the most part, have undergone little, if any, specific educational training (Loughrey et al., 1999). While Fullan (2001) presents research suggesting that some divergence between supervising and student teacher can lead to a productive Piagetian dissonance, there are also those who express concern about student teachers being socialized into non-exemplary teaching practices (Arends & Winitzky, 1996). This pedagogical 'gulf' is exacerbated by the political distance in a relatively stratified society, between the Emirati students and the majority of the teachers, who are non-Emirati, expatriate Arabs, since at present, the majority of English teachers in UAE schools are drawn from other Arabic-speaking nationalitites, such as Egyptians, Jordanians and Palestinians. These teachers were recruited in the early stages of establishing the UAE's education system because they were the most accessible and had cultural affinities with the Emirates (Findlow, 2000). The aim behind the HCT B. Ed. project is to decrease this proportion as part of the Emiratization, or nationalization of the workforce, process. This in itself is a source of potential tension as the expatriate teachers – the same group HCT relies on to supervise teaching placements – are the ones the students will eventually replace. This reflects wider tensions between globalization and nationalism which have been touched upon already and which are discussed below in the context of English education in the UAE.

Discourses of globalization and nationalism in UAE education

Tensions between nationalism and globalization are reflected in the UAE's policy of 'linguistic dualism', whereby English is associated with business, modernity and internationalism while Arabic embodies religion, tradition and localism (Findlow, 2006; Kazim, 2000). This dualistic approach is not made explicit in language policy documents but has evolved through practice, for as Karmani (2005b: 90) notes, in a society without substantial governmental accountability and with relatively weak society–state linkages, 'language education policy and planning decisions are liable to be a hit-and-miss affair'. This 'hit-and-miss' linguistic dualism partly explains the embracing of English as a global language that underpins, and is reflected in, the establishment of the Higher Colleges of Technology as an English medium institution in an Arabic-speaking society. But it is also important to recognize the contemporary 'nexus' between oil and English that underlies the UAE's current 'rentier' economy and lends as much, if not more, effective support to English as would more coercive approaches (Karmani, 2005b). Nevertheless, the important role English has to play in the region is only likely to increase in coming years; thus, a key challenge for the UAE, in common with other countries in the region, is how to resolve, or at least accommodate, 'ambiguities about English' (Ramanthan, 2005) and how to reconcile the competing demands of local, regional, national and religious identities with the homogenizing tendencies of globalization and English (Canagarajah, 1999; Mohd-Asraf, 2005). A solution urged by Karmani (2005b: 101) is 'to explore language education policy and planning solutions that are locally based and help maintain and indeed promote Arab-Islamic values ...

[while] expanding the hugely important role and contribution of bilingual Arab teachers of English.' The HCT B.Ed. programme can be seen as answering this last call.

A number of issues contribute to recognition of the potential significance of issues of language and culture for the students' identities as teachers of English, given the crucial place of identity in teacher education (Britzman, 1991; Danielewicz, 2001; Johnson, 1999; Mayer, 1999; Miller Marsh, 2003) and language learning (Norton, 2000). These include: the fact that the students' teacher education is completely in a language other than their mother tongue and their nation's language; the fact that they will be teachers of only that language and so will be identified as agents of its penetration/dissemination; the fact that they are entering the world of TESOL teaching which has been so dominated by the notion of the 'native speaker' as the ideal teacher (Holliday, 2005; Pennycook, 1994, 1998; Phillipson, 1992; Braine, 1999; Seidlhofer, 1999). Yet despite the prominence of these issues in the TESOL literature, they turned out to be of less significance in relation to the students' identity construction as language teachers – perhaps in part because 'native' English-speaking teachers are extremely rare in UAE schools that provide the context for the students' concerns – than locally salient constructions of nationality.

However, discourses of language and culture, globalization and nationalism are not the only areas of tension in UAE education. Others include discourses of gender and the role of women in education as both students and teachers, explored in the section below.

Discourses of gender in UAE education

There is no escaping the real limitations on women's lives in UAE society. A number of students commented that teaching was one of the few careers acceptable to their families while a few expressed concerns over whether their future husbands would 'permit' them to pursue a career of any sort. Such attitudes were cited by Lefrere as a possible source of the relatively higher unemployment rates among female school leavers and graduates across the Gulf region (2007: 210). In this context, one of the reasons Richardson feels reflective practice to be inappropriate for Emirati female student teachers is the traditional role of women in a 'male dominated society [that] still resists the idea of women thinking for themselves' (Richardson, 2004: 433). She describes the typical Emirati woman as one who is 'protected from public display and not often involved in the public arena' (Richardson, 2004: 432). Yet reality is so often more complex than such descriptions allow for. One recent commentator, while noting that the continued male domination of society 'remains a stumbling block to true equality', presents a far more optimistic picture of life for Emirati womanhood:

> Women are encouraged to become highly educated ... They are taking on new roles as teachers, doctors and leaders. One out of every three doctors, pharmacists, technicians and administrators is a woman. About twenty per cent of the total work-force are now women. However, in government the percentage is much higher. In this sector, the country's women form forty per cent of the labour force ... Over eighty per cent of the UAE employees within each of the Ministries of Health and Education are women. Many are heads of departments – at par with many Western countries. Strangely, when one thinks of how writers in the West portray Arab women as meek and servile, many UAE women are joining the military and police forces. (Salloum, 2003: 1-2)

Although these statistics are consistent with those available elsewhere (e.g. the United Nations Development Programme), the tone is perhaps overly optimistic. Women's personal status in the UAE is determined by Islamic law which circumscribes their choices in relation to men in numerous ways. While UAE men are allowed to marry non-Muslim women the reverse does not apply. Women are prohibited from leaving the country without permission from a male guardian and must gain written permission in order to work or gain a driving license. Even in aspects of life where the situation seems more equal, closer observation reveals further inequalities. Thus, while UAE men and women have the same opportunities for education in the UAE and while women account for approximately two-thirds of the higher education population, this is partly explained by the fact that men can more easily travel overseas to study at foreign universities. Yet despite their obvious social constraints, women still achieve greater success in education with indicators such as female literacy rates consistently exceeding those of men.

In addition, the scope of opportunities for women is increasing. The UAE government has recently encouraged women to become police officers and volunteers in the military, while the first female taxi drivers in the gulf region began service in the UAE in 2000. UAE women are able fully to own private businesses in the country, a fact that has facilitated their visible participation in the private sector. Most recently, the prominent female entrepreneur, Shaikha Lubna, was appointed as part of a cabinet reshuffle to preside over the Ministry of Economy and Commerce and the Ministry of Planning (Salama, 2004). Against this progress must be set the continued operation of a powerful gender discourse that holds women responsible for the family and the home, as well as for the moral behaviour of men, which combined with the structural limitations of the education system, continues to limit the full leadership potential of women in education as in other sectors. In this context the opportunities for women to aspire to leadership roles in UAE education offered by the HCT's teacher education programme take on special significance.

Discourse and Teacher Education

I discussed discourse earlier as a set of social practices that 'make meaning'. We also considered learning to teach as the process of forming an identity as a teacher. A discourse framework offers a productive model for discussing education, in general, and learning to teach, in particular, given the centrality of language and discourse in the construction of knowledge and the constitution of identities:

> Therefore a good pedagogy is one that recognizes the centrality of discourse and encourages its proliferation ... A pedagogy for learning how to be a teacher (and by extension for becoming a teacher) is characterized by discourse richness, situations that are structured to put into play all possible relations. (Danielewicz, 2001: 141–142)

One way of embracing this complexity is to recognize that education generally, and teaching specifically, is an 'amalgam' of discourses (Coldron & Smith, 1995) that are appropriated and synthesized in the process of learning to teach. In this view the task of learning to teach is to create, through this process of discursive appropriation and synthesis, a philosophy of education, an 'orientation to teaching' (Freeman & Freeman, 2001), in the broadest terms. Such a philosophy will include assumptions and beliefs: about the why and how of teaching and learning; about relationships to learners, to social and institutional contexts and to wider discourse communities of teaching and education; and the embodiment of all of these in a coherent 'teaching self' (Danielewicz, 2001: 117-118).

Coherence in this context does not entail elimination of conflict or seeking a tidy, systematic unity. Employing the metaphor of knowledge as a woven fabric, Buchman and Floden argue that 'educational coherence is found where students can discover *and* establish relations among various areas of sensibility, knowledge and skill, yet where loose ends remain, anticipating a reweaving of beliefs and ties to the unknown' (Buchman & Floden, 1993: 234, emphasis in original). The discursive 'threads' the HCT Emirati students are working with include the wider social discourses of 'conservatism', 'progressivism' and 'moderation' that were outlined in earlier parts of this chapter. The student teachers' discursive resources also include the 'traditional' model of teaching they experienced during their own schooling, and which they still observe in some classrooms at some point during their eight teaching practice rounds (totalling 36 weeks), as well as the 'progressive' models the students see in college, although it is important to realize that pedagogical approaches are not presented to the students in stark oppositional terms but rather as part of a methodological and historical continuum.

What the students are accomplishing in weaving these discursive threads into a coherent and meaningful pattern is a work of imagination leading towards the creation of new teaching selves as part of an evolving community of practice of new English language teachers in the UAE. In the following section I examine the discursive resources available to the student teachers in the specific content of the HCT's teacher education programme.

Student Teachers as Agents of Change

As outlined above, the challenges of improving the effectiveness of the UAE education system and raising student learning outcomes are considerable. In this context, the expectation on the HCT student teachers to contribute in significant ways to the national development and educational change in the UAE cannot be overstated. This, in turn, required a teacher education degree programme of internationally recognized quality and high impact. The design of the B.Ed programme resonates strongly with the nature and scope of language teacher education degrees undertaken in countries such as Hong Kong, Singapore, Canada and Australia, while the majority of the teacher educators – from a diverse range of linguistic and cultural contexts including Australia, Canada, Ireland, Lebanon, New Zealand, South Africa, Tunisia, the UAE, the UK and the US – have experience working in language teacher education and/or language education programmes designed along similar lines. An example of this resonance is the focus on social constructivist pedagogy, that is, on the notion that knowledge is constructed by learners through their engagement in thinking, rather than being transmitted to them by teachers, textbooks or the curriculum, within the enablements and constraints of the social context. A social constructivist approach to teacher education entails a focus on meaningful, purposeful classroom activities which provide opportunities for rich, complex and 'situated' learning and which bear some relation to the sorts of activities in which students and teachers engage in the wider social setting. It also implies a change in the role of the teacher, who becomes a facilitator of learning, assisting students' performance in socially valued, purposeful activities, rather than transmitting or dispensing knowledge. Students' roles also change in the social constructivist classroom, as they become potential sources of 'socially-embedded' learning for peers rather than just passive recipients of knowledge. Other 'change oriented' aspects of the HCT B.Ed. degree are outlined below (see also Clarke *et al.*, 2007).

A change in pedagogy

A repeated criticism of teacher education in the past has been that student teachers learn 'about teaching' rather than 'learning to teach' (Calderhead and Shorrock, 1997; Korthagen, 2001). To ensure that links are made between practice and theory, the *Teaching Practice, Preparation and Review* strand is deliberately constructed as the core of the HCT B.Ed. programme, with placements in schools in each of the eight semesters totalling 36 weeks of school experience over the span of the degree. This is where the learning that the students engage in at the college is 'realized', in the sense of being put into practice or made real. It is also where the college learning is tested so as to further inform ongoing learning in the college classroom. The teaching practice component increases through the degree, culminating in the final semester with the students undertaking a 10-week internship supported by a supervising college teacher-mentor (SCT), and a supervising school teacher-mentor (SST).

In order to enrich students' perspective on the classroom and teaching, the second strand, *Education Studies*, develops an understanding of the basic underlying principles of teaching, learning and schooling, including theories of child and human development, first and second-additional language development, theories of learning, including behaviourist, cognitive-developmental and social constructivist theories. Students also develop their understanding of how to plan for and teach a successful English programme in elementary schools, and analyse classroom management, curriculum development and syllabus design, and assessment and evaluation, while also considering the way in which the societal context of schooling affects what goes on in the classroom.

A change in the nature of the content and focus of English lessons

A third key strand of the B.Ed. degree comprises *English Language Studies*. Here, in addition to general language proficiency, students develop competence in specific classroom language including the use of language for explaining, monitoring, prompting, eliciting, encouraging, correcting, as well as for purposes such as telling stories and singing songs, chants and rhymes. In addition, students develop their knowledge of the nature of language and its uses, including formal language systems (phonology, semantics, grammar, genre and discourse) and related linguistic terminology, but also the social aspects of language, recognizing how the purposes for which it is being used shape the forms it takes and examining notions such as discourse communities, language variation and the links between English and globalization.

A change in the breadth of teacher knowledge

A fourth programme strand, *Complementary Studies*, involves an emphasis on broadening the students' general education while at the same time fostering awareness of potential links between a range of education-related topics and the English language classroom. Thus, for example, students undertake studies on special needs in education, children's literature, information and communication technology and design, media studies and social studies. These areas of study provide students with a broad repertoire of knowledge to draw on in their professional work with students in the classroom, as well as providing an initial foundation for further professional growth.

A change in mode of learning

The HCT has also been proactive in using – and modelling the utilization of – online technologies, such as Web CT. This has facilitated UAE-wide communication and sharing of ideas between students as a community of 'electronic collaborators' (Bonk and King, 1998) and encouraged the sort of socially embedded thinking aloud that precedes shifts in individual cognition. These strategies also encourage the reflective dialogue and considered rehearsal of positions that facilitate the development of an individual 'authorial stance' towards the multiple possibilities for development of 'teaching selves' offered by social and educational discourses.

It is worth emphasizing that online communication is not just a 'high tech' substitute for face-to-face interaction and discussion: 'New technologies construct a totally new environment and this radically alters the way we use our senses and thus the way we act and react to things' (Carter, 1999: 321–322). Online discussion forums from this perspective are an additional vehicle for teacher learning and identity development, through reflective dialogue involving new combinations of elements from existing modes of communication. As Carter goes on to state in the context of his research into using IT forums to extend 'supervisory reach' in the teaching practicum, 'It needs to be stated that the role of technology as an amplifier of human capacities is not to act as a surrogate for face-to-face interaction' (1999: 331). Rather, by utilizing and combining elements from existing communication formats in new ways, technology alters the very nature of our interaction and communication, offering ways of communicating and interacting that are more distributive, interactive and collaborative than would otherwise be possible (Bonk and King, 1998). The use of written forums for reflection and discussion resonates with Kramsch and Lam's (1999) emphasis on the particular suitability of the written mode for language learners.

Foundational-Overarching Principles: Vygotsky, Dewey and Bakhtin in UAE Teacher Education

The powerful theoretical insights of thinkers such as Vygotsky and Bakhtin that inspired the framework for identity development in the previous chapter, along with the seminal work of educators and linguists such as Dewey and Halliday, provide fundamental underpinnings to the HCT B.Ed. degree. To complement the content focus in the sections above, I will sketch out some of the ways that underlying theories have been incorporated into the HCT's teacher education programme.

Assisted performance

Assisted performance involves providing assistance to learners at points in their development where potential for learning exists but the learner is not able to achieve this learning alone; in other words by providing assistance in the learner's zone of proximal development. Teacher educators in the HCT's B.Ed. degree take on significant mentor roles vis-à-vis student teachers by enacting neo-Vygotskian principles of 'assisted performance' (Tharp & Gallimore, 1988), apprenticeship and guided practice within students' zones of proximal development, during visits to students on teaching placements in schools.

The practice of assisted performance is also facilitated by small student numbers. Classes are limited to 20 students and, for a variety of reasons including societal influences and the fact that students are learning in a second language, contact hours are considerably more than would be the case in a similar programme in the West. These factors facilitate a close working relationship between students and staff and among students themselves. The value of these close relationships between teacher educator and student was recognized by Dewey (see Whitcomb, 2003 for a recent discussion) and is still emphasized in the literature (Korthagen, 2001). Such relationships expedite successful apprenticeship through scaffolding strategies such as modelling, taking advantage of and creating teachable moments, providing feedback, instructing, questioning and cognitive structuring, as part of assisted performance (Tharp & Gallimore, 1988, 1990).

Situated learning

Student projects and assignments are closely linked to and draw on the school experience wherever possible, so as to emphasize inductive learning from practice rather than a purely deductive model of theory into practice. In addition, the curriculum and its assessment are linked through projects which form vehicles for learning. These projects are designed to offer students the opportunity to take over the teachers' tool kit of skills and knowledge that will enable them to work effectively in the classroom. Examples of such projects are developing an integrated thematic unit for implementation in the classroom or completing a diagnostic assessment of a school pupil. In order to link situated learning to students' level of development, student teachers are scaffolded into classroom teaching through incremental increases in responsibility, moving from a purely observational role, supplemented by peer micro-teaching, in their first semester, to full responsibility for the classes that comprise 60% of a full teaching load by the time of their final semester internship.

Social thinking

Vygotsky was interested in the social and cultural aspects of individual human development. His recognition of the social origins of higher mental capacities is captured in his argument that 'Every function in the child's cultural development occurs twice: first, on the social level and later on the individual level; first, *between* people (*interpsychological*), and then *inside* the child' (Vygotsky, 1978: 57). The small class sizes at the HCT facilitate educational conversations and dialogues through which student teachers can develop, share, process and appropriate ideas and theories. In addition, group project work encourages students to discuss ideas and represent their thinking to others.

As another part of this process, prior models are consciously explored, externalized and set side by side with alternative images and models of teaching. As Johnson (1999) urges:

> If teachers' epistemic beliefs are to be refined, expanded, or transformed, and teachers' projected or newly emerging beliefs are to become more dominant, teachers must become cognizant of their own beliefs; question those beliefs in light of what they intellectually know and not simply what they intuitively feel; resolve conflicting images within

their own belief systems; and have access to, develop an understanding of, and have successful encounters with alternative images of teachers and teaching. (Johnson, 1999: 39)

This encourages teacher educators to meet student teachers on their own terms and to acknowledge, validate, challenge and extend their previous experiences and current understandings. One of the key modes for this exploration within the HCT B.Ed. involves the use of online technologies, as discussed above.

Reflective dialogue

Another key principle of the HCT B.Ed. is derived from Bakhtin's notion of dialogue which complements a Deweyan emphasis on reflection, whereby knowledge is co-constructed by students and teachers during extended educational conversations, and whereby teaching selves are shaped and formed. This involves both interpersonal and intrapersonal dialogue. A critical component of the latter approach is to encourage students to infer personal theories from practice, for 'To theorize about one's experience means to engage one's reflective capacities in order to be the author of that experience' (Britzman, 1991: 50). Interpersonal dialogue involves conversations between two or more people and the construction, through this dialogic process, of self – what I think; other – what she thinks; and shared meanings, knowledge or understanding. That is, dialogue entails an utterance, a reply and the relation between them. As Holquist (1990: 61) writes, 'An utterance, then, is a border phenomenon. It takes place between speakers and is drenched in social factors.'

Dialogue also entails an ethical component in that students (and teachers) are 'answerable' for the thoughts and ideas they share and must take account of the responses and judgements of others. Holquist puts Bakhtin's notion of answerability thus: 'I am always responsible for the response that is generated from the unique place I occupy in existence' (Holquist, 1990: 30). To this end, while HCT teacher educators recognize their role as more experienced partners in the business of teaching and learning, and are thus answerable for the advice given to students, they also see themselves as learners in relation to the local context; and they seek to engage student teachers in reflective dialogues and provide forums for them to engage in similar professional dialogues with their peers. Faculty participation in these dialogues is encouraged so as to reflect the notion of teacher-as-student, student-as-teacher.

Overall, these approaches recognize the situated construction of knowledge within particular social and cultural contexts and acknowledge that both the individuals and the environment can and will change as a result of dialogic interaction. The conditions and approaches discussed above enable teacher and students to enter into the close and trusting professional relationships that facilitate extended and ongoing educational conversations, whereby students can experiment with and reorchestrate experiences and discourses in the process of developing their own philosophy of education, their own orientation to teaching and their own teaching self.

Researching Language Teacher Identities

The issue explored in this book concerns the ways in which the social and educational discourses that have shaped the contemporary UAE and the HCT's teacher education programme are taken up by the students, as they construct their identities as teachers and as a community of practice. This focus on discourse, community and identity has particular implications for the processes and methods of data collection and analysis, which are outlined in the following sections.

A key assumption of this study is that language – and conversation – is of prime significance in generating meaning: 'the conversation may be conceived as a *basic mode of knowing* ... When we understand knowledge as the social justification of belief rather than as accuracy of representation, conversation replaces confrontation with nature' (Kvale, 1996: 37, emphasis in original). Thus, it was a strategic decision to seek forums involving the 'social justification of belief' in online discussions and focus group conversations as the core data.

Research participants

The UAE study involved the first cohort of student teachers to complete the Bachelor of Education in Teaching English to Young Learners at the six women's colleges of the English language medium Higher Colleges of Technology. In each of the six women's colleges across the HCT, classes comprised between 6 and 20 students, usually around 12 to 14. In total, 75 students participated in the study. The women, all UAE nationals and all but two speakers of Arabic as a first language,[1] were mostly recent school leavers aged 20–22 at the time of the study, although there was at least one 'mature' student in her early thirties. The students were all studying full time and spent 30 hours per week studying together at their respective colleges, as well as completing 36 weeks of practicum in schools over the four years of their degree. As per the cultural norms of the UAE, the female students, depending on their marital status, lived with either their parents or their husbands, and many had children of their own. The research took place during the final two years of their Bachelor of Education degree.

Reflexivity

It is important to stress in this study, that the researcher, the research subjects and, indeed, the whole research process are all institutionally situated,[2] increasing the likely predominance of particular educational discourses and diminishing the odds against the appearance of others (such as a Marxist-inspired critique of schooling as a conservative force of social reproduction). However, the alternative of presenting the student teachers' 'true' voices is something of a chimera. Indeed, sensitivity to the potential problem of 'othering' research participants and imposing the researcher's agenda can be taken to patronizing extremes – in effect another form of 'othering' – where subjects are seen as passive cultural dupes rather than skilled users of culture (Holliday, 2002: 149). Such concerns have led some writers to emphasize the need for researchers to embrace authority and responsibility,[3] given the inescapably asymmetric nature of the researcher–researched relationship (Krieger, 1991; Phillips & Jorgensen, 2002). In this book, I propose a substantive and coherent line of argument while remaining tentative in my claims, in light of the recognition that we cannot know everything about the complex individuals who are our research subjects. This last point brings us into the realm of epistemology.

Epistemology

The recognition of the discursive constitution of reality puts the researcher in the position of constructing, rather than uncovering, knowledge. As Phillips and Jorgensen (2002: 210) put it, any 'unmasking' of reality that we are able to achieve entails replacing existing masks with new ones, rather than 'getting behind' the masks. Within this approach, all claims for a singular, correct way of representing experience are challenged and replaced by more modest claims to situated interpretations of experience. This is not necessarily a fatal flaw, tainting anything one might say with the charge of 'bias'. As Eagleton (1991) points out, it is not necessary to locate oneself at some Archimedean point outside of discourse as the only alternative to guilty complicity, in order to make a valid contribution. Indeed, posing such a dichotomy ignores the discursive plurality entailed by the multiple situations in which we are all inevitably positioned, hence Phillips and Jorgensen's (2002: 203–210) characterization of the process of writing research as a 'positioned opening for discussion'. In this sense, a key aim of this book is to initiate a dialogue about language teacher education from my position as interested researcher and to open up spaces for further discussion and research into teacher education in this and other contexts.

At a more concrete level a key epistemological issue with regard to the textual data in this book is the question *'How does the data mean?'* (Freeman, 1996: 744). Freeman elaborates two responses paralleling the differences we encountered in Chapter 1 between language as reflective versus language as constitutive of 'reality':

> In the representational approach to language, the emphasis is on individuals whose words are taken to represent their thinking. A presentational approach repositions individuals within language, to see users as participants in wider social systems. Language is a function of that participation. Words are not expressions of individuals, but rather statements of connections to and within these social systems. Language provides a map of these relationships. As research data, it offers an entry into the interrelationship of an individual user and the world. To gain entry, however, language data must be studied for what it is – language – and how it is presenting the world, rather than simply for what it says about the world. (Freeman, 1996: 744)

Freeman's presentational approach aligns with the constitutive view of language in this book, where language is seen as performing rather than just naming (Butler, 1997), as construing – that is both constructing and articulating – systems of knowledge and belief through its ideational function, intrapersonal identities through its identity function and interpersonal relations through its relational function (Fairclough, 1992; Phillips & Jorgensen, 2002). The specific ways in which language is studied 'for what it is' are outlined in the discussion of discourse analysis below.

Data Collection

The data for the UAE study was collected over a two-year period, during the third and fourth year of the students' four-year Bachelor of Education degree, through a series of 'conversations' in both the spoken and written modes, the former comprising focus group interviews, the latter comprising online Web CT discussion forums. The focus group interviews involved students from three of the women's colleges within the HCT, selected in order to provide a mix of urban and rural, large and small colleges, while the online discussions involved students from all six colleges. The focus group interviews took place during the third year of the students' degree, while the Web CT discussions occurred during the students' fourth and final year of study. Overall, this meant that the data were collected over a two-year period, representing a substantial chunk of the students' enrolment in teacher education.

Focus groups

The focus of the first set of discussions[5] was on the students' recollections of teachers and teaching from their own schooling (Johnson, 1999; Lortie, 1975; Mitchell & Weber, 1999; Roberts, 1998), while the second set of discussions focused on the students' thoughts and feelings about their emerging 'teaching selves' (Danielewicz, 2001), the ways their attitudes towards, and understandings of, teaching had developed due to their experiences on the B.Ed. programme and in schools, and any 'critical incidents' or episodes that had made a difference to their understanding of themselves as teachers (Day, 1999; Goodson & Sikes, 2001). The third set of discussions explored the students' memories of learning English both in and out of school and their recollections of English teachers and English teaching at school, as well as when and how they had made the conscious decision that they wanted to become English teachers, and what it was that made them decide they wanted to teach English in particular. These discussions also focused on issues of language and culture surrounding the teaching and learning of English in the UAE, including their attitudes to English and its implications for Arabic and Islamic cultures and societies in the global and local context of the early 21st century (Canagarajah, 1999; Eggington & Kelly Hall, 2000; Karmani, 2005a, 2005b; Mohd-Asraf, 2005; Pennycook, 1994, 1998; Tollefson, 1995).

Online discussions

The Web CT discussions were organized around seven broad topics. These broad topics were co-developed by B.Ed. faculty and student teachers (see Maxwell, 2004, for a discussion of this process). There were three topics in the first semester and four in the second semester of the students' final year of study. In the first semester the three topics were: 'Moral issues in UAE education'; Beliefs about teaching'; and 'A critical incident from teaching practice'. In the second semester the four topics were: 'Managing behaviour in the classroom'; 'Insights from the internship'; 'How teaching has changed my life'; and 'What I'm looking forward to in starting my teaching career'. Within each of the broad topics, the students initiated discussions, including selecting a title for their posting, or their discussion thread if they were initiating one, and responded to the postings of other student teachers. Students were asked to post at least one message and to respond to another student's posted message within each of the broad topics, each semester. In fact, the students, while still conscious of their teachers as a potential audience, quickly assumed ownership and wrote for a peer audience in the online forums.

Indeed, the Web CT data validated and amplified the findings from the focus group data. This is related to the issue of ownership mentioned above, which is in turn related to the potential of the online medium for fostering a shared space or 'sub-culture' that Chong (1998) identifies. But it is also related to the inherent nature of asynchronous, online communication using computer technology and the specific features of the online discussion forum.[5] Sustaining a long, complex argument in the spoken mode without notes is a challenge for most people in any language. This has been seized upon by advocates of asynchronous online learning as one reason for promoting the use of written online interaction between students and between students and teachers (Bonk & King, 1998; Le Cornu & White, 2000). Jonassen (1996) has commented on the increased time that learners have to develop their thoughts and arguments with online forums as compared with oral class discussions, while Geer and Au (1998) found that as a form of communication that utilizes the written mode, email has the potential within an educational context to increase interaction and encourage deeper understanding of the subject matter concerned, although such communication needs to be supported (Le Cornu & White, 2000) and structured (Schlagel et al., 1996). More recently, Walker (2003) describes the value of an electronic, shared communication environment within a teacher education programme as a means of fostering and modelling the communities of learning advocated by sociocultural theory. Similarly, Bloomfield argues that online discussions provide student teachers with new insights into the notion of a learning community, as well as offering spaces for the ongoing negotiation of identity that, drawing on Britzman (1991), she sees as fundamental to learning to teach (Bloomfield, 2000).

It is also worth noting Kramsch and Lam's (1999) emphasis on the particular suitability of the written mode for language learners in terms of its capacity for fostering a secure and confident identity in relationship to the foreign language and Norton Pierce et al.'s (1993, cited in Norton, 2000: 123) notion of the important role played by the 'locus of control' in confident, effective language use; in the online discussions the locus of control was firmly with the student teachers.

Overall, the spoken and written data can be seen as symptomatic of the process of the students' identity construction as teachers, in the way that these identities, instantiated in the students' discussions of the meanings of teaching and being a teacher, are developed in response to the prevailing discursive context. This can be seen, for example, in the way the student teachers position themselves as agents of change, bringing student or child-centred learning to classrooms and schools dominated by 'traditional teaching', as well as in references to the discourses of culture and national development that are so prominent in the UAE.

Discourse and Material Practice

It may be argued that data derived from discussions are just disembodied talk which bear no direct relation to practices in the classroom and to what student teachers are likely to do in their own classrooms. Behind this objection lies an assumption of the purely mental character of discourse underpinned by the classic dichotomy between a pre-discursive, objective reality and representations or expressions of that reality in thought, language and discourse. But as Laclau and Mouffe (1985: 108) note:

> This is, precisely, the dichotomy which several currents of contemporary thought have tried to break. The theory of speech acts has, for example, underlined their performative character. Language games, in Wittgenstein, include within an indissoluble totality both language and the actions interconnected with it ... It is evident that the very material properties of objects are part of what Wittgenstein calls language game, which is an example of what we have called discourse ... The linguistic and non-linguistic elements are not merely juxtaposed, but constitute a differential and structured system of positions – that is, a discourse.

Laclau and Mouffe draw two conclusions from this: first, that the subject cannot be the originary source of discourse, but rather, a discursive formation will be dispersed among a range of different subject positions; and second, a discursive formation is not just a matter of linguistic phenomena but will penetrate into practices, rituals and institutions at the same time. In the context of the discursive practices discussed in this book, we can see this reflected in the student teachers' frequent references to situations involving the 'material' matter of classrooms, books, students, teachers, lessons and activities, where their actions instantiate the discursive meanings reported in the data, and where language is performative in relation to the student teachers' practice. Indeed, during the course of the study on which this book is based, I visited student teachers during their teaching practice and while these visits were not part of the formal data of the study, many of the teaching practices I saw aligned with the predominant 'progressive' discourse we will encounter in subsequent chapters.

To cite a brief example, in one rural school I visited, two student teachers had transformed a previously bare and unstimulating classroom in which the eight-year-old male students were unengaged in learning and often 'off-task', into a print-rich learning environment where students' work was prominently displayed, where developmentally appropriate activities formed the core of the lesson, where routines and structures were balanced by purposeful cognitive challenges, and where students were encouraged to collaborate and take risks within a non-threatening and supportive classroom climate. One of the student teachers responsible for this transformation forms the focus of Chapter 6, where we will see that her discursive comments are aligned with this picture of her practice.

Data Analysis

There is no single agreed method for doing discourse analysis; analysts therefore need to adopt and adapt linguistic methods and tools (Threadgold, 2000) in order to analyse the ways in which discursive practices are embodied, or 'languaged', to borrow Stuart Hall's term (Barker & Galasinski, 2001: 156), in a particular situation or context. This view sees discourse and text as characterized by a number of key features. One key feature is the multifunctional nature of language where discourse is seen as constitutive at the levels of systems of knowledge and belief, interpersonal relations and intrapersonal identities. Another key feature is the 'intertextual' nature of discourse in that any text contains traces of other texts and other discourses. A third key feature is that text is a process involving meaning making practices in particular situations for particular purposes – though this does not preclude viewing texts synoptically for analytical purposes (Poynton & Lee, 2000). However, these features do not mean that discourse analysis is able to provide an exhaustive interpretation of a given text, given the 'excess' or 'surplus' which exceeds the text and leaves its mark within it, but which we cannot grasp in any fixed form outside some system of representation or textualization (Connolly, 2002).

Discourse analysis can appear as the quintessential example of a priori research insofar as the literature-derived categories exist and the data merely populate them. This, however, suggests a somewhat linear procedure, whereas the actual analysis involved a cyclical process of moving back and forth between the data, the literature and the research questions, leading to a gradual refinement and clarification of the key discursive themes structuring the data and enabling me to arrive at the categories that structure the following chapters. In this context, it is important to note here in relation to the two sets of data, that although there are differences in terms of mode and method of collection, the two sets have enough in common in terms of field and tenor – that is in terms of the fundamental discourses and the interpersonal relationships operating throughout and structuring the texts – that they can be treated as one set. The analysis of the data incorporated a range of technologies, from handwritten notes and annotations, manual coding with highlighter pens, as well as a qualitative data analysis software package, and a range of concepts and tools derived from Fairclough's work in critical discourse analysis (1992; 2003), as well as the discourse theory of Laclau and Mouffe (Laclau & Mouffe, 1985; Torfing, 1999).

Critique of discourse analysis

Discourse analysis has not been without its critics. Widdowson, in particular, has been a persistent and vocal critic of Fairclough's critical discourse analysis (1998; 2004). Describing Fairclough's theoretical underpinnings as an 'ad hoc bricolage', he consequently derides critical discourse analysis as a 'toolkit' that lacks rigour (Widdowson, 1998: 137). Widdowson also takes discourse analysts to task for reading a social phenomenon, i.e. discourse, into linguistic artefacts, i.e. texts (Widdowson, 2004: 21). Blommaert offers a somewhat opposite set of criticisms, arguing that far from not focusing enough on 'rigorous' linguistic analysis, discourse analysis has a 'linguistic bias' and is often so focused on textual minutiae and so 'aridly grammatical' that it misses the bigger social picture (Blommaert, 2005: 34). As MacLure notes, these comments can be read as reflecting a binary opposition between linguistic and post-structuralist approaches to discourse, each of which sees an irredeemable lack in the other. Combining these two approaches may appear to be attempting to combine 'incommensurable discourses' (Pennycook, 1989), in that the former derives from Anglo-American analytic linguistics while the latter is in the tradition of post-structuralist political philosophy; yet as MacLure notes, while there is no 'overarching, unified discourse theory that would regulate the traffic, so as to accommodate the concerns of those with an interest in discourse… there *are* connections between the fine grain of language and action ("what people actually say and do") and the broader sweep of Discourse with a "big -D"' (2003: 191). The analysis in this book seeks to trace these connections by moving back and forth between text and discourse and exploring the 'nodes' (to use Laclau and Mouffe's term) or 'folds' (to use Deleuze's term) that articulate their co-imbrications as they mutually 'incorporate without totalizing, internalize without unifying, collect together discontinuously in the form of pleats making surfaces, spaces, flows and relations' (Rose, 1996: 37).

A related criticism of discourse analysis is that texts, written or oral, are always interpreted through the filter of the analyst's subjectivity, though as has been argued above, the presence of the researcher's subjectivity in research is unavoidable while the alternative of writing from nowhere is simply unrealistic. A solution here might be to seek the text producer's intentions, but this merely defers the problem, since we are then just presented with another text. A potential alleviation of this problem lies in cross-referencing a given text or group of texts, with another source altogether, be it a written or an oral text as is the case in this study where oral focus-group texts are considered alongside written comments from online discussion forums.

Blommaert argues that CDA has been too focused on Western contexts and closed to other societies – a criticism echoed in the work of Shi-xu (2005; 2007) and one to which the study on which the current book is based can be seen as contributing a response. Shi-xu also argues that discourse analysis is of Western origin and orientation yet claims universal applicability in a range of cultural contexts; thus discourse studies need to be reconstructed in order to enable them to make sense of the culturally different 'other' and properly to recognize discourses 'as sites of cultural struggle' (2007: 3). Shi-xu's critique rests on the unfortunate 'culturalism' we encountered in Chapter 1, that 'uses "culture" indiscriminately to explain issues in colonial contexts' (McConaghy, 2000: 43) and privileges it as *the* tool for explaining difference. Aside from resting on a synoptic view of cultures as distinct 'things', such critique inadvertently undermines its own claim for the non-relevance of 'Western' categories and concepts to non-Western contexts in its deployment of binaries in the dichotomous distinction between the 'West' and the 'rest'. Thus, while agreeing that discourse is a space of contest, we need to recognize that this contest occurs across and within many sites, including those within the purported monolithic 'West', and resist seeing power and domination as following any simplistic predetermined lines. As we will see in the following chapters, the UAE student teachers can be seen as dominated by colonial and masculinist discourses, yet at the same time they construct and exercise a powerful dominance of their own.

Discourse analysis and social practice

Some of the issues considered in the analysis included questions of what wider societal discourses and orders of discourse a text instantiates; what hegemonic relations are being sustained or opposed; and what are the ideological effects in terms of systems of knowledge and belief, social relations and social identities (Fairclough, 1992: 238). Thus, using an example from the focus group discussions, in a statement asserting the need for more Emirati nationals to take up teaching positions in the nation's schools, we can note the presence of wider societal discourses of nationalism and Emiratization. The hegemonic status of these wider societal discourses plays a key role in sustaining identities premised on a discourse of difference. This discourse of difference, in turn, sustains and supports the operation of particular educational beliefs that operate via a dichotomized framework as we will see in Chapter 4.

Among the key features examined in considering the student teachers' texts are questions of purpose and audience and how this influences and constrains the construction of textual meaning. Of key relevance are the strategies of justification or what Fairclough (2003) calls 'legitimation'. These include such strategies as rationalization, involving references to the utility of a course of action or belief, and authorization, involving appeals to authority, tradition, custom or law. Such strategies serve the dual purpose of maintaining systems of knowledge and belief, as well as the interpersonal, social relations built around those systems of knowledge and belief (Fairclough, 2003).

The relevant factors to be considered also include what is taken for granted, what values are assumed to be shared in a given context, and what are the operating presuppositions. These assumed values and presuppositions can be seen in the way text producers frame their utterances with explicit statements such as, 'as we all know' and 'of course', as well as in less obvious ways, such as assuming the given-ness of claims that to others may be entirely contingent and contestable. These presuppositions, of both readers and writers, form part of the intertextual aspect of the text. When considering presuppositions and assumptions, often what is not said is as important as what *is* said, and so the silences in a text are as significant as the actual content (Holquist, 1990). Regarding presuppositions, Fairclough notes that they are very useful for manipulating readers because of the difficulty in challenging them (Fairclough, 1992: 120). He argues that presuppositions are a matter of relying upon or tapping into other discourses or texts and the same could be argued for 'condensations' (Lemke, 1995, see the section below) or expedient reductions in the complexity of a proposition. These may be examined in terms of what discourses are being drawn upon covertly by means of such reductions.

Discourse analysis and textualization

Specific linguistic features and strategies are examined in order to explore questions about how a representation of the world is being created through language, about how readers are being 'positioned' and how sequencing, logical reasoning and interaction patterns contribute to these effects (Janks, 1997). Salient linguistic features examined fall under the three main headings of vocabulary, grammar, and cohesion and text structure (Fairclough, 1992: 75). There is a progression here from smaller to larger 'chunks' of language.

In terms of vocabulary, my analysis looks at the ideological import of particular words or 'nodal points' (such as 'traditional' and 'modern' as adjectives to describe teachers and teaching) and at the way 'lexical chains' of words with similar ideological import are placed through a text, cumulatively reinforcing a particular ideological thrust (this is also an element of cohesion) and governed by what Laclau and Mouffe (1985: 127–134) describe as the 'logic of equivalence'.

These 'nodal points' are described by Torfing (1999: 98) as 'privileged discursive points that partially fix meaning within signifying chains ... The nodal point creates and sustains the identity of a certain discourse by constructing a knot of definite meanings'. MacLure (2003: 9–11) gives an example of this textual and ideological process at work in the binary framework structuring an article from the time of the first Gulf War, in which the positive terms used to describe British soldiers (e.g. 'professional', 'lionhearts', 'confident') were negatively echoed in those used to describe Iraqi soldiers (e.g. 'brainwashed', 'paper tigers', 'desperate'). This is a pervasive feature of many texts, particularly argumentative ones, and we will see examples in the discussion of the student teachers' texts. Highlighting the existence of such nodal points and discerning the ways they cumulatively form lexical chains that 'quilt' (Zizek, 1989: 95, cited in Torfing, 1999: 98) and discursively unify the text offers a linguistic means by which analysts can draw attention to the operation of particular discourses.

Another feature I examine at the level of text is what Lemke calls 'condensations'; these are when a set of complex and/or contentious issues is glossed over by the use of a single term (Lemke, 1995: 75). An example might be, 'Modern approaches have been proved to be the most effective methods in the language classroom' where issues of the specific approaches and methods under consideration, their suitability to the given situation and their actual effect on performance are suppressed by the uncritical use of this seemingly unproblematic term 'modern approaches'. Hence, condensations are useful for ideological purposes since they collapse distinctions and allow chains of ideas or ideals to be expressed and subsequently re-expressed by use of a seemingly simple catchphrase or term.

In terms of grammar the main feature I consider is modality. Modality is realized through a wide range of grammatical features and expresses the degree of 'affinity' or solidarity with either a proposition or a text participant. Modality is thus a useful ideological device, that can be employed in relation to a given notion or statement, to subtly, or not so subtly, cast doubt on it, or conversely to affirm it as solid, absolute 'truth'. Modality is often realized through modal verbs, such as 'should' and 'must' or modal adverbs, such as 'probably' and 'definitely', which indicate degrees of obligation or necessity. An example would be the comment, 'Effective teachers *must* cater to the different needs of all their students'. I also consider 'epistemic modality', where a statement assumes a putative 'truth' or 'reality' status by virtue of its existential expression. This is typically achieved through tense, as for example, when the choice of the categorical assertion 'is' expresses a high level of affinity with the truth of a proposition, for example, in statements such as, 'the teacher's responsibility *is* to create an active learning environment'. Such present tense statements also tend to attribute a universal, timeless quality to the processes in question.

In addition to seeking an affinity with truth, the desired affinity may also be with the text participant. Thus, for example, a tag question ('I think active learning is essential, don't you?') invites concurrence with the speaker/writer, and hence indicates a relatively high degree of interpersonal affinity. At other times, modality involves expressions of low affinity. One such device is 'hedging', which is a way of further distancing oneself from a proposition. It is often achieved through the use of tag questions, or qualifiers ('You still want to go, don't you?' 'She was about 40, at least I think so.').

Modality can also be realized through evaluation, involving either negative denial or positive affirmation. In my analysis of the data, numerous instances of explicit affirming strategies are identified, often involving statements such as, '*You are right*', as part of the students' responses to each others' comments about educational practice. Such emphatic affirmation of agreement serves to enforce both ideational and interpersonal solidarity, exemplifying the co-construction of community and communication.

Cohesion, in addition to the lexical chains found within a text and across texts as we discussed above, may involve looking at the way transitions in a text are effected, for example whether the conjunctions imply causal relations as with 'so that' and 'since'. Cohesion may also involve reference to other material (earlier or yet to come) in the text; or it may involve ellipsis, which is the leaving out or substituting with another word, of material which is recoverable from another part of the text. A further element of cohesion may be the silences and gaps in the text. These may allow a coherent effect to be achieved at the cost of omitting pertinent, perhaps crucial, ideas or information. A student may choose only to emphasize her differences with a supervising government school teacher, selectively ignoring the points of agreement in order to construct a discourse of difference. Cohesion shades into overall text structure, which will also look at text layout and format, and the patterns of argument and/or propositions in the text as a whole.

Discourse theory sees our identities and our communities as shaped by social and historical discourses. In the following chapters this process of discursive construction is explored in relation to the HCT B.Ed. student teachers from a number of perspectives. The discursive illumination of the ways in which the student teachers are constructing a community of practice forms the focus of Chapter 3. Following this, and drawing on Fairclough's (1992) three aspects of the constitutive effects of discourse, Chapter 4 explores the discursive construction of the community's systems of knowledge and belief; Chapter 5 focuses on the discursive construction of interpersonal, social relationships among members of the community; and Chapter 6 focuses on the discursive construction of intrapersonal identity through a focus on the construction of one student teacher. The overall conclusions and implications language teacher identities in relation to the co-construction of discourse and community are explored in the final chapter.

Conclusion

In this chapter I have drawn on the notion of discourse as socially valued ways of thinking, speaking, feeling and acting, to provide a discourse-based reading of UAE history and society. I have also examined discourses of education in the UAE and the related discourses of nationalism and globalization, as well as discourses of gender. Against this background, I have offered a view of teaching as an amalgam of discourses and provided an overview of the discourses students encounter as part of learning to teach in the HCT B.Ed. degree. I also made a link back to the previous chapter by exploring some of the ideas of the key theorists whose work underpinned that chapter in relation to the model of learning to teach that we have developed at the HCT. This chapter has also briefly outlined the methods of data collection and analysis employed in this study and discussed related issues of epistemology and reflexivity. We have seen how face-to-face focus groups and online discussion forums provided two sources of research texts and how, although the modes of these two sources are different, the commonality in the field and tenor justify the treatment of the two sets as one in an analysis of the discursive construction of the teaching identities, as members of an evolving community of practice, of the first cohort of Emirati Bachelor of Education students at the HCT.

Underpinned by a view of discourse as mutually constitutive of language and society we have seen how discourse analysis enables us to explore the effects of the discourses in terms of social identities, social relationships and systems of knowledge and belief (Barker & Galasinski, 2001; Chouliaraki & Fairclough, 1999; Edwards & Potter, 1992; Fairclough, 1992, 2003; Phillips & Jorgensen, 2002; Taylor, 2001). The discursive co-construction of community and identity, and the common understanding that binds the two, are explored in the following four chapters.

Notes

1   One student spoke English as her first language while another spoke Baluchi.
2   Were this book reporting an investigation into the 'quality' of the HCT B.Ed. programme, a reader might reasonably feel that my particular position at the time of the UAE study, as head of the HCT's education department, compromised the possibilities for *dis*interested critique to an unreasonable degree. As it is, the study seeks to explore the ways in which the students' teacher identities are being constructed, rather than to evaluate them for their educational or pedagogical merit, although in finding out about 'how' the B.Ed. programme works in terms of the professional teacher identities it constructs, the study inevitably identified issues for consideration in terms of programme (re)design; these are discussed in the final chapter.
3   The words 'authority' and 'responsibility' in the above section remind us that, as Lather points out, a post-structuralist framework "brings ethics and epistemology together" (1993: 686). In this sense the characterization of research as a "positioned opening for discussion" is at once an epistemological and an ethical statement. At a more obviously ethical level, I should note that the research was carried out with the informed consent of all participants and that permission was also given to use the data in any potential publication arising from the research. Participants were also assured that in the event of any publication of the research I would strive to preserve their anonymity, within constraints entailed by factors such as the relatively small size of the overall student body. However, aside from such risks the study has the potential to bring benefits, to future student teachers if not to the cohort in the study, by increasing levels of understanding of teacher education in an under-researched context.
4   Summing up the strengths of focus groups Morgan argues that their key merit is allowing the researcher to witness aspects of participants' experiences and perspectives that would not be possible without group interaction (Morgan, 1997). The most obvious examples of this are instances when participants agree, disagree, ask questions, provide additional comments, etc. The focus groups were semi-structured with broad topics predetermined, and some questions pre-scripted, to enable me to pursue a particular line of inquiry, while at the same time offering scope for the students to initiate topics and take the discussion in directions that reflected what seemed of importance to them.

5   First, there was an unconstrained alternation of 'speaker' in these online conversations which meant that each participant could contribute at any time to any other(s) and could make statements, ask and answer questions. Second, once a particular 'speaker' had the floor she could contribute without interruption to the conversation for as long as she wished; and of the more than 750 messages posted, some were over 500 words in length, a few over a thousand. Third, students could select and introduce topics of their own choice, as well as change topic if they wished. They could raise particular issues they felt needed airing and make connections between topics already under discussion and related topics or issues. And, finally, they could offer summaries and commentaries of the discussions conducted so far, offering their own interpretation of the issues and promoting their own reading of the community.

Chapter 3
The Formation of a Community of Practice

This chapter explores some of the ways in which the student teachers in the HCT B.Ed. programme formed a community of practice and the implications this had for them as teachers. The communities of practice framework recognizes the way we learn through participation in social practices; but it also acknowledges that the community whose practices we are learning has a reciprocal, and potentially transformative, effect upon us as individuals. Thus as we participate in and utilize the discourses and practices that embody the subject or content knowledge of the community, we are reconstituted as individual subjects, or to put it in more human terms, we grow and develop as we learn through joining in with others in socially valued enterprises.

In Chapter 1, communities of practice were defined in terms of mutual engagement in a joint enterprise involving a shared repertoire of discourse, with three modes of belonging: engagement, imagination and alignment, which we recognized as broadly congruent with the figurative, authored and positional identities, also outlined in Chapter 1. In this chapter we explore data from the student teachers, reflecting the formation of an evolving community of practice in terms of the three modes of belonging. In terms of engagement, we examine evolving forms of mutual engagement, developing understanding of the enterprise at hand and developing repertoires of styles and discourses. In terms of alignment, we look at matters of locality and the evolving community of practice's relation to other communities in their 'constellation', as well as exploring boundaries and border practices. In terms of imagination, we look at self-consciousness, reflection and creation as ways in which members continually reinvent their community of practice.

One of the fascinating aspects of the development of the HCT B.Ed. programme is that we are witnessing the evolution of a community of practice where none previously existed. In the first section below, I discuss a critical aspect of this evolution, the students' reasons for choosing teaching. This initial act of belonging is foundational in an obvious temporal sense for any teacher, but also because it involves all three modes of belonging. For this reason I am treating it as a separate section bringing together all three modes, before discussing each mode of belonging separately in the remaining sections of the chapter.

Choosing Teaching as an Act of Belonging

Choosing teaching is a particularly significant statement of 'belonging', even though here, as elsewhere, it occurred before the formation of the student teachers' community of practice as it later evolved. Choosing teaching potentially involves all three modes of belonging: it may involve alignment with the social purposes of teaching; it usually involves engagement with the practices of teaching; and almost by definition, it involves an imaginative casting of self into an envisioned future role as a teacher. Not surprisingly, however, and arguably reflecting what was referred to in Chapter 2 as the 'conservative' societal discourse, family influence was one of the most commonly cited factors in choosing teaching and this is where we begin exploring the students' formation of an evolving community of practice below.

Family connections

Families shaped students' choices in a variety of ways including through implicit approbation, explicit encouragement and sometimes disapproval and discouragement. In some students' experiences, family members who were or had been teachers provided potential role models. These family members were not always sources of unconditional encouragement, however. In some cases a family member's bad experiences of teaching were linked to their not having chosen it initially as a career:

> My sister's a teacher but she tries now for a long time to get out from the school; because she didn't study to be a teacher ... But I say to myself, maybe she's teaching older learners, it's different from young girls. So I'm enjoying what I'm doing, but she's saying terrible things about teaching. (*Maysa, FG 1*[1])

Aside from providing an example of the (declining) trend for UAE teachers to be employed without formal education qualifications, this message also reflects the relatively low status of teaching and the poor conditions in schools, a direct consequence of the underfunding of education noted in the previous chapter. Other family members also communicated the stressful nature of teaching in the UAE but balanced this with affirmation of the pleasures of working with students:

> The same, I have twin aunts who are both English teachers. At first they used to say good things about teaching but now they are saying terrible things. They are saying that teaching is not just teaching. They enjoy teaching and they enjoy the students, but the loads of work that the teacher has to do, that's what they hate. (*Amirah, FG 1*)

The reference to a past golden era in the twin aunts' previous enjoyment of teaching is at odds with the more frequent discursive construction of the past as an educational 'dark age' that we will encounter later in this and the following chapters. Another student had three sisters who were also teachers and disparaged teaching as a career: 'They were asking, "Why are you becoming a teacher? Being a teacher is a very stressful job"' (*Fawzia, FG 2*). There were also more positive and encouraging role models provided by some families. In some cases the influence of a positive family role model whose career choice already had family approbation led to further encouragement from family members:

> My sister is an English teacher and when I entered the programme she told me that teaching is not that bad. It's like, a good job ... Yes and many members of my family, when they saw how I'm learning to be a teacher, they're encouraged me to join this programme ... Yes. It's the same reasons; when my sister became a teacher my father was proud of her. So it's like, uh, go and get the same way. (*Zainab, FG 1*)

Sometimes family members' involvement with teaching offered opportunities for formative early experiences in working with children:

> My aunt, she's my aunt-in-law. She's American. She's not a teacher but she used to have a nursery where she gathered some children who were five years old or six and teach them English. And I used to teach with her and she used to use different things, different methods for teaching the students, for teaching the children how to speak English, the alphabet and that's what motivated me more to get into teaching. (*Amirah, FG 1*)

In this instance the student had an early opportunity to cast herself in the figurative identity of the teacher and engage with teaching, albeit in a supporting role. In other cases family encouragement was linked to unfulfilled aspirations of particular family members:

> I think I would consider the student teacher's background too, because in my situation, all my aunts are teachers too ... and my father wished to be a teacher and it's like I'm fulfilling his dream. My father wished always to be a teacher, but then he entered law school. All my aunts are

teachers of different subjects. They influenced me one way or another. I don't know how I came to this conclusion but it does [influence me]. *(Abir, FG 1)*

Here we get the sense that choosing teaching is not so much a rational choice as something intuitive and emotional that just feels right. The link to feeling is made explicitly by the following student teacher:

All of my aunts are teachers ... Well at home my mother did all the teaching and she was the best teacher I've ever had, so I'd like to be like her so that's why I chose teaching ... I saw the way my mother was happy when she was teaching us and how she appreciated when we ... when we learned and so on, and got high marks. I wanted to feel that too; that's why I became a teacher. *(Hadiya, FG 2)*

In this instance the student is being apprenticed into teaching through a powerful combination of personal role models at home who are at the same time acting as professional role models. There seems to have been every reason to choose teaching in this harmonious alignment between personal realization and professional fulfilment. In other cases, family encouragement came in the form of pressure, which was not focused so much on happiness and fulfilment but, rather, derived from discourses (again, reflecting what was referred to in Chapter 2 as the 'conservative' societal discourse) that position female students in particular ways in terms of what is or is not appropriate for a woman.

Discourses of gender

As elsewhere in the world, in the UAE teaching is widely constructed as a suitable career for women. As a student commented: 'And my father, he thinks like teachers are the best thing and teaching is the best thing for a woman' *(Fellah, FG 1)*. Sometimes this was linked to a desire for family prestige: 'My family, they badly wanted a teacher in the family so I decided I'm going to be the teacher ... In most families, women are encouraged to be teachers or doctors' *(Sabah, FG 2)*. In other cases, desire for personal fulfilment and pressures related to family prestige intersected in complex ways with other social and cultural pressures deriving from discourses about what is or is not an appropriate role for a woman:

It's a mixture, to me it is a mixture ... to make my family happy and make me happy. My parents wanted me to be a good doctor, but when I grow older they say that it's difficult for an Emirati woman to become a doctor because it requires many years working in this field. And then it's important to get married fast, and that contradicts with what I want, so I choose to be a teacher which is to me and to them is the next best thing. (*Hadiya, FG 2*)

When challenged about whether family encouragement might be a source of pressure, this last student neatly resolved any conflict between her wishes and those of her family in her mind by affirming the alignment between their wishes and her own desires: 'It's like first I have to please myself and then my family. Now, I'd have to say that my family cares about what pleases me first. So what pleases me first is what pleases them' (*Hadiya, FG 2*).

The notion of teaching as an appropriate career for a woman is intimately tied to religious and cultural discourses in the contemporary UAE, and a number of students in focus group discussions made explicit reference to Islam and its views about teaching. One student emphasized the value Islam places on education: 'Most books that outline the life of Prophet Mohammed have a section that discusses the emphasis on education - educating oneself and others. Teaching is the most highly regarded job in Islam' (*Sabah, FG Arabic*).

Another student offered a perspective reflecting contemporary discourses of 'new globalism' that challenges simple oppositions between discourses of Islam and cosmopolitan modernity and reminds us that it is impossible to talk about 'Islam' in the abstract, since we are always referring to someone's interpretation of Islam (Safi, 2003). 'One of the goals I want to achieve from being in this programme is to learn English and to teach it to children, because Prophet Mohammed encouraged us to learn languages so that we can travel and learn about other cultures' (*Nabila, FG Arabic*). Yet, in the following posting from the same student teacher, cultural discourses ostensibly derived from religion coalesce conveniently with socially constructed needs, desires and priorities: 'It's an all female environment ... even supervisors are all women now. Also the timings are good for mothers and housewives' (*Nabila, FG Arabic*). The contrast here with her earlier comment, in terms of the role being constructed for women as teachers, illustrates the ongoing negotiation of identity and the capacity of the student teachers, like all of us, for inhabiting multiple discursively constructed spaces. Another student was aware that a future husband may well be more conservative than her father, which might constrain her later options: 'Especially husbands, they want their wives to be teachers ... So my father he wants ... it's okay for him if I work in business or in teaching but if I got married my husband would want me to work as a teacher, because of the time and atmosphere in schools' (*Sabah, FG 2*). For this student, career choice may involve sacrifices to wifely duty. A metaphor of sacrifice as part of a discourse of service, possibly derived from religion, came through in another student's comment that drew on a metaphor of education as enlightenment: 'I have always believed that teachers have an honourable job and they have great responsibility because they are candles that burn themselves to light their students' lives' (*Kaneez, Beliefs about teaching, Teaching is an honorable job!!*). The honour associated with the public service of teaching is a pervasive discourse in education in the UAE as elsewhere, often linked to notions of sacrificing less elevated financial rewards for the incomparable and indefinable spiritual and emotional remuneration that comes from 'making a difference'.

In these comments we see the student teachers drawing on and interweaving a range of discourses to make their varied cases, reminding us that different influences can combine in many different and often unpredictable ways and thus, individual courses of action cannot just be attributed in simple fashion to any single influence. Rather, the students accommodate and/or utilize this range of influences and pressures as resources that shape the particular script they construct, within which they take on the role of a teacher. This work of imaginative self-casting is perhaps most obvious, however, in relation to the part played by past teachers as role models who inspired the students to envision themselves as future teachers, which is examined in the following section.

Teachers as role models

Family influences and discourses of what is and what is not appropriate for women were often supplemented with other sources of influence for these young Emirati women. For some students, inspirational models were provided not by family members but by teachers encountered at school, whom they subsequently aspired to imitate. For one student, positive role models combined with the discovery of pleasure in the ability to explain things to others:

> For me, when I was in preparatory school I have lots of good teachers so I wanted to be like them, to imitate them, that's why I wished to be a teacher. Even more, I noticed in myself that whenever I explain something for my … even my brothers or sisters or my friends at school, I explained step by step. They could understand … So I liked it, the idea that I can explain, so that's why maybe. (*Sahar, FG 1*)

For some students the role model teacher stood out in contrast to the majority of teachers, reflecting an opposition the students constructed between sensitivity and insensitivity that will be discussed in detail in the following chapter:

> When I was in preparatory school I had a history teacher. She was different because other teachers were strict with us and didn't give us the chance to discuss the lesson with them and give our opinions but this teacher she was very, liked to, she liked to interact with the students and give them more chance to participate in the lesson so that's what I like ... this. (*Fawzia, FG 1*)

Another student at the same college recalled being inspired by this same teacher: 'And the same teacher affected me also. Because me and Fadwa were in the same class and she taught us for four years and I really liked her and because of that I want to be a history teacher' (*Kamilah, FG 1*).

This factor of the inspirational school teachers is consistent with other studies that discuss students' reasons for taking up teaching (Calderhead & Shorrock, 1997; Danielewicz, 2001; Furlong & Maynard, 1995). In some cases the impressions made by inspirational teachers may lie dormant for a number of years until triggered by a particular combination of circumstances or events:

> In fact I remember one day at my secondary school I was thinking about being an English teacher because I liked my English teacher. So one day I went to her and asked whether studying to be an English teacher is difficult or not. So she told me that it might be a little bit difficult ... Then I forgot about that and I decided to join the HCT ... my fist choice in the HCT was to go into the technology section. But then they mentioned to us that there is a new programme that is teaching English. And then I thought more about working as a teacher; the work ... the work opportunities that I would have. And then I also remembered the day that I was asking my teacher and I remembered all my memories from the past and I was amazed that this came now and I thought that I'm really going to be a teacher. (*Shayma, FG 1*)

As we saw above choosing teaching in this case was not so much a rational choice as something that just felt right. However, things are rarely simple and straightforward; given our multiple identities it is quite possible to combine emotional satisfaction with other strategic calculations. Moreover, while for some students, like Shayma, past teachers offered positive role models, for many they provided negative ones that the students wished to surpass.

Surpassing past teachers

Discussions in the teacher education literature of reasons for choosing teaching as a profession, draw attention to the ways this choice is often connected to past experiences of teachers (Calderhead & Shorrock, 1997; Danielewicz, 2001; Furlong & Maynard, 1995; Johnson, 1999). This connection can involve wishing to emulate past teachers, as we have seen above. However, it can also involve a wish to improve on the model provided by past teachers; for many B.Ed. students this desire to do a better job of teaching than their own teachers had done was a particularly powerful motive. A number of students expressed this desire in general terms without focusing on a specific aspect of teaching they wished to improve: 'I wanted to be a better teacher than my teachers in school. I wanted to show them what a teacher is. What a teacher should be' (*Sabah, FG 1*). In this comment teaching is constructed as a competition with past teachers. A similar element of competition came through in the comments of another student who described how she held a negative image of past teachers in her mind to remind her of what she did not want to become: 'I'm putting the negative view of teachers in my mind, negative to prove that I'm doing the opposite of her and like, doing the positive things in my class and remembering what teachers did to us and we didn't like it so I'm doing something different' (*Zainab, FG 1*). The use of 'positive' and 'negative' is indicative of the oppositional framework that many students used to reconstruct their memories of school and the teachers who taught them in the past. The aspect of reviewing the past through the lens afforded by study in the B.Ed., implicit in this last comment, was an explicit feature of other students' remarks: 'When I joined this course, the first semester they taught us how good classrooms should be and I was interested in what they said. Why, when I was a student, why didn't we have that? Why?' (*Takiyah, FG 1*).

Other students were more specific in pointing out what it was about past teachers and teaching they – and it is noteworthy that this student speaks on behalf of the community through her use of the first person plural form – wished to surpass: 'We are not going to treat students badly like her, we've thought about that ... Because most of the teachers, we didn't benefit from them so we want to change the system' (*Fawzia, FG 1*). Another student also ascribed the stimulus for a personal agenda for change to the lack of learning that occurred at school: 'We didn't understand from them ... So I just thought about being a teacher to change what they did for us' (*Nabila, FG 1*). A number of students contrasted their teaching aspirations with characteristics of the educational practices they had observed in UAE schools, such as students being treated as homogenous. This resulted in suppression of individual pupils' talents and abilities in the classroom: 'During my schooling, I met some people with extraordinary abilities which were hidden; so I want to help those students improve their abilities' (*Adila, FG 1*); and it was manifested in a lack of attention to students' different learning needs: 'I think they didn't understand what the students need or how the students are different with different learning styles. So I thought that when I teach, I will try to understand what students need to learn' (*Maysa, FG 1*).

Such distinctions provided the material with which the students constructed their systems of educational knowledge and belief, which will be explored in the following chapter. However, while discussing the reasons for her choice of a teaching career, the same student who commented on the need for attention to individual learning needs, voiced awareness that surpassing past teachers might be more complicated that just expressing the desire to do so, as she noted the continuing influence of these past models on her own teaching: 'because maybe they influenced us and sometimes we teach in the way they taught us. So we think back and we try to change it' (*Maysa, FG 1*). This is another theme that will be picked up in later chapters.

The part played by teachers as positive or negative role models relates to teaching per se rather than to any specific pedagogical content. But for a number of students, English, the subject matter they would teach, was itself a motivating factor in joining the Bachelor of Education programme, as explored below; here again, we see an interweaving of motives as English conjoins with other factors influencing the decision to teach.

Choosing English

The perception of English in the students' wider communities, itself reflecting wider global discourses of global English as well as discourses of national development, intersected with other influences shaping the students' choices. For some student teachers, choosing teaching was linked to the prestige and practicality of English as an increasingly global language. In some cases this was linked to the presence of English in the global media: 'When I was a child I said to my parents I want to be a teacher. And especially English, because when I turn on the TV and see the movies, especially English movies, I want to speak like that ... that was my dream. And it's becoming real. (*Hanan, FG 1*). For some student teachers, the language is perceived as lending special prestige to teachers of English, as opposed to other teachers of other subjects. 'And maybe ... it's like special to be an English teacher. It's got advantages. And even your family look at you' (*Zainab, FG 3*). In some cases, prestige derived from scarcity value and challenge:

> And also there aren't many English ... national English teachers. And many ... I can say fifty per cent of the population in the UAE, look at English as a difficult subject. So if you are teaching English you should be like ... you have special ability or something like that. You should be excellent to be an English teacher. (*Adila, FG 3*)

Other students, foreshadowing a theme we will explore in greater depth in the following chapter, linked English to a discourse that constructed an opposition between new methods of teaching and traditional approaches in the classroom: 'There is also another thing that influences the choice. English was taught differently. It wasn't taught in the traditional way' (*Abir, FG 3*).

And reflecting the complex pattern we've seen already in the student teachers' choices, sometimes feelings and beliefs about English combined with family influences, which themselves involved complex mixtures of yearning for approbation and desire to surpass:

> One of our relatives, she's an English teacher. And we have an art teacher ... but the English teacher, she really ... because I like learning English and I saw that she's an English teacher and everybody's speaking about her and she's a good teacher ... I put it in my mind and I want to be better than her. (*Kamilah, FG 1*)

In other cases, the prestige of English aligned with family aspirations for the next generation to go beyond the parents' achievements. When this intersected with encouragement from other important role models it provided a powerful incentive:

> Actually my parents, especially my father, he really encouraged me to be an English teacher because he speaks English. But he can't write because he learned ... he was working in an American company, so he acquired the language. So his dream was for me to be a teacher and especially an English teacher. And I was interested and when I heard that there is a new programme at HCT, so I was interested to join. And my teachers in foundations also encouraged me. (*Hanan, FG 1*)

Given the importance of family in the discourses of UAE society it would be surprising if families were not frequently cited as a decisive influence alongside other reasons for choosing teaching. However, like the identity formation processes with which it is linked, choosing teaching is often, as we have already seen, the outcome of a complex interplay of factors and reasons, which may evolve and mutually shape each other over time, as we can see below with a student whose family had encouraged her to enter the programme and who later commented on how her family's understanding of teaching had altered as they had seen her grow and develop:

> Among my family, I think I have changed their idea about learning to teach. They have noticed the authentic and interesting way that we moved through the programme ... I believe in myself ... that we will all do something very special and effective in teaching in the UAE. (*Zainab, How teaching has changed my life, Teaching REALLY has changed*)

What Zainab's coments exemplify, in addition to the way ideas about teaching and motivating factors co-evolve over time, is the way that many students are also motivated by an altruistic wish to 'make a difference' to lives and to education. This was often connected to the way the students constructed their memories of past teachers as models to be improved upon, which we explored in the previous section.

At a number of points in the discussion in the above sections, we have encountered a discursive strategy involving categorizing teaching into 'good' and 'bad' and linking the latter with past teachers. This tendency echoes wider 'progressive' discourses of the benefits of social change and is something we will see again in the following chapters. However, more immediately, having examined choosing teaching as the initial act of belonging to the evolving community that involved all three modes of belonging, engagement, alignment and imagination, the following discussion explores each of the three modes of belonging in their own right, beginning with belonging and engagement.

Belonging and Engagement

Engagement as a mode of belonging can be explored through the student teachers' evolving forms of mutual engagement in learning to teach; through their development of common understandings of the joint enterprise of becoming teachers; and through the development and deployment by the community of a shared repertoire of styles and discourses in relation to education and teaching. Each of these processes, as part of constructing figurative identities by drawing on the discursive resources of the figured worlds of education and teaching, is discussed below.

Evolving forms of mutual engagement

The student teachers shared a number of common experiences. They were involved in the same input sessions, read the same chapters and articles, and, overall, encountered the same educational discourses. They worked on the same assignments, sometimes individually and sometimes as groups, and they shared the same daily routines including timetables, breaks, lunch times, etc. In addition, they went into schools at the same times with the same set of tasks centred on the English language curriculum and textbooks common to all government schools across the emirates, and generally encountered similar challenges in working in English language classrooms in UAE primary schools. All this was part of the experiencing and negotiating on a daily basis over months and years, entailed by being student teachers in the Bachelor of Education programme at the HCT in the context of the comtemporary UAE.

This common experience and engagement creates a shared history, which can be recalled and referenced in discussions. Thus, in a focus group discussion about language and culture, students were able to draw on classroom discussions with their college teachers from the previous year: 'Do you remember the example that Alice gave about the French word ... they don't want to use the word "Walkman"™'. The online discussion forums were another means by which the students were able to engage with students from their own college community of practising student teachers as well as with students from other colleges, drawing on common experiences from school and from the programme.

Mutual engagement entails responding to others as part of the process of establishing relationships of mutuality. One way the students developed these mutual relations was by offers of assistance to each other concerning the challenges of student teaching. As an example of this, a student teacher initiated an interaction by voicing a request: 'Really listen to the story of this girl who is in grade one and I hope to have solutions and suggestions from you' (*Madidah, A critical incident during TP, NEED HELP*). This elicited three responses, all opening with empathetic expressions of shared concern: 'I think this is really a difficult situation' (*Zainab*); 'It really is a problem, but each problem should have a solution' *(Adiba)*; and 'I really felt sad when I read your story about this girl' *(Mayyadah)*.

Another aspect of establishing relationships of mutual engagement is recognizing and being responsive to the needs of others, even when these are not stated explicitly, or expressed as an overt request for support or assistance: 'Thank you so much for sharing with me your experience. I want to give you a solution for the problem that you had with the little student in grade' (*Adiba, Dealing with challenging behaviour, Hi Warqa*). Mutual engagement can also involve collegial empathy and approbation: 'Hello Asiya, Your posting is very interesting. I was impressed with the way you dealt with that difficult unprofessional situation with the supervisor. I think that I would have done the same if I were in your place' (*Fellah, Dealing with challenging behaviour, Re: Oh my God*). The recognition here of what constitutes a 'difficult unprofessional situation' reflects a level of connection between the participants that is characteristic of a community of practice. Mutual engagement also comes through at times through the choice of vocabulary, as in the explicit use of 'connect' in the following: 'I really like your posting Maizah. I especially connect with your opinion that learning to be a teacher makes you think twice about ... how individual decisions affect the children' (*Farida, How teaching has changed my life, Re: 180 degrees*).

Mutuality can also be seen in the cumulative development of issues and questions between community members within their dialogues. The following is an example involving four student teachers in which the argument moves through stages of assertion, complication, challenge and synthesis. The first student, Nabihah, begins the dialogue with a concern based on her observations in schools: 'What concerns me most is the teacher herself. Some teachers teach the students without being concerned if they understood the lesson or not' (*Nabihah, Moral Issues, Teaching without having a conscience*). A second student responds in agreement but adds another dimension to the issue: 'I agree with you Nabihah, this is what we see and observe in our schools ... On the other hand, I think there are some good teachers who do give their lessons in the best way they can' (*Adiva, Moral Issues, Re: Teaching without having a conscience*). A third student enters the discussion with a counter-opinion that offers a possible explanation of the issue in terms of the organizational structures teachers have to work within: 'Why do we always blame the teachers?!! I disagree with teachers who do that, [i.e. ignore student learning] however this happens because of lack of time and supervision pressure to finish off the textbook and teach every word in it' (*Farouz, Moral Issues, Re: Teaching without having a conscience*). A fourth student enters, diplomatically finding points of agreement with both sides of the discussion: 'I agree with you Nabihah, that it is the teacher's responsibility to teach with a conscience, but I strongly agree with Farouz that "we can't blame the teacher only"' (*Samihah, Moral Issues, Re: Teaching without having a conscience*).

In discussions like this students are sharing experiences, trialling points of view, working through issues and responding to each others' perspectives, while at the same time establishing and maintaining relations of mutuality through this shared engagement with common issues. While the engagement with common issues is reflected in the shared lexis, the mutuality is reflected in the use of names and the use of the inclusive 'we' that embraces the community within an individual's speech acts.

Finally, mutual engagement can also be seen in the detailed responses students offered to the multiple points made in each other's messages. One student raised the issue of children's differing needs and argued that teachers need to plan their teaching taking into account the different levels of their learners. In her response, another student moves back and forth between the originator's viewpoint and her own, weaving them together as a dialogue within her own words:

> The issue you're raising is very important ... You've talked about looking at individuals' specific needs; this is necessary, nevertheless it takes time. What I suggest is looking at needs in terms of groups ... You also mentioned starting from where the learner is and I totally agree with you. (*Fellah 449, Beliefs about teaching, Re: Different Learners, Different Lessons*)

Overall, the shared history, support, empathy and connections between students are persuasive indicators of a considerable degree of mutuality, but this mutual engagement rests on a common understanding of their shared enterprise. The student teachers relate to each other, in part, because they are all interested in the common set of issues, questions and challenges defined by their joint enterprise and constituted within a shared discourse. It is to the notion of developing a common understanding of the community's joint enterprise that I turn next.

Developing a common understanding of the joint enterprise

By developing a history of common practice, including working together on common tasks, co-constructing new forms of knowledge, sharing experiences, aims, hopes, fears and dreams, the student teachers have developed a common discourse as well as a sense of community, of shared identity, which allows members of the group to feel able to speak for the group. Whether in fact the students are justified in claiming to speak on behalf of the group is not so much the point, though as discussed in the section above, the students do share a great deal in terms of educational histories; rather, the fact that they do feel justified is indicative of a sense of common understanding. Jenkins makes the point thus in relation to social identities: 'What is significant is not that people see or understand things in the same ways, or that they see and understand things in ways which differ from other communities, but that their shared symbols allow them to believe that they do' (Jenkins, 1996: 107).

In many instances the students' understanding of the enterprise they are engaged in is energized by a common vision for the future outcome of that common enterprise. In such cases a common belief in a shared vision of the community's future mission is implicit within their understanding of what they are currently doing. The following is typical in its assumption of this common sense of mission and vision for the future:

> Hi everyone ... I know that we are all looking at our future in an optimistic look [sic] ... all of us feel that we are ready to face the challenge and hopefully we will be ... BUT never say that we are taught everything that makes us perfect teachers, learning never stops at a specific stage or degree. Learning is a long life journey. (*Adiva, What I'm looking forward to in my teaching career, Be a good teacher*)

After an initial introductory statement using 'I' Adiva quickly positions herself as speaking for the wider community of practice as she pronounces that *we* are all optimistic about the future and are ready for its challenges. There is also an element of establishing the scope of the enterprise here, flagged by the capitalized 'BUT', followed by two negative imperatives summoning the community to embrace an ethic of continuous learning and improvement.

Shared thinking can also be evidenced by the assumptions that are made about what is, or can be, taken as understood by a 'speaker' as they address an audience. In the following posting, a student teacher refers to the purpose of the students' common enterprise, in terms of implementing 'the much needed changes', with no preliminary introduction or explanation:

> The B.Ed. programme has given me a great deal of knowledge, such as the importance of learning styles, multiple intelligences, orientations to teaching, classroom management, lesson planning and successful strategies for teaching EFL learners. In my opinion, progress and change in teaching will come slowly in the UAE but we must remember that Rome wasn't built in a day and be thankful that we as the first batch of TEYL graduates will be instrumental in implementing the much needed changes. (*Sara, Beliefs about teaching, Then and Now*)

In addition to the condensation of meaning evident in 'the much needed changes' and the common understandings about purpose, assumed to be shared among 'we as the first batch of TEYL graduates', there is a great deal of specific educational discourse and terminology here, such as 'learning styles', 'multiple intelligences', 'orientations to teaching', 'classroom management', 'lesson planning' and 'EFL learners'. These are all part of the bank of shared styles, practices and representations that is another defining feature of a community of practice.

Developing a shared discourse repertoire

Common participation and common understanding shapes and is shaped by common styles, common practices and common representations. In other words, partly enabling and partly reflecting the shared foundation of understanding that we have observed above, is a common pool of shared language and shared representation, a shared discourse which co-constitutes community and communication.

Sometimes the language that comprises the shared discourse derives from organizational factors such as course codes and titles, assignment titles and the shorthand labels for roles and people, such as SSTs for supervising school teachers. At other times it derives from shared stories or common narratives that come to form a communal semantic framework of shared understandings and assumptions. This can be seen in the following exchange between two students from different college communities.

> Since joining the B.Ed., I realized that some of the ways I have been taught through the English subject during school are not the only and appropriate one to the teaching and learning cycle. This is according to the input and discussions about different teaching and learning theories that we've had in the programme. These theories supported me to build up my own beliefs about teaching and learning. (*Areebah, Beliefs about teaching, Before and After!*)

> I strongly agree with you Areebah because the B.Ed. Programme has changed my beliefs about teaching English to young learners because as you know, we were taught English in inappropriate methods. However, the programme tried to develop us professionally and prepared us to be English teachers for the future based on different teaching approaches and assumptions. As a student teacher, I have been influenced by some of these approaches and they really made changes for my teaching. (*Madidah, Beliefs about teaching, Re: Before and After!*)

One of the consequences of the establishment of a shared discourse repertoire in a community of practice is the quick setting up of a problem or issue to be discussed, with little in the way of introductory preambles and formalities, reflecting assumptions about a shared base of knowledge and understanding. In the exchange above, we see common references to the input of the B.Ed. degree and the assumption of a shared understanding of the students' negative school experience, flagged by the preliminary 'as we all know'. Such features form part of the stories which, through a performative of telling and retelling, come to comprise the community's shared repertoire.

Sometimes the community's shared repertoire derives from the common knowledge base the students are being inducted into. Thus we see shared references to terms like: *group work, team work, scaffolding, print-rich environments, individual learning needs* and *individual learning styles, multiple intelligences, formative* and *summative assessments, curriculum, lesson plans, misbehaviour, classroom management, the teaching and learning cycle, teaching strategies* and *feedback*, to list just some items of this shared discourse repertoire, many of which we have seen already in this chapter. The shared discourse may also derive from and reflect a shared world view or narrative that has been constructed. One example of such a shared narrative is the journey from experiencing old-fashioned, 'traditional' ways of teaching while a school student, before encountering 'new' or 'modern' methods of teaching at college.

However, while contributing to the sense of shared purpose that is vital to the establishment of a community, such markers can also serve as deterrents to communication with those beyond the community's boundaries, in part because those outside lack the specialized discourse, and in part because as the discourse becomes reified it may be difficult to acknowledge the potential value of perspectives couched in language outside the discourse. As Mercer puts it:

> Trapped within their technical vocabularies, ways of organizing texts and contextual frames of reference, members of particular discourse communities may find it hard to represent and share unconventional ideas about their shared area of interest – and so find it hard to conceive of radical alternatives to conventional views, or to develop new, fresh perspectives on the problems and issues with which they are dealing. (Mercer, 2000: 115)

This is something that we will discuss further in this chapter under the topic of alignment and is also something that will emerge as a key theme in Chapters 4, 5 and 6.

In the preceding sections we have seen how the development of an evolving community of practice has been effected through the development of mutual forms of engagement, characterized by a common discursive repertoire reflecting and shaping a joint understanding of the student teachers' common enterprise. Yet, as discussed in Chapter 1, the student teachers' evolving community of practice is embedded within a wider 'constellation' of communities of practice. Having established the contours of the student teachers' engagement as one mode of belonging to their evolving community of practice, we can revisit the notions of 'locality', 'constellations' and 'boundaries' in relation to communities in more detail as part of belonging through the mode of alignment.

Belonging and Alignment

Alignment entails looking beyond the boundaries of a particular community of practice and considering its relations to other related communities and its place within wider communities. Alignment transcends the here and now and focuses on coordinating and synergizing a community's energies with those of other communities. This work is more outward looking than the work of engagement, involving social relations with other communities and groups, and is thus of a more political nature. In terms of identities, alignment has particular importance for positional identities and the ways individuals are positioned within unequal social relations, since the configurations between communities, like all social relations, inevitably involve relations of power (Foucault, 1997a).

Part of the challenge of alignment is 'to give members a legitimate role in society by linking their ideas with those of the broader educational community' (Buysse et al., 2003: 274). As such, the work of alignment involves recognizing the location of a community and its members within the wider community; it involves formulating, articulating and sharing principles and objectives in terms of the community and its members' relations to other communities and their members; and it involves negotiating, arguing and persuading others as part of developing strategies for putting these principles and objectives into place. I begin by using the notion of locality to consider some global–local tensions and then go on to explore some of the border practices that are occurring around the boundaries of the evolving community of practice.

Locality

We saw in Chapter 2 how the student teachers' identities are being constructed in a context that draws on both local and global discursive resources. This reminds us that in working on this project of creating a teaching identity, they are not creating something out of nothing; they are not able to forge new meanings of 'teacher' and 'teaching' that bear no relation to meanings of teacher and teaching in wider social and historical contexts. Rather, their professional identities are constrained in terms of pre-existing, 'global' and 'local' discursive configurations. The student teachers' work involves relating these to each other and to their own experiences as they negotiate the meanings of being a teacher and teaching in this particular place and time.

We can see this happening in the following discussion about whether there is such a thing as a universally appropriate method of teaching, or whether all methods need to be contextualized if they are to be effective, because of cultural differences between children. One student, using a somewhat behaviourist image of children, argued for minimal differences between global and local meanings:

> Teaching is still the same; the children, all of them are children, native or non-native. I feel that maybe ... the children are like clay. The teacher can do whatever with them ... the children are the same but the teacher ... they have the same thinking ... still they are children. We can do whatever we want with them. (*Takiyah, FG 1*)

The line of argument is that since children are made up of the same malleable material the world over, teaching is fundamentally the same job regardless of the context. This view was challenged in the discussion by another student: 'The method that they are using to teach English in the UK; if we want to use it here we have to modify it' (*Kamilah, FG 1*). For this student, the gap between the global and the local was far wider though not unbridgeable.

A related tension centred on the relative use of English and Arabic in English language classes. One student, reflecting the 'English only' views prevalent in communicative language teaching, argued for the need 'to teach our students English, not to emphasize their Arabic language' (*Nabila, Moral issues, I'm an English 'Arabic' teacher*). However, others challenged the transposing of practices from global EFL teaching into the local context without considering other factors, such as the lack of focus on speaking in the curriculum, the lack of opportunities for students to practise English outside the classroom, the weak relationship between school and home and the lack of time devoted to the English curriculum, all of which led to the conclusion that the teacher should 'try to use simple English which is suitable for the standards of the students' (*Maitha, Moral issues, Re: I'm an English 'Arabic' teacher*). Maitha insists on connecting classrooms to the 'real world' of the local context, rather than seeing them as 'closed boxes' or 'isolated spaces' for learning (Pennycook, 2000), as tends to be the case when we only adopt a macro, global perspective. The topic of language and culture appears again in Chapter 4 within the discussion of the community's discursively constructed systems of knowledge and belief.

Boundaries and border practices

In conceptualizing the student teachers' community of practice within the wider set of communities of practice that comprise the enterprise of education, the issue of boundaries must inevitably arise, involving in particular the shared objects and shared practices that provide connections across communities. For the student teachers, education books and classroom resources originating in other education communities, or portfolios and laminated teaching materials that are taken from the college to schools, are examples of the former; while drawing on international education literature as part of researching and writing projects, devising lesson plans in college that will be implemented in schools and negotiating the content of a lesson with a supervising college teacher and a supervising school teacher, are examples of the latter.

Hand in hand with these objects and practices, members cross boundaries by being members of multiple communities and in so doing have the potential to be a source of continuity across different communities and practices. In terms of other communities, it is clearly the community of college teachers that the students value most highly and who play the most significant role in shaping their practices. The educational discourse the student teachers subscribe to derive from the college classroom; but this discourse finds its fulfilment, in the sense of being both tested and realized, in the school classrooms.

Thus the 'border practices' that inevitably occur as part of the students' movement between these worlds, are a significant aspect of their development. Indeed, although the initial conscious shaping of practice occurs in the college classroom, it is expected that much of their learning to teach will be achieved in this arena of boundary-crossing practices through participation in the college *and* the school communities. The power relationships in these situations and the expectations of the students' roles – elements of positional and figurative identities – have very real implications in terms of the purposes and possibilities of these border practices. These implications can be played out as both sources of opportunity for growth and as limitations upon that growth. Examples of the latter were evident in comments where the students voiced frustrations about working with their supervising school teacher as can be seen in the following in which a student laments the limiting effect her supervising school teacher's approach has on her ability effectively to implement her own preferred approach to behaviour management:

> I tried different ways of using signs and gestures and body language but it did not work and this is because of my SST. She doesn't have

management rules in her class. So I cannot apply what I want and believe that it will work if my SST is using her own methods, which are beating them or shouting at them. (*Karimah, Dealing with challenging behaviour, My SST is the problem*)

Karimah is grappling with the complex difficulties of crossing borders and trying to establish one's own teaching personality in a classroom that is already populated with someone else's teaching personality, someone else's teaching style, someone else's classroom practices and someone else's educational beliefs (Britzman, 1991). But she constructs the situation in simple oppositional terms: 'I tried different ways ... but it did not work because of my SST' and 'She doesn't have management rules ... So I cannot apply'. The following response to Karimah's posting also demonstrates this division between 'good' and 'bad' as well as reflecting the overriding significance of the college teachers and the beliefs shaped in the college classroom in the eyes of most of the community:

Try not to let your SST's attitude influence you in a negative way. If you believe that there are other ways to manage the students' behavior then you should look for them. I think you can always ask for help from your SCTs and peers ... Make a classroom rules chart. Read it with the students whenever they misbehave or in the beginning of each session. Try to use child-centred activities and group work where each child has to do something. Use TPR activities to get their attention. (*Asiya, Dealing with challenging behaviour, Re: My SST is the problem*)

The SST is constructed here as a potentially contaminating influence, while the references to the community-building practice of developing a 'classroom rules chart', to 'child-centred activities', 'group work' and 'TPR' remind Karimah of central elements of the community's beliefs. However, the SSTs were not always constructed in this negative light. Sometimes they too were recognized as sources of positive influence. We can see this in the following comment from a student teacher who was also having problems managing student behaviour in the classroom:

So, I spent some time with my SST talking about this problem and she gave me some advice which was, at the beginning of the class, talk with the whole class about the behaviours that I want to see in the class and we were able to set class rules that we must all follow. (*Azziza, Dealing with challenging behaviour, Big students*)

Another student commented, in a useful reminder that the negative stories about what is going on in school are not universal, 'I am gaining lots of experiences in teaching, in getting feedback from my SST by listening to her ideas and suggestions to improve my teaching' (*Madidah, Insights from the Internship, Goodbye TP*). Indeed, part of the value of the school experience is to give the student teachers insights into the roles and responsibilities of those in the teaching community, which comes through in the following excerpt:

> This internship is really different from the previous teaching practices. It provides me the opportunity to feel like a real teacher since I have a lot of responsibilities related to teaching inside the school and outside the school and I am teaching 60% of my SST's load. I start my school day by attending the assembly, starting my lessons on time, checking students' books, planning for the next day, helping the teachers for their lessons by giving them different ideas and activities, helping the SST if she needs any help and taking the students in to the cafeteria to have the lunch and do their homework in the homework session. (*Farihah 499, Insights from the Internship, Re: Goodbye TP*)

Another valuable aspect of the teaching placement is gaining a sense of the school as a community. This discovery came about through the border practices of teaching practice for the following student teacher:

> Through this internship I have established different relationships with other staff members, not only my SST and other English teachers. To elaborate, I had the chance to talk to the social worker, nurse and other teachers. This helped me to understand different roles and responsibilities within this community that I didn't recognize before. (*Zainab, Insights from the internship, Internship experience*)

Indeed, student teaching placements are border practices in a rich variety of senses. Sometimes student teachers have successfully brokered new practices to school communities:

> It's a great success when people believe in you and follow your way of doing things ... That's exactly what happened to me this week during teaching practice ... During this week I started to use different activities and strategies ... my SST started to change her way too and started to follow my lesson plans and materials ... Even in using English in the classroom. My SST used to speak Arabic with the students most of the time. However, when she saw that I am using English all the time and encouraging the students to do the same things, she started to use less Arabic in the classroom. (*Maysa, A critical incident during teaching practice, Copycat*)

Here the teacher approves of the practice the student introduces. Such approval is not always the case and sometimes new practices are rejected and become a source of conflict: 'I have problem with my SST she doesn't like the new strategies of teaching, she always complains that this not useful and the students will be confused' (*Almas, What I'm looking forward to in my teaching career, Learning lessons from bitter past mistakes*). Such conflicts highlight the inherent challenges, in addition to the opportunities, for the student teachers as they engage in border practices. As Britzman (1991: 76) argues, the very business of student teaching 'is about struggling between tradition and change, of having to negotiate one's own territory and construct one's own intentions amid pre-established spaces already "overpopulated" by the intentions and practices of others.'

These potential difficulties of the students' boundary crossings can sometimes be eased by their bringing artefacts as well as new practices with them into the school classroom. The sharing of carefully and lovingly crafted teaching materials can offer a focal point for negotiation and enable the student to be perceived as bringing added value to the situation, particularly in a context like the UAE where government schools are generally equipped with limited resources. Indeed, students commented that teachers on the whole value the colourful resources they were able to bring from college, though even the most attractive materials could be dismissed by the conversation-stopping discourse of 'real teaching':

> I remember, not a teacher telling me something, a supervisor. She told me that 'Now you are young and enthusiastic and you want to do a lot of things. And these are all great things that you have produced.' They were materials and stuff. 'But when you will be a real teacher you won't do these things.' (*Nabila, FG 2*)

Overall, we need to note that boundary practices can be both a source of transformative connections as well and a source of risk, insofar as they have the potential to lead to conflicts that stifle those same transformations. This is a theme that will be examined later in the context of the discursive construction of the community's systems of knowledge and belief and in terms of the construction of intrapersonal identity and interpersonal relations. However, before we look at these issues in the following three chapters, we need to examine the third mode through which student teachers can be seen as belonging to their evolving community of practice, imagination.

Belonging and Imagination

Imagination is fundamental to being human in terms of moving beyond the immediate world of experience. As we saw in Chapter 1, imagination is key to cognitive tools such as language and to our ability to cast ourselves into social roles. Thus, 'It follows that teacher education, the process of becoming a teacher ... is in part a journey of imaginative development. Students come to imagine teaching and themselves as teachers in new ways' (Fettes, 2005: 3).

Imagination does not imply a retreat from reality into a realm of fantasy, but rather a process of creating new *images* and new connections that reach across trajectories of time and space as part of the ongoing negotiation of identity (Wenger, 1998). 'Imagination can exceed what everyday thought tolerates as normal' (Britzman, 1998: 61). Imagination is both retrospective and prospective in that it draws on the experiential and narrative resources of the past to narrate a vision of the future (Bernstein, 1996: 78–79, cited in Sachs, 1999: 3) as part of an ongoing process of (re)creation. In this section we look at some of the ways the student teachers are accomplishing this ongoing reinvention as part of the third dimension of the work of belonging to the evolving community of practice.

Self-consciousness and reflection

In order to move from the given to the possible, individuals need to develop conscious and objectified conceptions of their emerging selves, as part of identity-as-self-consciousness, that can be used as reflective heuristic tools (Holland *et al.*, 1998: 40). For the student teachers this involves standing back and making observations or comments about the self, objectifying it for purposes of discussion and analysis, as part of a process of 'seeing themselves as teachers' (Danielewicz, 2001), developing an identity of 'me-as-teacher' (Furlong & Maynard, 1995) and 'feeling like a teacher' (Calderhead & Shorrock, 1997). Such work can be seen as a process of self-conscious consolidation, which provides a platform for further growth and development. In the student teachers' context, personal realization and professional fulfilment are often intertwined, in that much of the personal development they describe, for example, in terms of her confidence to stand in front of people and discuss issues, are also key professional qualities for teachers.

Thus, in the following posting a student discusses these changes both in the context of the college classroom, working with peers and college teachers, and in the context of the school, working with schoolteachers and students. The frequent use of 'I', 'my' and 'myself' reflects the self-consciousness which culminates in the final sentence when she refers to herself in the third person in what can be read as an explicit act of self-authoring. I have quoted this posting in full, since it summarizes many of the themes and issues touched on in other postings and can be seen as representative of the wider community of practice:

> Teaching has a great impact on my life in a variety of ways and I can clearly see this in my personality and how it has changed since I entered the programme. During the first two years I was known as the calm and shy student in the class and as well; this was obvious through my teaching style. Moreover, even though I had good communication skills with my peers, I found some difficulties while working in groups in a particular project in a way that I can't express my opinions to my peers and I used to accept most of their ideas even I was disagreed with some of their points. This was also obvious during the class time (input sessions) with our teachers, while discussing an issue I used to have something to say or commenting on their ideas, but …… ??
>
> Now I can see the difference in my personality, attitudes and my teaching style. I think being at different schools and working with different people is the main factor that has changed my personality. Moreover, reading different theories and attending different conferences are also other factors that played an important role in the process of change. Now I really find my self an adaptable and a flexible person, who can work independently or in groups and in different environments. Regarding my communication skills, I can deal with a wide variety of people such as teachers and children and being a diplomatic person helped me to express my opinions without hesitating.
>
> Furthermore, teaching has changed my life in a way that I feel responsible for each child in the class by selecting appropriate strategies in order to allow students to meet their needs. Dealing with different behaviors, selecting appropriate assessment strategies, implementing different theories and preparing resources are all part of the teacher's responsibilities. Moreover teaching helped me to be a reflective person, in a way that I always think in depth (what, why and how), especially after giving a lesson and implementing a new strategy I ask my self, did it work well? Why? Why not? What do I want to change or add? etc … What is more, teaching allowed me to feel that being a teacher does not mean I have to stop learning. In other words, the teacher is the one who is responsible for their own professional development. As I see it, teaching helped me to develop my professional language as an English teacher, through the use of appropriate language (clear instructions,

good voice level and appropriate questions) with the students, which allows me to feel confident throughout presentations.

All in all, I can clearly see the difference between Rukan now and four years ago, which is noticeable from both my SST and SCT comments. (*Rukan, How teaching has changed my life, A great change!*)

This posting illustrates how learning to teach – indeed learning generally – has the capacity to make a student feel their identity has been transformed. We can see evidence of self-consciousness, of learning and development, of change and growth, at many levels: at personal levels of confidence and assertiveness; at professional levels of knowledge, communication skills and teaching strategies as well as in terms of less tangible qualities of understanding, responsibility and reflection. The student explores where she has been ('during the first two years I was known as … four years ago') recognizes where she is in the present ('Rukan now') and looks to the future ('being a teacher does not mean that I have to stop learning.'). It is important to note that in talking about trajectories over time, it is a narrative-focused notion of time that is important – as Bruner puts it, 'time that is bounded not simply by clocks but by the humanly relevant actions that occur within its limits' (Bruner, 1996: 133). The key to the events comprising the students' identities over time is not so much whether they occurred before or after some other event but that they endure meaningfully in the particular student's narrative construction of their development as a teacher. As a part of this development, the sort of self-conscious exploration we see above can be a source of re/inspiration, re/invention and re/fashioning of both the community of practice and individual identities.

A particular form of self-consciousness that Rukan highlights in her personal and professional growth is reflection, which she links to thinking in depth and asking questions. Reflection can be seen as another form of imagination in the sense of stepping back, even if briefly, from immediate concerns and realities as part of a process of self-conscious, deliberative, problem-solving (Roberts, 1998: 53) within a holistic orientation to teaching – a way of being a teacher that entails open-mindedness, responsibility and wholeheartedness (Zeichner & Liston, 1996: 9–10). Reflection in this sense is something that was significant to a number of community members. Again, the way it is linked with both the personal and the professional shows how integrated these two domains are for the students and how central teaching is within their overall identities:

> Teaching enhanced my critical thinking skills. It made me a reflective person who reflects constantly on everything, not only on the incidents

that take place in school but also on every article I read or programme I watch. I just feel that reflection deepens my understanding of certain things and strengthens my beliefs about teaching. I know that what I am going to say might seem odd to some of you, but I feel that reflection, somehow, makes me a better person! (*Asiya, How teaching has changed my life, A positive change*)

Asiya uses a series of 'I' statements here to connect the reflection she has learned to do in her teaching, with activities in her wider professional practices and her personal life. The habit of making connections like this across time and space enables teachers to see endless potential for classroom learning in the their own wider lives and those of their students; it also helps them to see what they do in the classroom within wider social and political contexts. Another aspect of making new connections is conceiving of and creating different futures, which is the focus of the following section.

Creation

Creativity is not so much about creating something out of nothing as about seeing and creating new connections, looking at familiar things in a new light. According to John-Steiner (1997: 51–52), 'creativity lies in the capacity to see more sharply and with greater insight that which one already knows or which is buried at the margin of one's awareness'. In this sense, creation is akin to Foucault's (1997a) notion of ethics as self-formation: both involve seeing and indentifying new patterns among existing ideas or experiences, developing new models, new representations and configurations, becoming animated by ideas, seeing the past as contingent and the future as shapeable, generating potential scenarios, improvising new practices and envisioning possible future practices, identities and communities. Creation can thus be a potent and energizing force, as experiences and ideas come together, with transformative effects in terms of identity development:

> When I entered this programme, there was something in my mind and heart refusing the situation in UAE government schools and my goal was to help change this situation. Therefore the TEYL programme was my hope to seek the knowledge and learn some strategies and methods to make some changes … How/when did I start developing and improving? … It was at the beginning of this programme when our teachers were introducing new concepts or theories like the ZPD or social theory. We all in the class agreed that we had thought about and applied this idea before and were surprised that there were some

psychologists who studied the same thing we are thinking about. From that moment, I felt that the change happened to me and in my friends. I started to learn with high ambition and be open-minded to the different opinions and theories that helped me to develop, improve and find my own road in teaching. (*Samihah, Beliefs about teaching, Three words to describe the changes*)

Here, teaching is perceived as a creative act through the authoring of fresh links and combinations between knowledge and experience, leading to a capacity for transformation. We can also see the student orienting herself within the landscape of UAE education and reflecting on her own trajectory – 'my own road in teaching' – moving from a vague sense of refusal ('something in my heart and mind') to an articulation of 'high ambition' and an intention to 'make some changes.' Creation in the sense of conceiving of different futures can also come about through an imaginative empathizing with others:

Imagine yourself in the classroom just to receive orders from the teacher without any normal interaction, how would you deal with it? ... if the teacher deals with the students as their mother or at least their friend, she will get a nice result at the end. Close relationships between the student and teachers help them to explore their learning more as they have a chance to ask for clarification, to ask for teachers' guidance and they have the freedom to give their opinion. (*Nashita, Beliefs about teaching, Re: Interaction (formal and informal chat in the classroom)*)

The student teacher here uses imagination, in the form of empathetic identification with others, in order to author possibilities beyond the realm of here and now experience, where closer, more human relationships between students and teachers in turn open up new potentials for learning. As a strategy, the rhetorical question, inviting, and at the same time presuming, active sympathy with students in government school classrooms, serves to monitor and maintain the commitment of the community to a particular set of educational beliefs. In this sense, it exemplifies the discursive co-construction of community and communication. The message also reminds us that imagination is a mode of belonging to a community, for we can see in this posting each of the three dimensions that are the source of coherence for a community of practice: mutual engagement is evident in the direct address to peers through the rhetorical question; joint enterprise is evident in the element of negotiated response to the ongoing situation of student teaching, that both defines the situation and is part of what makes the situation theirs; and shared discourse repertoire can be seen in the educational lexical choices and in the assumed understanding of a difference between the ways that teachers usually deal with students and 'normal interaction'.

Conclusion

Communities of practice offer a way of looking at the learning that occurs when people are working together as part of a socially valued enterprise. In this chapter we have explored the ways the HCT B.Ed. student teachers can fruitfully be conceptualized as a community of practice via an examination of their developing teacher identities in relation to the 'work of belonging' to this evolving community of practice. This entailed considering the students' figurative, positional and authored identities within the three broad modes of belonging of engagement, alignment and imagination. In achieving this 'work of belonging' the students are negotiating their way among a range of powerful and sometimes conflicting influences including those associated with family expectations, past experiences of teachers and teaching, discourses of gender and the discourses associated with the English language. Yet out of this mix, these young women are able to forge something that is their own, exemplified in Zainab's statement cited above in the section Choosing English:

> Among my family, I think I have changed their idea about learning to teach. They have noticed the authentic and interesting way that we moved through the programme ... I believe in myself ... that we will all do something very special and effective in teaching in the UAE.

Learning to teach and becoming a teacher clearly offers these young women scope for agency in a context where women are usually perceived as constrained and repressed. In this they seem to echo Mahmood's (2005) argument that agency can just as much take the form of finding creative, and potentially transformative, ways to inhabit norms as it can of openly resisting them.

Having explored reasons for choosing teaching as a foundational act of belonging that involved all three modes, we looked at the work of belonging through engagement in terms of the student teachers' mutual engagement in a jointly defined enterprise in which they employ a common discursive repertoire. We also examined some of the ways in which the students are aligning their community of practice and its enterprise with other communities within the 'constellation' of communities comprising UAE education, and, in particular, in relation to the schools where they engage in 'border practices'. In addition, we explored some of the ways the student teachers are engaging in the work of imagination through practices of self-consciousness, reflection and creation.

A number of factors have coalesced in the formation of a remarkably cohesive community of practice. Yet the same factors that underlie this coherence are also sources of potential conflict and exclusion. A number of tensions were touched on in this chapter that will be explored in greater depth in later chapters. These include the inherent limitations in the establishing of a shared discourse repertoire that reifies and temporarily fixes particular understandings and particular ways of looking at the world, and so by definition excludes other, potentially equally valid ways because they do not make sense within the dominant discourse. This is related to another source of tension discussed in this chapter, which was the conflict that can potentially occur as part of border practices when members of one community of practice take objects, practices and discourses from their community and transpose them into another community. Both these tensions are also evident in the vein of antagonism towards the teachers and the teaching of the past that has emerged in this chapter. These tensions will be explored in the following three chapters where we examine the discursive construction of the community of practice in terms of its system of knowledge and belief, interpersonal relations and intrapersonal identities .

Note
1. Data from the focus groups are referenced as *FG 1, 2, 3*, or *Arabic*. Data from the WebCT postings are referenced using the format: *Student* (pseudonym), *Topic title, Thread title* ('*Re*' indicates response).

Chapter 4
The Discursive Construction of Systems of Knowledge and Belief

The analysis in this chapter examines the discursive construction of the community of practice in terms of the first of the three constitutive effects of discourse noted in Chapter 1: the construction of reality as reflected in systems of knowledge and belief. The notion of systems of knowledge and belief refers to the rhetorical schemata that link statements and make them intelligible within a given field. It relates to Halliday's ideational function of language. In considering the discursive construction of an evolving community of practice we need to take account not only of the explicit utterances, interactions, attitudes and beliefs; we also need to locate these within wider social structures and practices, as reflected in the relevant social, historical, cultural and political discourses. Thus my analysis of texts will aim to 'examine actual patterns of language use with some degree of detail and explicitness but in ways that reconnect instances of local discourse with salient political, economic and cultural formations' (Luke, 1996: 11). I should note at the outset that this chapter's analysis of the pedagogical discourses structuring the student teachers' system of knowledge and belief follows Foucault (1980: 118) when he writes 'Now I believe that the problem does not consist in drawing the line between that in a discourse which falls under the category of scientificity or truth, and that which comes under some other category, but in seeing historically how effects of truth are produced within discourses which in themselves are neither true nor false'. That is, I am not so much concerned to judge the 'truth' value of the discourses discussed as to explore the ways in which they are used by the student teachers to construct particular language teacher identities. I return to this point at the end of the chapter.

Constructing the 'New' Teachers of the Present/Future Against the 'Traditional' Teachers of the Past

> Moving towards a more student-centred, active approach in all aspects of teaching is I believe the mission of the B.Ed. programme. In this way students take 'ownership' of their learning, which has the potential to make them more motivated, pro-active and interested learners. Passive learning belongs to the past. (*Sara, Dealing with Challenging Behaviour*)

One of the most characteristic discursive strategies employed by the B.Ed. students is the setting up of a series of strong binary oppositions that serve to define, establish, maintain and monitor the community. The binaries revolve around a core opposition between the 'new' teacher, who uses 'new' or 'modern' teaching methods and approaches, defined against the 'traditional' teacher using 'traditional' methods and approaches in the classroom. The 'traditional' teachers include both the majority of the teachers the students experienced in the 'then' of their own schooling, as well as the majority of the supervising school teachers (SSTs) they have worked with during their teaching placements, in the 'there' of government schools; while 'new' or modern' teaching is defined in terms of the approaches they have encountered during the 'now' of their years of study on the HCT B.Ed. degree, within the 'here' of college, and which they intend to implement in UAE government schools. Hence, this is also an opposition between 'them' and 'us', which involves the students investing significantly in a discursive divide between themselves and the teachers they are and will be working alongside. In fact, such is the prevalence of this commitment to the 'new' and the personal and professional passion with which the students testify to their belief in it, that it is possible to talk in terms of a 'conversion'.

A number of further distinctions support this major discursive opposition between the 'traditional' teachers of the past and the 'new' teachers of the present and future. Students are treated with 'insensitivity' or 'cruelty' in the 'traditional' classroom whereas 'sensitivity', 'kindness' and a concern for the 'whole student' and their individual needs is the modus operandi for the 'new' teacher. In 'traditional' classrooms, learning is 'passive' and learners display low motivation and self-esteem, whereas 'new' classrooms involve 'active' learning by motivated learners with positive self-esteem. Other oppositions focus on the way that the 'new' classroom is characterized by 'equality', whereas rigid hierarchy dominates the 'traditional' classroom. Teaching in the 'traditional' classrooms is an 'easy', straightforward business involving transmission of knowledge, whereas in 'new', learner-centred classrooms it is complex and challenging and the teacher is a facilitator. These binary oppositions, as represented in the discourse of the student teachers in the HCT's Bachelor of Education, are outlined in Table 4.1.

I explore the distinction between past and present in more detail below before going on to examine the other distinctions.

Table 4.1 The discursive construction of the 'traditional' versus the 'new' teacher

Traditional paradigm	New paradigm
The past – 'traditional' teachers and teaching – 'them'	The present/future – 'new' teachers and teaching – 'us'
'Insensitivity' / 'cruelty'	'Sensitivity' /' kindness'
Learners as a homogenous collective – children as 'empty vessels'	Learners as presenting individual styles, strengths and needs – children as 'geniuses'
'Teacher-centred'	'Student/learner/child-centred'
'Passive' learning	'Active' learning
'Low' motivation and self-esteem	'High' motivation and self-esteem
'Hierarchy'	'Equality'
Teacher as 'transmitter'	Teacher as 'facilitator'
Teaching as 'easy'	Teaching as 'complex'

Past versus present/future

One of the most frequent discursive strategies the student teachers employ in establishing the parameters of their community of practice is the drawing of a sharp dividing line between the past and the present/future. This usually entails a fierce rejection of the past in favour of the present. As one student in a focus group discussion put it, 'I just ... threw out everything I had about teaching from the past and I just acquire what I have ... what I'm learning now and what I'm doing at schools' (*Sahar, FG 1*). Many students gave a little more acknowledgement of the influence of past teaching approaches, while still insisting that they have moved irrevocably beyond these approaches. Linguistically the members of the community of practice establish this distinction by repeatedly contrasting then and now:

- '*I had always* thought ... *However* in the first few months of B.Ed.... .'
- '... *most of us started* ... however now ... '
- '*I never thought* ... however now ... '
- '*In the first stage* I viewed teaching as a matter of imitating other experienced teachers ... *Now I know* that learner-centred classes are the best ... '
- '*When I started teaching* I used all the ways I was taught with in the schools, such as the teacher speaks all the time and the students listen ... *Now I feel like a different person* ... '

The emphasis in these constructions is on a clean break with the past rather than a more evolutionary change or developmental growth in understanding. It is worth noting in this context, that most of these constructions occurred in the discussion board with the broad topic, 'Beliefs about teaching'. There was no suggestion that in discussing their beliefs, the students should contrast the past and present; rather, this seems to have been a construction that the students were particularly drawn to. In the following posting, a student's poem is fairly typical in its employment of this discursive strategy of establishing a clear opposition between 'then' and 'now' to emphasize the decisive nature of the break with the past:

> I never thought that teachers should have their own orientation to teaching and learning, however now I am quite sure about my orientation towards teaching and learning English.
>
> I never thought that students are different, however now I realized that each student has her own learning styles and different intelligences.
>
> I never thought that there are different approaches to teaching and learning English, however now I got a broad image of several approaches to teaching and learning English with knowing my preference.
>
> I never thought that clarifying the purpose of the task is important in students' learning, however now I would never give a task without identifying its purpose.
>
> I never thought that group work or cooperative learning plays an essential role in students' intellectual and emotional development, however now if you would have a chance to look at my lesson plans you will know that group work is my first concern.
>
> I never thought that motivating students towards learning has a significant effect on their studying, however now I can see clearly that my job is to motivate every single student in the class.
>
> I never thought that teaching is fun, however now since I practiced teaching, I notice that doing what you like is actually more than having fun.
>
> Finally, I believe that teaching comes equally from heart and mind. (Falak, Beliefs about teaching, I never thought!!)

This poem, with its seven stanzas reciting the same refrain, has a revelatory quality, evident in the repeated admission of dramatic change and in the passionate commitment to the newly adopted views. Yet while the description of change is intensely personal, it is also a public testimonial, exuding confidence in the newfound beliefs. Other students similarly described how 12 years of belief in what were once viewed as 'perfect methods' were overthrown in just a few months of study:

> Throughout twelve years of being a student in school, I had always thought that the best methods in making the students understand the lesson were through using the traditional methods such as memorizing … However, in the first couple of months in the B.Ed., all my beliefs about these perfect methods changed. (*Nafisah, Beliefs About Teaching, What are the appropriate methods to use in our classrooms?*)

The above comments, though passionate and personal, are focused on professional beliefs. In the following posting the student's comments about feeling 'like a different person' offer a similarly passionate testimony of change that even more explicitly suggests the convert's wholehearted and personal embrace of a new present/future and rejection of the past.

> When I started teaching I used all the ways I was taught with in the schools, such as the teacher speaks all the time and the students listen … Now I feel like a different person and I cannot believe that I was doing so with the students. (*Nabila, Beliefs about teaching, Re: My beliefs have changed in stages*)

We can also see this intensely personalized conversion in other postings, for example, in Nashita's opening line, 'Now I can say it and I can say it in a loud voice MY WHOLE LIFE HAS CHANGED' (*499, How Teaching Has Changed My Life, I Love Teaching, emphasis in original*). Some students, however, while still embracing change wholeheartedly, did present their conversion to new teaching beliefs in less dramatic fashion, as implied by the title of the thread 'My beliefs have changed in stages'. The initiator of this thread contrasts her teaching approach during the first year of the B.Ed. with her current views:

> My beliefs at this stage were somehow old-fashioned approaches that school teachers used to utilize. Lessons were viewed as teacher-centred classes where the teacher dictates the knowledge to students. Now I know that learner-centred classes are the best environments to improve students' learning in which the students are allowed to expand and explore their own knowledge. (*Halma, Beliefs about teaching, My beliefs have changed in stages*)

Despite the more measured tone, the elements of revelation and testimony with regard to past errant beliefs and wholehearted acceptance of new beliefs ('now I know') are still present here. The response below recognizes the testimonial aspect of the initial posting and offers supportive empathy ('most of us started in the same way') and optimistic solidarity ('now each of us had the opportunity to enter … ') that helps constitute the community as one of enthusiastic converts, whose passionate conviction is all the stronger for being in stark contrast to the beliefs of the past: 'To be honest with you most of us started in the same way … However, now, each of us had the opportunity to enter the 'teaching/learning world' and explore many theories, approaches and methods of teaching' (*Samihah, Beliefs about teaching, Re: My beliefs have changed in stages*).

What we see here is that these revelatory testimonies are part of a discursive strategy that involves drawing a passionate and personal, as well as professional, 'line in the sand' between the 'new', teachers that characterize the B.Ed. student teachers' community of practice as defined through their shared discourse repertoire, and the school teachers of their past and current (i.e. during teaching practice) experience.

An additional element in the students' distancing of past from present is their rejection of the emotional, as distinct from pedagogical, approaches of their past teachers. This comes through strongly in the posting below in the description of the teachers as being 'like monsters' and in the emphatic final words:

> In my opinion, this belief comes from our childhood education where the teachers are like monsters, they didn't care for our feelings and they were treating us like adults without any sense. I hope that those days don't come back again and I hope that these kind of teachers DON'T EXIST AGAIN IN THE WORLD AT ALL (*Nashita, Beliefs About Teaching, Re: Change of name, emphasis in original*)

Even more so than the passionate embrace of 'new' teaching approaches we saw above, statements like 'I hope those days don't come back again' and 'I hope these kind of teachers DON'T EXIST IN THE WORLD AT ALL' convey an epic, epoch marking, almost apocalyptic (with its emphatic capitalization) wish to break with the past that preceded engagement with learning to teach and the establishment of the Bachelor of Education students' community of practice. There is also a powerful sense of relief in these comments, perhaps best captured by another student's comment in a focus group discussion, 'We thought that we would be as our teachers but thanks, no: Thanks to God we are not like them' (*Nabila, FG 2*). But a number of the comments also indicate, particularly, for instance, in descriptions of past teachers as 'monsters' with no consideration for children's feelings, an almost visceral rejection of the past that has a strong emotional aspect related to the treatment of learners. I will explore this further in the section below.

'Sensitivity' versus 'insensitivity'

The distinction between insensitivity and 'cruelty', as opposed to 'sensitivity', kindness and understanding towards learners in the classroom, is another powerful binary opposition constructed in the student teachers' discourse. The majority of the teachers that the students recalled during the focus group discussions were remembered with fear and/or resentment for their loud voices and frequent use of punishment, rather than for any pedagogical inspiration they provided. The following comment was typical: 'I remember my first English teacher. She really was horrible. She always shouted at us. Even the good students she always shouted at them and hit them. She didn't consider if they were good or bad. She always was angry, upset. Because of that I really hate her' (*Moneira, FG 1*).

Another student made the point that this was not a matter of the odd 'bad apple' or teachers having the occasional bad day, but rather this was the common pattern among teachers in UAE government schools across the whole school year. 'I might sympathize with them if they were only bad for one day or one week, but not for the whole year. Not giving anything and always in a bad mood and always punishing students and always shouting. That's not a good excuse' (*Sabah, FG 1*).

The best that the students usually had to say about a past teacher was that, in contrast to the norm, she was kind; though interestingly it was often this rare, 'kind' teacher who inspired the students to first think about teaching: 'I remember my teacher when I was in grade four ... she was very helpful. She tried to make the lesson interesting ... so .... from grade four I put the English course in my mind ... because of her and her methods. (*Takiyah, FG 1*)

The experience of harsh teaching seems to have been so widespread to be taken as given among the students, reflected in the use of the inclusive 'we'. Thus in empathetic response to the above posting, another student replied:

> Your issue made me really sad because it reminded me of the days where in some subjects *we* memorized things without having any idea or understanding of these things ... some teachers think that students are machines ... they don't think of the students as humans who have needs and interests. (*Nashila, Beliefs About Teaching, Re: What are the appropriate methods to use in our classrooms?*)

The use of machines to describe students, suggests a metaphor of the school as a factory, and is reminiscent of the inhuman grind of education in Dickens' *Hard Times*, as indeed are a number of the student teachers' anecdotes of their experiences in schools.

Looking in hope to a different future, Sara commented that 'in years to come, students will hopefully gain an education that is free of discrimination, corporal punishment, sarcasm, de-motivation and cruelty' (*499, What I'm looking forward to in my teaching career, Re: When will September come?*). Many other students commented critically on the ongoing prevalence of these 'cruel' approaches to working with children in UAE classrooms. A posting about 'The Physical Punishment' for example, received nine replies. On a less dramatic level, one of the students cited in the section above about the past and present dichotomy, noted that whereas in the early stages of learning to teach she refused to listen to students who had problems understanding the lesson, she now employed strategies that are far more sympathetic to students: 'Now I give the students time to express themselves and encourage them to use English and to help each other, even if that means they will take the whole class to say their sentence' (*Nabila, Beliefs about teaching, Re: My beliefs have changed in stages*). There is a clear sense of 'now I know better' here, evidenced by the student's earlier remark in relation to her previous approach that 'I cannot believe I was doing so with the students.'

Associating 'insensitivity' with 'ignorance' and 'sensitivity' and 'kindness' with educational 'enlightenment', the students' criticisms are often supported by references to educational theory underlining how the 'new' teacher is able to support her views by appeal to the literature. Thus Asiya, refers to Gardner's (1983) multiple intelligence theory, as she laments the way in which students with non-linguistic intelligences are 'verbally attacked' for not doing well (*Asiya, Beliefs about teaching, Re: different learning styles*). Criticizing the ongoing practices of physical punishment in UAE schools, Manal notes, 'If we think that corporal punishment is an appropriate strategy to make students behave well, we are wrong because corporal punishment has both short term and long term consequences which affect students emotionally and physically' (*449, Moral Issues, Some of my moral concerns about education and teaching in the UAE's schools*). Drawing support from the education literature, she goes on in the same posting to point out that 'short term consequences are 'pain, fear, humiliation and even physical injury' and long term consequences include 'desensitization to violence, learning that physical violence solves problems, and even posttraumatic stress syndrome' (this is stated by Eggen and Kauchal: 289).' The employment of references to the education literature and technical terms like 'posttraumatic stress syndrome' reinforce the student teachers' sense of distinctness as 'enlightened' practitioners in contrast to what they see as the 'ignorant' practitioners of corporal punishment. The posting concludes with the rhetorical question, *'are our roles to teach these children positive morals which increase their self-esteem and moral self worth ... or are we as teachers preparing criminals to be well prepared for their world of crime?'*, the either/or form of which serves to underline this constructed binary division.

The opposition between 'kindness' and 'cruelty' that the student teachers establish indicates that the internal persuasiveness of the 'new' paradigm of progressive education might lie at least partially on an emotional level. The students' previous common experience of superficiality and meaninglessness, often coupled with emotional stress, during their schooling may well have provided particularly fertile ground for engaging with content that places considerable emphasis and value on the learner, such as child development and recent learning theories that the students encounter in the first two years of their degree, described in Chapter 2. Whatever the reason, the changes that the students testify to are dramatic at both personal and professional levels. We see this, for example, in Nashita's statement cited above, 'Now I can say it and I can say it in a loud voice MY WHOLE LIFE HAS CHANGED' or less dramatically in Shayma's statement that 'The B.Ed. programme hasn't only changed my beliefs about teaching, but it also changed my personal life' (*449, Beliefs about teaching, The impact of the B.Ed. programme on my life*).

As we shall see below, however, even in less dramatic examples of the students' written and spoken comments, there is considerable evidence of the deep investment the students have made in the particular discourses of teaching and learning they have encountered in their degree. One of the most prominent of these, and one that relates strongly to a preference for 'kindness' in the classroom, is focused around an opposition between a classroom where learners are seen as a homogenous group and classrooms where learners are recognized as bringing individual strengths, needs and learning styles to the educational enterprise.

Learners as homogenous 'empty vessels' versus heterogeneous 'geniuses'

Literature on learning to teach notes that at early stages learners are often viewed collectively as 'children' without awareness of their individual differences and learning needs (Furlong & Maynard, 1995; Korthagen, 2001). As one student teacher put it, 'our view of children and teaching were very shallow ... now they're more complex' (*Hadiya, FG 2*). The students' recognition of complexity in learners is reflected in statements, such as the following, which acknowledges that students have different needs: 'If we look at the classroom of 25 students, each one has his/her own strengths and needs' (*Zainab, Beliefs about teaching, Re: Different learners, different lessons*). This is again constructed in oppositional terms against the 'traditional' teachers found in UAE schools: 'All over the UAE schools, many teachers are not even aware that they should bear in mind the students' weaknesses and strengths' (*449, Beliefs about teaching, Re: Different learners, different lessons*).

Again, the negative side of the opposition (prior to the adversative 'whereas') is often linked back to the teaching practices observed during the students' own schooling:

> In addition my way of viewing children has been changed. I viewed them as being fed with information, because this was my situation, when I was in school. Whereas now I view the learners as explorers who actively try to make sense of the world. (*Hanan, Beliefs about teaching, Joining the B.Ed. programme*)

The suggestion here of learners being fed with information seems to make reference to behaviourist theories of learning. Another student employed the 'empty vessels' metaphor in contrasting the views of teachers in schools as compared with her own views of children after studying child development: 'Well, you see, traditionally, they would look at children, who are as ... as empty vessels. But uh ... from what we learned here, children are like uh ... like mysterious ... they're actually geniuses locked in small children' (*Hadiya, FG 2*). In contrast to the 'traditional' teacher, the ideal 'new' teacher that the students are constructing recognizes complexity in learners in terms of their strengths and weaknesses, their learning styles and needs and their potential for achievement.

For many student teachers a consequence of recognizing differences among learners is taking the different learning needs of individual students as the starting point for teaching, constructed in opposition to beginning with the demands of the textbook or the curriculum. Unfortunately not many of the teachers the students experienced in either the past or were working with in the present lived up to this ideal in their eyes:

> I agree with you on this point because from my childhood education and from my experience in schools in the last three years, I found that there are teachers who teach without any background knowledge about the students' level ... [but] if she takes into consideration the individual differences, EVERYTHING WILL BE ALRIGHT. (*Nashita 449, Beliefs about teaching, Re: Different learner, different lessons*)

We can see just how 'internally persuasive' the notion of beginning with learners' needs, a key part of the student-centred discourse of education, has been for the students in the specific linguistic choices in these two postings, such as 'I *strongly* believe' and even more obviously in the capitalization of 'EVERYTHING WILL BE ALRIGHT'. Ironically, these linguistic choices, which seem to testify to the strength of the students' convictions, may also be indicative of a lack of confidence in the position being expounded; in this light they can be read as evidence of the students' fervent, if anxious, need to constitute themselves as a distinct community in *contra*-distinction to the past/present community of teachers in UAE schools.

The frequency, in both spoken and written discussion forums, of the theme of different learners having different learning needs reflects how eagerly the students appropriated a 'learner/student centred' discourse that is typically reflected in adages like 'teach the child, not the subject'. Typical is the following (an excerpt of which was cited at the beginning of this section), which argues for taking account of the inevitable differences among learners that will exist in any classroom, and reiterates the discursively constructed distinction between the 'enlightened' views of the B. Ed. students as opposed to the 'ignorance' of the current teachers:

> I think this is an important issue that many teachers are missing. If we look at the typical classroom it contains about 25 students, each one has his/her own strengths and needs. They are different in their abilities, personalities and performances. This is one of the many important things I have learned in this programme and which I totally agree with. I think teachers have to know about multiple intelligences and different teaching styles and try to plan activities and tasks that match with different levels and needs. (*Zainab Al H. 449, Beliefs about teaching, Re: Different learners different needs*)

Recognizing differences in children is a step towards believing that teaching and assessment need to take account of these differences. As a student in the same thread as the above puts it:

> It is more important to ensure that a learner's ability [is evaluated] against him/herself as he/she grows and develops, more that his/her ability against other learners. We must provide specific ways for each individual to learn as deeply and quickly as possible without assuming one student's road map for learning is identical to anyone else's. (*Meera, Beliefs about teaching, Different learners, different lessons*)

The approach advocated here emphasizes differences between students in that their abilities are to be defined in terms of an 'ipsative' model (Black, 1998: 73–74), i.e. one where students are evaluated against their own past progress, as opposed to a 'normative' model of evaluating students against each other, or a criterion model of evaluating students against external standards. In opposition to the teachers we saw chastised above for 'not taking account of any background knowledge of the students', here the message is that 'we must provide specific ways for each individual to learn'. As the thread title implies, in the students' discursively constructed system of knowledge and beliefs different learners may require different lessons. The reference to students having an individual 'road map' for learning both reinforces this 'learner-centred' emphasis and makes a probably unconscious reference to Bruner's discovery learning (Ormrod, 1995) in the use of a journey as a metaphor for learning. This posting received five supportive responses.

Another posting drew on specific educational content from the degree to make the distinction between views of teaching that acknowledge learners as heterogeneous and approaches that see learners as homogenous. Focusing on students' different learning styles, the following posting critiques the current school teachers while offering another opportunity for the community to constitute itself as 'enlightened' in contrast to the posited 'ignorance' of current government school teachers:

> My belief about teaching is that teachers should consider different learning styles while teaching children ... Before I entered the B. Ed., I didn't know that teachers have to consider different learning styles in order to improve learning, and even in my teaching practice I have not seen teachers plan or give lessons to cater for different learning styles. (*Rida, Beliefs about teaching, Different learning styles*)

This posting received seven responses, all agreeing with the need to acknowledge learners' different learning styles and many reiterating the critique of government school teachers. The following throws multiple intelligences as well as learning styles into the critique:

> I agree with you strongly that every teacher has to cater for different learning styles and multiple intelligences ... In fact I did not see any teachers in the government schools know about each individual's learning styles and multiple intelligences because they use the same materials with all learners. (*Manal, Beliefs about teaching, Re: Different learning styles*)

The thread was also referred back to in later postings, for example, in the following where a student was offering support for Manal's emphasis on learners rather than lessons (implicit in the title of her thread *'Is teaching a lesson to be taught?'*): 'Discussing the different learning styles, if you go to Rida's issue 'Different learning styles' you'll find that some other student teachers and I do believe that we should really consider students' learning styles when teaching' *(Fellah, Beliefs about teaching, Re: Is teaching a lesson to be taught?).* This sort of cross-referencing can be seen as evidence of the depth of the students' engagement in the discussions and the ownership that they took of the online discussion forum as a vehicle for their self-constitution as a community. It also indicates how interconnected many of the topics are. Indeed, many can be related back to a core distinction the students constructed between 'student-centred' and 'teacher-centred' approaches to teaching, examined explicitly in the following section.

'Student-centred' versus 'teacher-centred' teaching

The discursive distinction between 'student-centred' and 'teacher-centred' teaching is one that pervades the students' comments. The remark of one student teacher that 'Moving towards a more student-centred, active approach in all aspects of teaching is I believe the mission of the B. Ed. programme' would probably be endorsed by most of the student teachers' community. Indeed, a number of discussion threads posted under the broad topic of 'Beliefs about teaching' in Semester 1 of Year 4 were devoted to describing the changes the students' beliefs had undergone as part of the conversion to 'a more student-centred, active approach in all aspects of teaching' as Sara described the 'new' approach in the posting cited at the beginning of this chapter. The frequent use of oppositional language to describe these changes reflects the students' discursive investment in particular ways of talking about teaching and learning.

Typically, as we have seen in the opposition between past and present, this discursive investment involves drawing an opposition between the traditional, teacher-centred practices witnessed in schools and the learner-centred approaches the students had encountered during their time in the B.Ed. degree. Thus under the thread, 'Change of name', a student wrote:

> When I entered the B.Ed. programme I thought or I believed that the teacher should teach and the students should listen but while I'm studying this course I've changed my belief and I realize that the teacher should be a guide to the students and assist them to learn. *(Takiyah, Beliefs about teaching, Change of name?)*

The shift here is from a classroom dominated by the teacher to one where the students are foregrounded. This thread involved nine postings all reaffirming this message of changed beliefs about learning and teaching. In a focus group discussion, one student proposed a distinction between the community, who focus on children, and teachers in schools, who focus on the lesson: 'So our view and viewing the children, the students, I think, is different from our teachers. I mean our teachers may be think about the lesson only and teaching ... So I think this is the difference between us and our teachers.' (*Hanan, FG 1*). The language of student-centred teaching is not used here but is implicit in the contrast established between focusing on children and focusing on lessons. The following posting explicitly uses the language of 'teacher-centred' and 'student-centred' teaching to trace this same transition:

> In previous years I had this concept that the teachers are the only ones that should direct the teaching and learning cycle, in other words, teaching and learning is teacher-centred. However, throughout my studies in the B.Ed. programme my beliefs have changed and have been replaced by student-centred where the students are the main core of the teaching and learning cycle. (*Farah, Beliefs about teaching, Teacher vs student*)

What we see here is a clear opposition between approaches to teaching and a complete turn around in the student's views, as the earlier 'teacher-centred' beliefs 'have been replaced' by a belief in a 'student-centred' approach. Echoing the theme of a distinction between a teacher-centred versus a student-centred approach, the former associated with UAE schools and the latter with the B.Ed., another student teacher observed that: 'Now we build a clear picture of what is really meant by a 'teacher' and I think this view has changed gradually since we entered this programme ... this view fosters the shift from teacher-centred class to encourage a student-centred class' (*Rukan, How Teaching has changed my life, Before X After*).

Although the student's views have changed 'gradually', there is no doubt as to where she is now positioned in terms of the teacher-centred / learner-centred opposition. One student, however, offered a hint of doubt about the feasibility of actually being on the right side of the learner-centred / teacher-centred opposition in practice. She confessed that while 'I totally agree with you', nevertheless,

> I myself have difficulties planning a lesson that is totally student-centred. I do not know if you agree or not that planning a lesson always seems to be teacher-centred at first, but then when you think more of it, it tends to shift from one approach to another. (*Malak, Beliefs about teaching, Re: The successful lesson*)

This posting foreshadows something that we will examine later in Chapter 5, involving the tempering by a small number of students of the community's sense of mission grounded in the dualistic 'student-centred' / 'teacher-centred' framework that so much of the students' discussions about teaching and learning operated within. More common, however, was an unconditionally emphatic response such as Nashita's that blamed the failures of UAE schools on the wrong teaching approach:

> Yes I STRONGLY agree with that in most of the schools and especially the government schools, the students are not learning anything because as you said, the classrooms are teacher-centred where the teacher is the important part and the students are just following without any objection. (*Nashita, Beliefs about teaching, Re: The successful lesson, emphasis in original*)

It is worth noting here that the somewhat extreme assumption that the students in government schools are not learning anything is a clear indication of how absolute the opposition between 'teacher-centred' and 'learner-centred' approaches has become in the appropriated discourse that constitutes the students' community of practice.

Indeed, the opposition between 'student/learner centred' teaching, and 'teacher centred' or 'traditional' teaching, is one of the key articles of faith defining and maintaining the HCT B.Ed. students' community of practice. But the distinction also encompasses, as we shall see below, differences in the roles of students in the classroom, differences in notions of what it means to be a teacher and differences in the nature of knowledge. For students the distinction entails a more active role in the classroom. This key tenet of the student teachers' beliefs is explored below.

'Passive' versus 'active' learning

Another element of the student teachers' discourse of 'new' versus 'traditional' teachers and teaching is the role of the students in the two environments. As one student put it 'the child-centred approach focuses on cooperative work and developing active learners who will make sense of the world' (*Rida, What I'm looking forward to in my teaching career, My own classroom*). Implicit in this statement is the notion that 'teacher-centred' classrooms promote passive learning. In other examples, an explicit opposition is established in which the students are perceived as 'passive' in the 'teacher-centred' classroom whereas the 'student-centred' classroom environment expects them to be 'active':

> There are different beliefs that underlie teaching. One of the beliefs that I noticed during my teaching practice was giving the students 'teacher-centred' lessons. In these types of lessons, students act as 'passive

learners', where they just have to sit and listen to the teacher explaining the lesson with little involvement ... Therefore, in order to overcome this problem, I think that lessons need to be 'learner-centred' rather than 'teacher-centred', where the students act as 'active learners'. (*Atifa, Beliefs about teaching, The successful lesson*)

The comment above establishes a binary opposition around different beliefs underpinning teaching approaches. The student notes how in the 'teacher-centred' lessons she has observed the students 'just have to sit there and listen', implying that they should be doing far more. The solution to this 'problem' is therefore to develop 'learner-centred' lessons that encourage students to be 'active'. Another student teacher offered a similar message in even more imperative terms. First she recollects her own specific experience of delivering lessons where learners had a 'passive' role: 'I remember a lesson in which I spent the first part of the lesson introducing new vocabulary words through drilling, my students nearly slept... '. As a result of this experience her advice to peers is couched in uncompromising terms: 'always think how you can make your students active.' (*Adila Insights from the internship, Re: Yes I did it!*). The comment about students falling asleep is indicative of another opposition the students draw as part of the overall 'student-centred' versus 'teacher-centred' binary, this time centred on motivation, explored in the following section.

'Low' motivation and self-esteem versus 'high' motivation and self-esteem

In the 'learner-centred' classroom of the student teachers' discursively constructed system of knowledge and beliefs, students are also perceived as having a valuable contribution to make in terms of their background knowledge and experience, and this has significant implication in terms of student self-esteem, motivation and responsibility for their own learning. Specifically, classrooms that display the features they view as 'teacher-centred' are not likely to be environments that provide students with high motivation or positive self-esteem. At one extreme are the classrooms where physical and verbal abuse is common practice: 'In some schools corporal punishment is still being used to deal with boys' behaviors or even some students who don't know how to answer. Attacking the students verbally really decreases their motivation and self-image and self-esteem' (*Manal, Insights from the internship, Re: MODEL SCHOOLS !?*).

The lexical choice of 'attacking' indicates condemnation of the teacher's actions. Another student noted that such practices were part of her own schooling and again made the link between 'verbal attack' and students' self-esteem as well as motivation:

> The moral concern I would like to discuss is tightly linked with children's self-esteem. This is a problem that I experienced as a student and it can be observed in many schools. The issue is some teachers' use of discouraging language (verbal attack) such as 'you are stupid', 'you'll not understand', 'your mind doesn't work' or other statements like that as a way to punish students. I noticed that teachers don't understand or see the harmful influence they leave in their students' self-esteem and confidence ... In addition, that makes them feel unconfident to try. (*Adila, Moral issues, Verbal attack*)

The teachers perpetuating such practices are clearly constructed as 'unenlightened' (they 'don't understand') in contrast to the student teachers who see how detrimental 'verbal attack' is to motivation and self-esteem. These teachers are clearly at the outmost edges of the 'traditional', 'teacher-centred' versus 'new', 'student-centred' continuum. However, even less extreme examples of 'teacher-centred' practices are viewed as detrimental to student motivation and self-esteem. Criticizing teachers in government schools for spending too much lesson time in explanations, one student commented that: 'This way affects the students, as it decreases their motivation and self-esteem ... I believe that students learn best by getting them involved in the lesson and making them feel responsible for their own learning, which will increase their motivation' (*Atifa, Beliefs about teaching, The successful lesson*).

Focusing on the affirmative side, another student drew a connection between teachers providing positive, constructive feedback and students' motivation and self-esteem: 'Providing the students with positive feedback is considered as a vital tool to increase students' self-esteem and learning motivation' (*Faizah 499, Insights from the internship, Communication skills*). Another student drew the familiar broad distinction between the 'traditional ways of teaching' and her belief in 'the new strategies and approaches that we have learned' and linked the latter to increased language development and student motivation:

> I hope that we'll have the green card from the zone supervisors to stop emphasizing using traditional ways of teaching, because we believe in the new strategies and approaches that we have learned through our study and practiced in TP and we want to have the chance to develop our students' language and increase their learning motivation through the implementation of those strategies and approaches. (*Faizah 499,*

What I'm looking forward to in my teaching career, Re: Theories into practice)

Here, just as 'new' approaches are linked to increased motivation, so implicitly 'traditional ways of teaching' are linked to lower motivation. Another student referred to motivation as part of an even broader discussion, making a link between classroom atmosphere, motivation and language learning:

> Making the learning environment fun and relaxed will benefit the learning process and increase language acquisition, whereas making students feel isolated as you mentioned will de-motivate and de-moralize them, resulting in limited language growth. Let's all aim to be 'student-friendly' teachers, as the current way of teaching in many schools (sarcasm, nastiness, de-motivation and a promotion of passive learning) doesn't seem to produce fluent users of the language. (*Sara, Dealing with Challenging Behaviour, Re: Dealing with misbehaviours*)

Here an opposition is set up (flagged by the words 'whereas' and 'as') between the classrooms of 'student-friendly' teachers which are relaxed and fun, promote successful language learning and are presumably motivating for students (though this is not explicitly stated) and the 'current way of teaching' which does not produce fluent language use and is characterized by, among other negative qualities, 'de-motivation'. The 'invitation' to be student-centred ('Let's all aim to be student-friendly teachers') places considerable moral pressure on other students and is a clear example of members monitoring the community's discourse. At the same time, by its wide ranging nature, linking different parts of the community's discourse together (this posting could have been discussed in many of the above sections and the above is only an excerpt from the posting) it has considerable constitutive force.

Thus, high versus low motivation (and self-esteem) can be seen as part of a broader set of oppositions including 'student-centred' versus 'teacher-centred', active versus passive learning, 'student–friendly' versus 'cruel' that make up the overall distinction between the 'traditional' and the 'new' worlds of teaching in the community's discursive world. Implicit in this distinction is an issue of student-teacher relations in terms of hierarchy versus equality. I explore this in the section below.

'Hierarchy' versus 'equality'

Another opposition that some of the students constructed related to the recognition of individual learning needs and a concern for students' motivation and self-esteem, was centred on a concern to establish a classroom environment based on 'equality' rather than 'hierarchy'. One student teacher described the link between individual needs and equality thus: 'Just deal with the children as individuals ... don't treat them ... treat them equally but according to their individual needs' *(Meera, FG 2)*. Another student was emphatic in her idealistic, if naive, conviction that there must be no hierarchy in the classroom: 'Students have to feel that they're equal; no need to have leaders' *(Nabila, FG Arabic)*.

The concern for the classroom as a community of equals has implications for what it means to be a teacher and for the teacher's role. In connection with equality, one student argued that 'I think the teacher's main role is to involve all students in all classroom activities and discussion as well as helping them to be proud of abilities even if they are not good' *(Rashida, Moral issues, The relationship between a teacher and her students)*. This concern for all students follows logically from the shift the students have constructed from a 'teacher-centred' to a 'student-centred' paradigm. Another aspect of the teacher's role that changes with that paradigm is in relation to the learning process, which is examined next.

Teacher as 'transmitter' versus 'facilitator'

The 'paradigm shift' from a 'teacher-centred' to 'learner-centred' approach as the operative model in the students' minds was often linked to a desire for a 'change of name' as 'teacher' was felt to connote 'traditional' approaches and roles in the classroom, as can be seen in the following posting and the response it evoked. As Nashita commented in a posting already cited above: 'In my opinion, the teachers should understand that they are teaching to facilitate students' learning, not to give orders in the classroom without any care for the students' understanding or not' *(Nashita, Beliefs about teaching, Re: The successful lesson)*.

Others agreed that a different conception of the teacher is required, one that emphasizes a supporting, facilitating, caring role:

> When I was young I had the view that 'teacher' is that person who stands in front of the classroom that talks & talks & talks & plays with kids, this view has somehow changed. When I got enrolled in the teaching programme, the view of a 'teacher' has changed. It is now person who talks for only 5–10 minutes and spends the time facilitating, monitoring and supporting students while working through stirred/settled activities. *(Farah, How teaching has changed my life, before x after)*

Exemplifying how the various discursive strands of the community's construction are interwoven, another student responded, linking the shift in what it means to be a teacher, to the difference between 'teacher-centred' and 'student-centred' approaches to learning and teaching:

> I had the same idea of the teacher's role, where she is the one who stands in front of the students for 45 minutes explaining, talking and checking students' work. But now we build a clear picture of what is really meant by a 'teacher' ... In my opinion, this view fosters the shift from teacher-centred class to encourage student-centred class, hence we came up with a conclusion that says: 'the teacher's job is to be as a facilitator and a guide for students' (*Rukan, How teaching has changed my life, re: before x after*).

Another student linked the shifting conception of the teacher to a shift in emphasis from teachers to students in the classroom: 'I had a similar view, that a teacher is the only person who talks, writes and does everything in the classroom. But now I realized how important students' role in the classroom' (*Basha 499, How teaching has changed my life, re: before x after*).

The difference the student teachers are constructing in these postings, between the teacher as 'facilitator of learning', as opposed to the 'traditional' teacher, who 'stands and delivers', reflects the same discursive polarization between elements of 'new' versus 'traditional' education that we have already encountered above. In both cases, the conversion from acceptance of the traditional approach to embracing progressive education occurs as part of the journey from uninformed school student to 'enlightened' student teacher. Another element of this transition is reflected in the contrast between the students' early images of teaching as relatively simple as opposed to their later recognition of teaching as complex, explored below.

Teaching as 'easy' versus 'complex'

Lortie (1975) reminds us that although students have a great deal of experience of teaching by the time they leave school, the perspective of the student is quite different from that of the teacher. In the case of the B.Ed. students, many of them came into the degree with a view of teaching as relatively undemanding and uncomplicated, in contrast to their later recognition of teaching as both complex and demanding, requiring teachers to balance multiple activities and groups at the same time. The students' earlier standpoint is reflected in how often the word 'easy' appears in the students' recollections of their original views of teaching. Initially the students assumed that teaching was contained within the confines of the classroom: 'When I was a student I thought that teachers had it *easy*, that they just went into the classroom, taught a lesson and forgot all about it after they left' (*Sabah, FG 2, emphasis added*). 'In the past, I used to believe that teaching is just about teaching a lesson at school and then it's over, so it's an *easy* job' (*Adila, Beliefs about teaching, Teaching lessons and more, emphasis added*). This meant teaching did not impinge on life beyond school:

> When I was a student in school I thought that being a teacher is a very *easy* job and the teacher's responsibilities end with her work time, so she has plenty of time to do whatever she likes to do. (*Abra, Beliefs about teaching, Teacher's responsibilities, emphasis added*)

The students therefore assumed that teaching did not involve much in the way of effort or hard work:

> One of my beliefs that has completely changed since I joined the B.Ed. is the complexity of the teacher's job. I considered teaching as one of the *easiest* jobs and it did not require a lot of hard work. (*Warqa, Beliefs about teaching, Complexity of teaching, emphasis added*)

> Since I joined the B.Ed. programme lots of my beliefs about teaching have changed. In the beginning I thought that teaching is a very *easy* job, which doesn't require lots of effort and work. (*Rashida, Beliefs about teaching, Using a variety of activities, emphasis added*)

Based on their experiences of observing teaching from the perspective of the pupil they assumed that all teachers had to do was to go into class and open the textbook:

> One of my beliefs that changed most is that any one could come to any class and teach so *easily* without using any thing except a textbook … Actually I was thinking this way because this is the traditional way of teaching that most of our teachers used to use. (*Rashida, Beliefs about teaching, Using a variety of activities, emphasis added*)

Here we see that the student's viewpoint reflects the predominant style of teaching the students witnessed during their schooling, which was a textbook-dominated, 'stand and deliver' approach. However, experience of teaching during teaching practice led to recognition of the range of tasks teachers have to accomplish, the difficulties teachers face and the complexity of the teacher's role:

> I learned that, I don't know, it's a little bit complex. It's not an easy thing to do … (*Zainab, FG 2*)

Since my first few day in the classroom, I realized how difficult is to be a successful teacher: understanding the students, planning your lessons, giving instructions which suit each student's needs, managing the classroom, etc ... These responsibilities make me respect the role of a teacher in educational society. (*Mayyadah, How teaching has changed my life, Develop my teaching philosophy*)

The common view expressed here reflects the transition from a view of teaching as a trouble-free, straightforward and relatively relaxed working life that is contained within the limits of the classroom and ends with the conclusion of each day's lessons to a view of teaching as complex, challenging and extending far beyond the boundaries of the classroom walls. The students' comments reflect Mary Beattie's observation that, 'Prospective teachers are often shocked at the levels of adaptability, problem solving and managing of dilemmas that are required to deal with the realities of classroom life' (Beattie, 1997: 4). This is unsurprising and gels with the findings in much of the literature on teacher formation. As Feiman-Nemser and Buchman point out, 'Looking at teaching from the perspective of a pupil is not the same as viewing it from the pedagogical perspective of a teacher' (1987: 257, cited in Furlong & Maynard, 1995: 176). In the case of the B.Ed. students this simplified view found further support among the students' perceptions of 'traditional' teachers as transmitters of information to a homogenous and largely passive body of students. Experiencing the pressures of being on the other side of the desk in the classroom, as well as coming to view learners as having different learning needs that require 'new' teachers to adopt a 'student-centred' perspective and encourage active learning, has changed this view. As another student put it, 'I can't mention all the responsibilities the teacher has, nevertheless they are massive' (*Najah, Beliefs about teaching: Re: Teachers' Responsibilities*).

In the above sections we have seen the student teachers employing a series of binary oppositions, within an overarching distinction between the 'them' of the 'traditional' teachers of the past (which includes many teachers currently working in government schools) and the 'us' of the 'new' teachers who utilize 'new' teaching methods and approaches underpinned by 'new' theories. We have seen how, under this broad distinction between the 'new and the 'traditional' teacher, a series of further oppositions are operating such as: sensitivity versus insensitivity towards students; learners as heterogeneous versus homogenous; 'student-centred' versus 'teacher-centred' teaching; active versus passive learning; low motivation and self-esteem versus high motivation and self-esteem;

equality versus hierarchy; the teacher as facilitator versus the teacher as transmitter; and teaching as complex versus teaching as easy.

Operating here is a powerful ideological positioning that largely constructs the students' community of practice, through this set of binary oppositions, in contradistinction to and at times in antagonism towards, past and present teachers in government schools. The 'new' practice of teaching that the B.Ed. students construct themselves as representing is associated with the college experience and specifically with the theoretical knowledge the students have encountered in their degree. As we have seen in the above discussion, the discourses associated with 'new' teachers and teaching have achieved a powerful and hegemonic ascendancy over what is constructed as 'traditional' teachers and teaching.

So far we have been looking at the discursive construction of the community in opposition to the predominant practices in government schools. However, there was considerable discussion of another issue on which many of the student teachers were aligned with the views of many teachers in schools. Interestingly, this was also an issue on which there was disagreement among the students themselves. This issue was the relationship between the textbook series used in the English curriculum and the cultural traditions of the UAE, which I explore in the following section.

Discourses of Language and Culture in the Classroom

The issue of language and culture arose under the Semester 1, Year 4 online discussion topic, 'Moral issues'. In a posting whose title, 'English textbook versus our tradition and culture', immediately frames the discussion in oppositional terms, a student asserted 'it is a fact that some of the English textbooks used in some of the government schools are not relevant to the learners' culture and traditions.' The discursive strategy of prefacing of this statement with the authority of fact rather than opinion is an indication that we are dealing with an ideological argument, if we accept Thompson's gloss on ideology as 'meaning in the service of power' (Thompson, 1984, cited in Fairclough, 2003: 9). This is borne out by the supporting text which expresses concern over the possibility of children imitating cultural aspects represented in the textbook:

> These books present some information and ideas about other cultures, which might affect negatively the students' behaviour. By this I mean that the names of the characters are completely different than the learners' names. Besides that, these books present the characters in different clothes than the ones the learners wear and their foods are different as

well. So the child will be shocked about their own culture and traditions … Therefore the child will try to imitate whatever interests him from these books even if he is not sure about it. (*Sahar, Moral Issues, English textbook versus our tradition and culture*)

Ignoring for the moment the question of whether cultural appropriation operates this simply, a key issue at stake here is who has the right to say what children should or should not appropriate. The concern that a student might 'imitate whatever interests him' reveals anxiety as to whether students will know what is best for them in terms of cultural purity. There were seven responses to this posting, some in agreement, some sympathetic but playing down the originator's concerns and some in direct disagreement.

In agreement with the original point, one student argued 'It is completely unfair to teach students knowledge that is foreign to their culture and society and expect students to have background knowledge of it' (*Halma, Moral Issues, Re: English textbook versus our tradition and culture*). Another student added that because the foreign culture did not relate to students' lives it was potentially 'boring and meaningless'. These students seem to be wary of what Block (2002), drawing on Ritzer (1995), refers to as English language teaching as 'McCommunication', 'which reduces human existence to the principles of efficiency, calculability, predictability, controllability and standardization' (Block, 2002: 132). They are also voicing concerns about 'the ways minds, selves, and worlds are (re)organized and (re)structured' through 'second culture acquisition' (Lantolf, 1999: 45).

In the middle ground, one respondent while sharing the concern noted that 'this is where the teacher's job starts as a professional … [the teacher] will ensure that certain contents are made relevant to our culture' (*Kamilah, Moral Issues, Re: English textbook versus our tradition and culture*). Another student, while broadly sympathetic, moderated the concern with the reminder that 'there is no perfect textbook to be used.' She also noted that 'the teacher plays a crucial role in this. She can draw the learners' attention to the good things and avoid others which are not suitable for them' (*Warqa, Moral Issues, Re: English textbook versus our tradition and culture*), while another, although sympathetic, agreed with the point made above that teachers had the potential to introduce elements of the local culture into the curriculum and draw cultural comparisons.

Opposing the original point, a student tentatively argued

> I don't really agree with you in all aspects. It is important that children see and read images related to their own culture … on the other hand I

don't see any harm in getting students to learn about other cultures. The points you made about names and clothing are not really aspects that conflict with our culture. Course books can represent other cultures so long as they don't conflict with our culture. (*Adila, Moral issues, Re: English textbook versus our tradition and culture*)

It is interesting to observe how tentatively the first student directly to disagree with the original point enters into her argument. And she is keen to make the point that while cultural difference is not necessarily bad, cultural conflict definitely is not okay. The exact difference between cultural difference and cultural conflict is left open. Supporting this argument that cultural difference did not necessarily equate to cultural conflict, another student offered detailed advice on how to capitalize on cultural differences in the language classroom:

What we are supposed to do is adapt and relate to our culture. For example a lesson on clothing can easily be related to our students by asking them to compare their clothing to the characters in the book and explore the differences and similarities and which style they prefer. The key here is to adapt and look at the book as a window to a culture that speaks English because I always say that learning a language is learning a culture so that once we learn a language and its culture we'll understand the people who speak this culture [language?] and hopefully teach them in return about our culture. I don't believe in sheltering our students from western culture and I don't believe in making them accept it without questioning. What we should do is show them the bad and good of it and provide them with the knowledge and thinking skills that they need to make their own judgment about it and choose what's useful and reject what's not. (*Sabah, Moral Issues, Re: English textbook versus our tradition and culture*)

The general thrust of Sabah's argument here reflects Thanasoulas's point that 'We cannot teach culture any more than we can teach anyone how to breathe. What we can do though ... is to teach *about* culture' (Thanasoulas, 2000: 24). The detailed reasoning in Sabah's response utilizes what Lim (1991) refers to as 'cultural equivalencing' or a 'systematic promotion of the local culture in an English Language teaching programme ... with the aim of putting it on the same level of significance as Western Culture' (Lim, 1991: 66). Sabah also recommends what Pennycook (1994) describes as encouraging students to 'talk back' to the foreign culture.

The need for 'talking back' to and through English language and culture emerged as a theme in one of the focus groups at Sabah's college, as the students recollected the way English was presented at school:

> So the English language is linked to always English people ... I mean European people who are ... who speak English ... are portrayed as intelligent ... as more productive ... as the best people in the world and we cannot be like them. They used that just to encourage us but they don't understand that they are discouraging us. (*Adila, FG 3*)

Sabah made the same point in the discussion thus: 'When we were in schools, we were told that we should learn English because it would make us better human beings.' She then went on to argue for the need to learn English so as to use it to talk back to English language cultures: 'Now what I want to do is teach my students English so they can tell others that we are good human beings ... I want them to communicate our ideas, our culture.'

In relation to the English textbook, the points about inaccessibility of foreign cultural models and practices was reiterated by other students from the same college as Sahar, the originator of the posting above expressing concern about the cultural aspects of the New Parade textbook, in a further series of threads consisting of eight postings. Such comments included: 'there is a big gap between the culture of the characters in New Parade and the culture of the students' (*Nafisah 449, Moral issues, The English coursebook in the UAE*) and 'the pictures and topics in the books are not related to the UAE culture' (*Akilah, Moral Issues, The English coursebook in the UAE*).

This was often coupled with the perhaps contradictory point about the possibility of students being overly influenced by these foreign cultural models: 'the gap between the culture and the characters in New Parade and the Emirati students' culture can have a huge influence on the life of the Emirati students ... ' (*Nafisah 449, Moral issues, The English coursebook in the UAE*); 'I agree with what you said about the negative effect of this book on the children's ideas and traditions' (*Fadwa, Moral issues, The English coursebook in the UAE*). The one dissenting opinion came from a student from another college as the last word in the discussion. This student, while agreeing that we should not ignore the cultural aspects of language learning, made the point that 'we should give our students the opportunity to learn and widen their knowledge about the world' (*Nuha, Moral issues, re Textbooks used in the UAE*). The majority of the students in this discussion seem to hold a view of English as incapable of representing anything other than a Western ideology, a view which might be described as somewhat overdetermined (Canagarajah, 1999). An alternative perspective would be to recognize the applicability to the teaching of English, of the argument Luke and Luke (2001: 292) put forward with regard to globalization: 'the effects of globalization unfold locally, regionally and nationally in uneven and not always centrally predictable ways'. Rather than blanket refusal, it may be possible to work with and through available discourses, seeking to use them critically and creatively for one's own interests (Canagarajah, 1999).

Discourses of Gender in Education

Interestingly, another discussion occurred within the same college's student teachers about the influence of education on women. The initial posting in this thread of four postings began with the generalized assertion that 'Some people believe that the UAE education system is not playing the expected role in enhancing the students' knowledge ... I strongly agree with this opinion.' She then went on to outline the specifics of this concern:

> First of all, our grandparents think that educated women become more open. By this I mean that some women lose their traditional values, such as the way of dressing. For example, nowadays women are wearing trousers. In addition women are influenced by western style, like going shopping anytime, and paying a lot to buy things that are not necessary, just because they saw an attractive advertisement. Moreover the women's attitudes towards people have changed, for instance when they greet their relatives or grandparents they use inappropriate words, for example, they mixed some Arabic words with English and it makes it look like they are showing off. (*Fadwa, Moral issues, Concerns about education and teaching in the UAE*)

The initial charge, that women are becoming 'more open' derives authority from being attributed to grandparents who are seen as custodians of cultural values from a simpler, purer time, drawing on the respect for elders that characterizes this and many other regions. However, given that the specific points supporting the charge of openness are in no way unique to women, and given that UAE men are breaking cultural boundaries in far more spectacular ways by virtue of their greater social and economic freedom, it is difficult not to read this as an expression of a discursive pattern, in no way unique to the UAE, of holding women responsible for the moral status of society and blaming them for moral breaches in situations in which they are often the less empowered victims.

The only reply which could be construed as fully supportive to this posting made the following comments which, again, could equally well be applied to men in the UAE:

> I totally agree with you ... about how education has influenced and changed women. It is noticeable that a lot of women never knew the precious value of education; they never understood that education is not how you look or what you say in some event; they never tried to discover that education is beyond that. Education is how you think and what you believe in and much more. (*Nafisah 449 Moral issues, Re: Concerns about education and teaching in the UAE*)

Even this supporting voice hedges somewhat as the student goes on to remind the audience that, 'however, we should not forget that there are women who had a huge influence on education especially in the UAE.' Another student made the general point that 'we have to take the good points from other cultures' (*Kamilah, Moral issues, Re: Concerns about education and teaching in the UAE*). The final posting on this topic conceded that 'education has influenced some women badly' but argues that 'we should look at the good side'. The student sees her and her peers as a resource for hope as she makes the point that 'we didn't forget our traditions' and urges her audience to focus on being good role models so as to counter any potentially negative effects of education on women (*Akilah, Moral issues, Concerns about education and teaching in the UAE*).

The discussions about the cultural influence of the English textbook and about the influence of education on women can be viewed as reflecting aspects of the wider dialogue in the UAE that Kazim (2000) outlines, between the discourse of cultural conservatism and tradition and the discourse of progressivism and openness to global influences. More specifically, the concerns expressed about the influence of cultural models in the English textbook and about women becoming 'more open' can be viewed as representative of counter-discourses that reflect wider anxieties about the rapid social changes that have accompanied development and the emergence of new globalism in the past few decades. In this context, Kazim notes how:

> Within the last twenty years, many fragmented new social movements have emerged within the contemporary UAE's civil society in relation to the increased percentage of educated citizens, the variety of occupations they hold (especially at the middle level), the growth of immigrant labour population, new globalism, and consumerism. (Kazim, 2000: 430)

However, without diminishing the concerns expressed by some students in relation to cultural changes, it is worth noting that in relation to the overwhelming concern expressed about the detrimental effects of 'traditional' teaching approaches on educational achievement in UAE schools, these concerns can be described as a subsidiary, and to some degree divergent, theme in the community's discursive constitution.

Conclusion

In this chapter we have been looking at the discursive construction of the student teachers' community of practice in terms of systems of knowledge and beliefs. We have seen the student teachers who constitute the evolving community of practice constructing the community in terms of its system of knowledge and beliefs through a powerful series of binary oppositions. These oppositions are organized around a basic division between the 'traditional' teachers of the past – 'them', and the 'new' teachers of the future – 'us'. Fleshing out the details of this overarching opposition we have seen a series of further oppositions such as that between 'sensitivity' and 'insensitivity' in the classroom and between a vision of learners as homogenous versus viewing learners as heterogeneous. We have seen a critical distinction between 'teacher-centred' teaching as opposed to 'learner/student/child-centred' teaching. And as part of the latter we have seen an emphasis on 'active' learning, high motivation and self-esteem as opposed to 'passive' learning, low motivation and low self-esteem which are constructed as characteristics of the former, 'teacher-centred' classrooms. Finally, we have seen a distinction between the types of classroom culture with 'new' classrooms characterized by equality whereas 'traditional' classrooms are hierarchical. And within these classrooms we have seen a distinction between the traditional teachers' 'easy' role as a transmitter of information versus the teacher as facilitator accomplishing a complex and multifaceted role in the new classroom.

These dichotomies, which provide much of the material for the evolving community's discursive self construction, are characterized by a startling degree of consensus. This consensus is supported and reinforced by the shared discursive repertoire of the community that we examined in the previous chapter, which reifies particular ways of understanding teaching while at the same time excluding others. The effect of these patterns is a discourse characterized by a powerful differentiation between 'us' – the members of the community and 'them' – the government school teachers, involving an 'otherization' that, at times, takes the form of outright antagonism and hostility. William Connolly captures this drive that lies at the heart of identity construction:

> Identity is always connected to a series of differences that help it to be what it is ... there is a drive to diminish difference and to complete itself inside the pursuit of identity .... a pressure to make space for the fullness of self-identity for one constituency by marginalizing, demeaning, or excluding the differences on which it depends to specify itself. (2002: xiv–xv)

We will explore this phenomenon, including looking at practical possibilities for transcending it within teacher education contexts, in greater detail in the final chapter.

An aspect of the community's discursive self construction, where beliefs were more divided among the members, was related to issues of language and issues of culture. Here, we saw some members advocating practices reflecting a 'conservative', 'traditional' discourse of protecting and preserving UAE cultural values in the face of outside influence while other members recognized the value of practices reflecting a 'progressive' discourse of, if not embracing then at least pragmatically utilizing, the potential benefits offered by external cultural influences. We have seen how these two lines of argument reflect wider discursive 'conversations' in the UAE community.

But returning to the main focus of the chapter, the fact that the 'progressive' discourses of education were taken up so enthusiastically is no proof of their value and the book is in no way arguing or assuming that. Nonetheless, this enthusiasm raises complex issues – and this is where I return to the point made at the onset of the chapter about analysing the 'truth effects', rather than the 'truth' per se, of the educational discourses drawn upon by the students in constructing their identities – for a teacher education programme like the HCT B.Ed. for the following reasons: On the one hand, to state – one way or another – that the discourses the students are using to shape their identities are good or bad is to naturalize and reify these discourses; in this context it is worth noting that the HCT B.Ed. programme did not employ the dualistic, binary framework for thinking about curriculum and pedagogy, whose use by the student teachers is reflected in the discourse analysis in this chapter. On the other hand, there is clearly some connection between the HCT programme and the students' identities, since the students are drawing on aspects of the HCT B.Ed. programme, outlined in Chapter 2, in constructing their discourse of 'new' pedagogy. But to argue that this directly caused the discursive construction of knowledge and belief reflected in this chapter would be to position the student teachers as cultural 'dupes' (Holliday, 2002: 149). The situation – and social reality generally – is more complex than this; the student teachers' appropriation of progressive discourses to construct a sense of themselves as teachers that was wildly beyond what was expected is linked in interesting and powerful ways to discourses of Emiratization and national development, as well as to processes of identity formation per se. These links will be discussed more fully in the final chapter, but they relate to a key argument of this book about the way in which the student teachers took up particular notions encountered in their B.Ed. degree, within the wider context of salient local discourses such as UAE nationalism. This brings us to another key point made in the book, i.e. that the strength of these discursively constructed identities cannot be separated from the strength of the community the student teachers created. With this in mind, the next chapter examines the discursive construction of the community in terms of interpersonal relations and looks at the ways many of the themes discussed in the current chapter are also evident in the strategies and approaches through which the community is achieving coherence among its members.

Chapter 5
The Discursive Construction of Interpersonal Relations

The development and maintenance of an evolving community of practice has implications for the ways in which student teachers relate to each other. Indeed, as Dewey (1963 [1916]) recognized, the very act of participating in the community entails a certain degree of alignment in terms of communication, including thoughts, ideas, values and beliefs. Ideational and interpersonal realities are co-constructed through statements and utterances that achieve the dual discursive ends of construing social events *and* social actors. Once established, this alignment between the community's members and its beliefs needs to be monitored and maintained. This monitoring and maintenance work implies that the particular interpersonal relations that have been discursively constructed between the community's members also need to be maintained through the continual reiteration and reaffirmation of beliefs.

Thus the student teachers' ongoing self-definition requires considerable coherence and cohesion within the community in terms of their common purpose, beliefs and values. However, the need for a 'constitutive outside' leads to their 'us' being defined in opposition to the 'them' of the 'traditional' teaching, which they construct as characterizing UAE government schools. This is reflected in a tendency towards the discursive construction of antagonistic relations between the community of student teachers and the government school teachers. In this chapter I explore some of the ways in which this work unfolds: through the use of particular forms of interpersonal address; through statements that serve to monitor and maintain the community's beliefs and coherence; and through statements that serve to set the agenda for the community's future mission. I also discuss some examples where the evangelical sense of mission and the consequent antagonism towards the school teachers that often emerges, is tempered in the reflections of some student teachers.

Interpersonal Address

One of the most characteristic features of the student teachers' interpersonal communication is the frequent use of an introductory 'I agree with you' or an equivalent statement. In the first thread posted in *449 (Change of name*) four of the eight response postings began with offers of support, such as: 'You remind me of my belief ... '; Your belief about teaching is similar to mine ... '; 'You are right and I strongly agree with you.'; and 'I strongly agree with your point of view ... '. Similarly in the next thread (*Before and after!*) four of the five response postings began with affirmations: 'I also was like you when I first joined the programme'; 'I strongly agree with you ... '; and two postings beginning with 'I agree with you ...'. Indeed, in the 750 postings over the year, 'agree' (without negation) appeared in the first sentence 143 times. Variations included: I *totally* agree, I *do* agree, I *certainly* agree, I *firmly* agree, I *completely* agree, I *really do* agree and I *also* agree. Other supporting phrases were:

- 'I appreciate your comments' (*449, Beliefs about teaching, Re: Complexity of teaching*)
- 'You raised a good point' (*449, Beliefs about teaching, Re: My new thoughts*)
- 'I have the same thought as you' (*449, Beliefs about teaching, Re: Teacher vs Student*)
- 'The issue you're discussing is really important' (*449, Beliefs about teaching, Re: Different learner ... different lessons ...*)
- 'You have chosen a good topic to post' (*449, Beliefs about teaching, Re: Different learning styles*)
- 'I like what you wrote' (*449, Beliefs about teaching, Re: Different learning styles*)
- 'I liked what you said and your belief is similar to mine' (*449, Beliefs about teaching, Re: My beliefs ...*)
- 'YOU ARE RIGHT' (*449, Beliefs about teaching, Re: Teaching is an honourable job!!*)
- 'I totally agree with you sister' (*449, Beliefs about teaching, Re: The teacher or the book, which makes the subject interesting*)
- 'You've really raised some significant points that I also realized when I joined this programme' (*449, Beliefs about teaching, Re: My beliefs about teaching and learning*)
- 'What a good point' (*449, Beliefs about teaching, Re: Teaching boys or girls*)
- 'I am with you' (*449, Beliefs about teaching, Re: What are the changes??*)
- 'I have the same opinion as you' (*449, Moral Issues, English textbook versus our traditional culture*)
- 'I find myself in agreement with you' (*449, Moral issues, English textbook versus our traditional culture*)

- 'Yes you are right' (*449, Moral issues, Re: Textbooks used in the UAE schools*)
- 'What you mentioned is completely true' (*499, Insights from the Internship, Re: What is an effective learning environment in views of the principal and teachers in the school?!*)

These phrases exemplify the bolstering and support the students offered each other as they mutually co-defined the joint enterprise and the shared discursive repertoire of their community of practice. Indeed, this could be considered part of the generic structure of the responses, in that the social function of community building is construed in the statements of agreement. By contrast, expressions of disagreement were far fewer, totalling only 12 over both semesters with an additional 11 postings where initial agreement was followed by a qualified expression of disagreement with an aspect of the original message. Moreover, expressions of disagreement were often couched in tentative terms, such as: 'I don't really agree with you in all aspects' (*449, Moral Issues, English textbook versus our traditional culture*); 'I don't really agree with you ... however, yes, I agree with you that sometimes ... ' (*449, Moral Issues, Re; What would you do??!!*). Only occasionally was there more overt disagreement such as, 'It seems that you did not get my point of view very well' (*499, Insights from the Internship, Re: What is an effective learning environment in views of the principal and teachers in the school?!*); and this was part of an exchange between two students from the same college who knew each other very well.

It is interesting to note that the majority of the disagreements and qualified disagreements (14 of 23) occurred in the topic about moral issues in UAE education. One of the main focal points for this disagreement was issues relating to language and culture that we discussed in Chapter 4. Overall though, the expressions of dissent are outnumbered by the comments offering support and agreement. Indeed, the overwhelming impact on reading through the postings is that the students are working extremely hard to establish and maintain the common boundaries of their evolving community, embodied in a shared sense of purpose and enterprise, and agreed parameters in terms of their beliefs about students and learning, teachers and teaching and schooling and education.

However, the construction of interpersonal relations was often conducted through other means than the overt statements of agreement above. One of these ways is through a strategy of inclusive embrace of other community members in statements made by one member. Thus, for example, in one such posting as she reflects on the value of the internship experience a student offers the following: 'Well, in fact the internship was a valuable chance for all of us to show that this new generation of teachers are capable of being teachers' (*Amani, Insights from the internship, Re: Goodbye TP*). Here, the use of 'all of us' which then equates to 'this new generation of teachers' works as a discursive strategy for making the statement applicable to all the community's members. We see the same strategy in the following:

> I think we as teachers, are partners with parents and other community members in raising the new generations. We are part of a big community and are participating in promoting education, values and principles that everybody should respect and share. (*Adila, What I'm looking forward to in my teaching career, Making a difference*)

Although in the first sentence the statement about teachers being part of a wider community is hedged by the personal 'I think', which dilutes the affiliation with truth to some degree, in the second sentence the same comment is made as a categorical assertion of present reality that embraces the members of the community through its use of the inclusive 'we'. At other times students addressed the others in the second person. The following is a particularly strident example in which a student responded to another's description of her realization of the complexities involved in teaching: 'IF YOU LOVE YOUR JOB, YOU'LL DO IT even if it is very hard' (*Nashita, Beliefs about teaching, Re: Complexity of teaching*). Although the 'you' here is ambiguous in terms of whether it is the generic 'you', akin to 'one' (i.e. if one loves one's job), or whether it specifically addresses the originator of the posting or the wider community, the strategy here is to place the audience under a moral obligation to work hard since none of them would want to admit to not loving teaching. The force of the message is rather unsubtly underlined by the capitalization, perhaps suggesting that the wider audience is intended.

Other postings made reference to a common future destiny shared by members of the community: 'most of us will manage to be very good teachers and we WILL make a difference in schools because of our qualifications' (*Nuha, Beliefs about teaching, Re: My new thoughts*). The use of three inclusive pronouns, 'us', 'we' and 'our' in this brief statement shows the student teacher working hard at the ongoing task of maintaining the community while the capitalized WILL serves to underline her determination to fulfil the common mission that holds the community together, only softened by the concession to reality in 'most of us', acknowledging that they may not *all* go on to be exemplars of excellence. The theme we have seen so often already is present here again as the schools are constructed as in need of the reforming efforts of the student teachers. The following remark from the same discussion thread is another example of the discourse of difference working to cement the unity of community while at the same time emphasizing its distinction from the school teachers: 'I totally agree with you and that is what I found is the difference between our SSTs and we as trainee teachers ... I believe this happened because we had the practice and got the experience and reflected on our work more than the SSTs' *(Nabila, Beliefs about teaching, Re: My new thoughts)*. The discourse constructing 'we' the community works here to also construct an other-ization of 'them', the SSTs. A similar, simultaneous co-constructing of the community and its mission, is achieved by the title of another posting, 'It's us who will make the change' *(Malak, Beliefs about teaching)*. In the next section we examine the contours of this key aspect of the discursive constitution of the students' evolving community of practice as inclusive of all members in further detail through other more subtle discursive strategies.

Maintaining and Monitoring the Community Beliefs

At times students took on the role of holding others accountable for maintaining the commitments of the enterprise, by reminding them of their responsibilities to uphold the practices of the community. In one fairly explicit instance of this, a student teacher wrote about the difficulties of teaching practice when 'you are not in the mood today' and asked others for their views of what they would do on such occasions. The only response that came was one of chastisement: 'I don't really agree with you because as student teachers, we have to be prepared for our lessons because when you are teaching you are responsible for that' *(Madidah, Moral issues, Re: What would you do??!!)*. Clearly, anything less than full commitment is not part of the common understanding of this community's joint enterprise. However, the work of maintenance and monitoring was often conducted in less explicit ways.

As argued above, a statement representing social reality or events works simultaneously to construct identities and interpersonal relations. In Hallidayan terms, the ideational, interpersonal and textual meta-function all operate concurrently within any text, or as Volosinov (1973 [1929]: 41) puts it, 'Thus the psyche and ideology dialectically interpenetrate in the unitary and objective process of social discourse'. We have seen how the community can be characterized by a set of beliefs that can be grouped together under the label 'new' teaching, defined by characteristics such as belief in student-centred teaching, in active learning, in sensitivity to learners, in learners as heterogeneous, in a concern for high motivation and self-esteem, and in teaching as complex. To ensure the ongoing loyalty and adherence of the community, these beliefs need explaining, justifying and defending – what Edwards and Potter (Edwards & Potter, 1992; Potter, 1996) describe as 'warranting' – as part of the ongoing work of legitimizing both the beliefs and the community. Below we will look at some of the ways this purpose was achieved.

Legitimation

Fairclough (2003: 98) outlines four strategies for the legitimizing of beliefs: *authorization, rationalization, moral evaluation* and *mythopoesis*. Below we see examples of how each is employed as a legitimizing strategy by members of the community, to justify and maintain the values and beliefs that bind them together *as* a community.

Authorization is the justification of a belief by an appeal to an authority, be it tradition, custom, law or a person who has the authority of expertise in the field in question. An example of this is the following taken from a discussion about how to put 'theories into practice':

> No one at this level [year four] didn't use the social interaction through small group, pair and whole class interaction. If yes then you did it ... you managed to promote useful language and general knowledge learning through enhancing a helpful social interactions as *Vygotsky* stated that 'language develops entirely through helpful social interaction' (Lightbown and Spada, 23). So this is really an important goal that we have to keep in mind for our career as a teacher. (*Rukan, What I'm looking forward to in my teaching career, Re: Theories into practice*)

Rukan derives legitimacy for interactive approaches in the classroom from the authority of Vygotsky (referenced to a course text) and then rationalizes a conclusion, framed as a 'goal' that the members of the community 'have to keep in mind for our career as a teacher'. The rationality of the argument is signalled by the word 'so' which indicates that the conclusion follows legitimately from the preceding discussion. The use of academically authoritative sources was a common strategy, which is not surprising given that the students have been trained to rely on academic sources of authority in their coursework in the degree. It is important to note that the legitimacy deriving from a reference to authority does not require the originating source to be explicitly cited. Numerous forms of knowledge are accepted in the discourse community and only require the relevant lexical items as proof of authority:

> My belief about teaching is that teachers should consider the different learning styles while teaching children as some of them are more visual,

some are more kinesthetic and some are more auditory. Therefore teaching materials need variety of content and approach to cater for the different learning styles. (*Rida, Beliefs about teaching, Different learning styles*)

Here the lexical items – visual, kinesthetic and auditory – refer to Gardner's (1983) theory of multiple intelligences, which provides the implicit authority for Rida's conclusion. The causal conjunction 'therefore' indicates to her audience that she is moving to this stage in her argument, which also references learner heterogeneity, one of the key tenets of the community's belief system.

Rationalization involves drawing legitimacy by reference to the utility of a course of action or recommendation or by reference 'to the knowledges society has constructed to endow them with cognitive validity' (Fairclough, 2003: 98). In progressive education, as well as in the students' community which draws many of its beliefs from progressive education, one source of cognitive validity is whether a classroom activity leads to 'deep', meaningful and lasting learning as opposed to short-term memorization of information that is quickly forgotten. Longevity of learning as an indicator of meaningfulness is the source of legitimation in the following excerpt:

> I will ask all of you two simple questions:
>
> Do you remember Cinderella, Snow White and the Sleeping Beauty?
>
> Now do you remember any lesson in any subject we had in the secondary schools?
>
> I assume that most of your answers will be yes for the first question and no for the second.
>
> This shows that we learn more from stories ... so why do we forbid students from learning through an interesting and useful way such as stories and songs? (*Nabila, Beliefs about teaching, Re: Teach lessons through stories*)

The questions here, as Nabila acknowledges, are rhetorical as are most questions asked within the community. This in itself is an indicator of their role as devices mutually to check beliefs rather than as genuine heuristic devices – interrogatives in the sense of 'interrogate' rather than the sense of 'seek information'. Rationality is again foregrounded with the phrase 'this shows' indicating the move from premise to conclusion. The final rhetorical question serves to distinguish the 'enlightened' insights of the community in contrast to the predominant approach in the government schools.

In another example, a student draws on the community's belief about the need for students to be motivated in order to rationalize her argument for the related community belief in the need for sensitivity towards learners in the classroom: 'In my opinion one of the teacher's responsibilities is creating an understanding and comfortable educational environment for the students. This will lead the students to be more interested and motivated to learn' (*Abra 449, Beliefs about teaching, Teachers' responsibilities*). The rationality in terms of utility is flagged by the phrase 'this will lead to'. In another example, two 'desirables', one a teacher attitude and one a teaching approach, are rationalized on the basis of their utility in relation to outcomes that have educational validity in the community:

> Teachers must remember that hard work and planning at the beginning will pay off dividends at the end and if students are allowed and encouraged to work in their preferred learning mode, they will ultimately reach their full potential and develop a lifelong love of learning. (*Sara, Beliefs about teaching, Re; Different learning styles*)

The necessities, indicated by 'must', of hard work on the part of teachers, and of letting students work in their preferred learning style are rationalized respectively in terms of 'dividends' and of the legitimized educational value of lifelong learning. This type of argumentative strategy, often relating the students' classroom experiences to notions that have educational validity in the community, is one of the most commonly used as part of the ongoing maintenance of the community and its belief system.

However, it is worth noting that the very persistence of rationalization strategies, as well as maintaining the coherence of the community, is also indicative of a discursively contested terrain:

> Giving claims a basis is a sign of dispute rather than harmony; warranting is an occasioned phenomenon, done when it is considered to be needed and shaped for its occasion ... factual discourse is constructed to be apparently factual and resilient to rhetorical onslaught. (*Edwards & Potter, 1992: 152*)

In the case of the students' community of practice, much of what we might describe as 'factual rhetoric' is aimed at securing the ongoing cohesion and commitment of the community *against* the potential claims of 'traditional' teachers and teaching.

Moral evaluation involves legitimation though appeal to value systems. An example of this is the following excerpt in which a student argues for putting up displays in the classroom that include all students' work rather than just the pieces judged by the teacher to be the best. The student teacher relates an incident when a teacher threw most of the class's work in the bin and makes her appeal in the form of a series of rhetorical questions: 'What is your reaction going to be if you knew that she is going to throw the rest of the displays in the bin? ... Doesn't she know that these students have feelings? ... What are the students going to do with this teacher?' (*Amirah, Moral issues, Teacher's morality*). Here the student invites her peers to put themselves in the position of the relatively powerless students in the classroom and uses rhetorical questions to appeal to moral values, as indicated by the posting title. The argument here is for sensitivity in the classroom which, as we have seen, is one of the community's core beliefs. In another posting arguing for sensitivity, a student mixed an appeal to moral values with an appeal to utility, in terms of conduciveness to learning, to argue against hitting students:

> ... all teachers should understand that discipline has psychological effects on the students; in many cases it can stop the students from learning and producing ... Teachers should use many strategies to communicate with their students rather than hitting them. I totally believe that teachers should never think of hitting the students. They should remember that these students are still young children who do not mean to misbehave in the classroom. (*Nafisah, A critical incident from TP, Discipline versus learning*)

The moral appeal is to values of non-violence and the innocence and vulnerability of children. Not surprisingly, such appeals to moral values as a source of legitimacy were particularly used in relation to the community values of sensitivity towards learners, although values such as student centredness were also sometimes justified on moral grounds.

Mythopoesis refers to the legitimation that is derived from narratives. This can take the form of a shared narrative interpretation of events. We saw this in Chapter 4, where the role of a communal interpretive resource was served by the story of how the student teachers, having experienced the 'bad' ways of 'traditional' teaching, including passive, teacher-centred learning, in classrooms characterized by insensitivity, low motivation and low self-esteem, achieve a redemption through their encounter with the paradigm of 'new' teaching. Such narratives serve both to establish common beliefs and understandings, and to consolidate the interpersonal connections based on shared experiences among members of the community.

Narrative legitimation can also take the form of on an individual story. In the following example the student teacher employs a narrative genre in her posting (*Sabah, A critical incident from TP, The model lesson!!!!!*) to relate the experience of losing her students because they were taken by a science teacher for two days to prepare a model lesson that was to be observed by a local education zone supervisor.

> Contemplate this scene …
>
> The poor English teacher (me) goes into 4/2 classroom fully equipped with materials and worksheets to be met by 10 students out of 24 which is the total number of students. When she asked about the rest of the students she was told that they are 'rehearsing' the science lesson in the school resource center.

Having set the scene, Sabah then goes on to describe what she saw when she went to find her missing students:

> She made the students memorize the answers to the questions she's going to ask during the 'model' lesson and gave them worksheets to answer. She even rehearsed facial expressions and gestures … She threatened the students that if they misbehaved or didn't follow the 'script' of the lesson, they would lose marks.

Sabah goes on, after relating more details of the event, to conclude the story and draw the moral implications:

> After two days of 'rehearsal', the visitors came and the lesson was perfect, the students were perfect and everybody was smiling and happy. The poor English teacher was shocked and speechless and stunned and flabbergasted. She was also disappointed and thinking that there should be something to stop this madness and nonsense. The teacher is saying that lying, deceit and cheating are ok. Is this what we want our students to learn?

It's a very self-conscious performance, reflected in the initial instruction to 'contemplate this scene', the scare quotes around 'script' and 'rehearsal', the ironic tone in the description of the 'happy', 'smiling', post-lesson scene, the cumulative build-up of adjectives to describe her reaction, the choice of vivid, colourful words like 'flabbergasted' and the use of the third person for the part of the author, the 'poor' English teacher. The humour plays an important part, uniting the audience in their common understandings and values through ridicule of the *ridiculous* perpetrators of the 'model lesson'. In addition, the vivid description serves to create a sense of perceptual re-experience and to underline the writer's qualifications as an observer of verbatim reality (Edwards & Potter, 1992: 161). The overall discursive strategy is to build up a description of 'madness' and 'nonsense' that functions as a moral, cautionary tale. This moral evaluation becomes explicit in the student's summary of what has occurred as 'lying, deceit and cheating', as well as in the concluding rhetorical question.

The overall effect is an underlining of the beliefs of the community through a form of member checking that reinforces the common attunement of the community's values. Such legitimating of beliefs serves the ongoing co-constitution of the community in terms of both ideational and interpersonal meanings. Having looked at ways the community maintains its interpersonal bonds – interestingly, a term with both positive and negative connotations – through ongoing explanation and justification of its belief and value systems involving various legitimating strategies, we will go on to look at the interpersonal responses evoked by a student teacher who admitted to difficulties in living up to the beliefs and values of the community.

Embracing a struggling soul

We have seen in the preceding chapters how 'student-centred' teaching is one of the key tenets of the community's educational creed. Many of the students in the focus group discussions and in the postings above convey a sense of confident excitement about the progress they are making towards improving and gaining control over their teaching in terms of making their practice increasingly 'student-centred'. The following comments from a student in a focus group discussion reflecting on her teaching during the second semester of Year 3 exemplify this confidence:

> Maybe this practice that I had is the most interesting and the most invaluable for me because I felt like I took students ... I made a change instead of having teacher-centred learning, to children ... students where they are bringing the language and working on research projects ... and ... I found ... this is me; this is what I wanted to be happening in the future is having students doing the ... most of the job and working and researching and questioning. (*Fawzia, FG 2*)

However, not all the students were able to report such positive results. In the online posting below a student teacher is particularly candid about the difficulty she had in making the journey from 'teacher-centred' to 'student-centred' practice:

> Throughout my previous practicums, I was suffering from one problem which was being a traditional teacher who always uses the teacher-

centred way more than student-centred. And believe me, I tried and tried and tried, but I found my self coming back again to the traditional way of teaching. Any way, after 4 years of experiments and experiences, I did it this semester and I want to say it loudly YES I DID IT. I feel that I changed 100% than the previous time. I am a little bit sad because I changed in the last TP, but when I thought about it I saw that it is better to change now than after graduation. Now I am not the traditional teacher who lectured the students and giving them instructions, BUT I am the facilitator who supports my students and help them all over their learning. (*Nashita, Insights from the Internship, Yes, I did it …*)

The sense of achievement and relief, after 'I tried and tried and tried' is palpable, literally embodied by the capitalized words 'YES I DID IT'. It is almost as if to remain a 'traditional' teacher would have amounted to a gross moral failure. Like a lost soul, struggling to be a good member of the community, this student is clearly under immense emotional pressure to be a 'progressive' teacher. Again, this reflects the extent to which the students have internalized the discourses of contemporary education as part of the construction of their community of practice. Moreover, the disciplinary capacity of the discourse that forms the shared repertoire of this community can be seen in the difficulty any of these students would have in posting a message saying 'I'm a traditional teacher and what's more, I'm proud to be one.' This would be tantamount to pedagogical heresy and is clearly not an option in this community of practice. As another student commented in a focus group discussion, in a remark we noted in Chapter 4 which brings an explicitly religious discourse to bear on the issue, 'We thought that we would be as our teachers but thanks, no. Thanks to God we are not like them' *(Nabila, FG 2)*.

The relief expressed as the student proclaims that 'Now I am not a traditional teacher' is concomitant with the critical stance the students have adopted towards the predominant approaches of their former school teachers, but it is also evidence of the regulatory power of the discourse of 'new' teaching among the community's members. This regulatory dimension is evident in the moralizing tone of a posting written in response to the one above.

> I think that identifying that you already had a problem with your teaching and trying to do things to improve it and make it more child-centred indicates that you have been reflecting on your teaching which is good because not many teachers reflect on their teaching styles … Not many teachers would admit that it is their traditional teacher-centred way of

teaching that makes the students passive learners, but you did and that illustrates that you really wants to change for the better ... Keep up the hard work Nashita and I am sure you will do just fine. (*Asiya, Insights from the Internship, Re: Yes, I did it* ...)

Here, despite her difficulties, Nashita's willingness to change is seen to elevate her above the majority of teachers. This response can be read as the caring pastor responding in somewhat sanctimonious fashion to the struggling 'lost soul' of the 'repentant sinner' ('not many teachers would admit ... but you did and that illustrates that you want to change for the better.'). The final words about keeping up the hard work 'and I'm sure you will do just fine' make it clear that student-centred teaching is the only acceptable option and it is incumbent on Nashita to ensure that she lives up to this standard. Not that one would want to belittle or cast doubt upon the genuine feeling that characterizes these postings. Indeed, balancing the wish to treat the students' words with respect, with the desire to draw conclusions from texts whose meanings – like those of any text – can never be fully exhausted, reflects one of the inevitable tensions in analysing discourse, particularly when the social and cultural distance between the analyser and the 'analysees' of the text is as wide as in this case.

Another respondent welcomed Nashita back into the fold if in slightly less moralizing fashion but with some advice couched in the imperative mood to make sure that there is no slipping back:

> I am really happy for your great achievement. Don't worry about changing your teaching style 'late' as you said. It's still a positive change you could achieve and you should be proud of your self. It's still a learning experience ... always reflect on what you do in your classroom and see what works best for your students ... I remember a lesson in which I spent the first part of the lesson introducing new vocabulary words through drilling, my students nearly slept ... always think how you can make your students active. (*Adila, Insights from the Internship, Re: Yes, I did it* ...)

Along with the advice, the student teacher extends empathy by relating her own experiences of slipping into 'traditional' mode. The 'better late than never' message came through in another response and again the respondent offers empathy as she confesses that she too was a late developer: 'Congratulations. Well done Nashita. Really I am so happy to hear that and am glad that you did it. I was facing the same problem since first year but I have changed last semester' (*Farida 499, Insights from the Internship, Re: Yes, I did it* ...).

All these responses convey a sense of genuine concern for Nashita's pedagogical 'soul' and express relief that she has lived up to the expectations of the community as they welcome her into the fold. In this sense the respondents are playing a monitoring and gate-keeping role of the community's values and beliefs.

Another strategy for fulfilling these functions is through the setting – and policing – of agendas (Fairclough, 1992). This was a feature of a number of the student teachers' interactions, particularly in the final semester as they prepared to go forward and carry their ideals into the world of full-time teaching in UAE government schools and classrooms.

Setting the Agenda for the Future

In one of the postings under the broad topic of 'What I'm looking forward to in my teaching career', a student teacher focused on teachers' relationships with students as the aspect of educational practice in which she was most looking forward to implementing change. 'I am looking forward to change first the way teachers look at students. That is, I have seen almost all of the teachers who I dealt with have negative ideas of the students' (*Nafisah, What I am looking forward to in my teaching career, When will September come?*). In her response to this posting, another student, Sara, used her own offer of support as an opportunity to remind the community members of the long term nature of their commitments and responsibilities.

Sara begins by reminding the community that 'Teachers ... need to always remember that their actions have profound effects on young lives. Teachers leave imprints on their students that can last a life time'. The language here is categorical: 'teachers *need to always remember*'; 'their actions *have* profound effects'; 'teachers *leave* imprints'. Only with reference to the prospect that these imprints '*can* last a lifetime' do we get any concession to modality. This reminder of the serious nature of their joint enterprise functions to focus her audience's attention on what follows as Sara proceeds to formulate an inclusive agenda on behalf of the members with whom she assumes a high degree of affinity ('let's' i.e. let *us*), seeking their implicit commitment to the priorities she outlines:

> Let's make those imprints possess the following qualities: a love of lifelong learning; a love of the English language; consideration of other's feelings; concern for people's problems (both locally and globally); a liking for teamwork and co-operation; an ethos that promotes caring, doing good to and helping others; tolerance to others.

This agenda is mainly focused on sensitivity to learners, self-esteem and motivation, which we have seen are key features of the community's systems of knowledge and beliefs. Moral obligation to live up to these beliefs is then placed on the community members (*'our* B.Ed. girls'): 'I hope that our B.Ed. girls will bring to the teaching profession a promotion of the above qualities and from all the postings I have read I feel really optimistic that this will happen'.

After letting them know that she has read their postings, Sara conveys her confidence that they will live up to these expectations. The final sentences echo the solemn responsibilities of the first two sentences by reminding the community members that it is *students* (and the community is, as we have seen, *student-centred*) who will be the beneficiaries of this commitment, *when this happens*, i.e. if the community members fulfil their obligations and meet Sara's high expectations: 'In years to come, students will hopefully gain an education that is free of discrimination, corporal punishment, sarcasm, de-motivation and cruelty. When this happens students' potential to learn will be limitless'.

Sara took on the role of simultaneously maintaining and monitoring the community's agenda in another posting entitled 'Engaging environment'. In a message addressed 'To all', she begins with a reminder that as the completion of the degree approaches, 'we have to keep in mind that this is the start, not the end.' The categorical assertion of necessity ('we *have to* keep in mind') serves to remind members that this is not the time to be letting their guard down. The implicit danger here is made explicit when, after referencing many of the key tenets of the community's beliefs that should be part of their future classrooms such as 'print-rich' environment that 'build self-esteem' and involve 'student-centred activities', she reminds members that 'the potential is there, to be influenced by traditional teachers who favour an audiolingual approach to teaching'. She then goes on to point out that whatever the commitment of the Ministry of Education to change – and such a commitment is explicitly stated, as Sara mentions, in the Ministry's Vision 2020 policy, as well as in recent statements by the Minister of Education (Al Nowais, 2004) – the responsibility and the opportunity to improve practice, as the student teachers have constructed it, is clearly theirs for the taking. It's an extraordinary rallying cry:

> Anyway, the onus will be on us, as the first batch of English teachers qualified from the HCT, to improve primary education throughout the country. Are we up to the challenge? You bet we are. Good luck and go forth with optimism and pride (we all have the potential to contribute

successfully to the educational process in the UAE). (*499, What I am looking forward to in my teaching career, Engaging environment*)

Again the combination of moral pressure with assurances of capability is a potent mix. The message is all inclusive – only first person plural pronouns are used. And the bar is set very high – the student teachers are to 'improve primary education throughout the country' even though they will only be responsible for one aspect of the curriculum and their number is relatively small. Taken together, these aspects provide another example of the community constructing itself in opposition to a system in need of reconstruction.

Another message (within the broad topic, *'What I am looking forward to in my teaching career'*) which took the form of a call to arms, outlined an agenda addressed to the members of the community in a posting with the imperative title, 'Be a good teacher'. Adiva begins by emphasizing the inclusiveness of the community, addressing 'everyone' and using 'we' and 'all of us' to imply that she is speaking for all the members: 'Hi everyone ... I know that we are all looking at our future in an optimistic way ... all of us feel that we are ready to face the challenge and hopefully we will be'. This is followed by an emphatic contrastive conjunction, after which comes a reminder against complacency: ' ... BUT never say that we are taught everything that makes us perfect teachers; learning never stops at a specific stage or degree; learning is a long life journey ...'. Adiva goes on to remind the community members that they have been well prepared for the challenges that lie ahead:

> As we all know, we are very well prepared young English teachers. Moreover, through out the four years in the B.Ed programme we learned all the teaching essential skills from A to Z. We've been taught about children's psychology, language theories, teaching strategies, classroom management, teaching language to ESL learners, different types of assessments ... etc.

This list is followed by another emphatic 'but' and a few words of praise to the students and their teachers before our gaze is directed forward to the responsibilities that lie ahead and the question of what qualities, abilities and skills will be required to fulfil them:

> When you read this huge list of the things that we've been taught you will be astonished BUT that's the fact we deserve to be proud of our selves, college and staff ... I'm looking forward to being a good teacher so I need to ask my self 'what makes a good teacher?'

Having reminded the members of how fortunate they have been and how well prepared they are, the scene is now set for Adiva to outline the main points of her agenda as to what is required from the community members in order to fulfil the roles and responsibilities of the 'good teacher'. The list includes mainly affective qualities and interpersonal skills though knowledge is stressed too. Many of these requirements are cast in obligatory terms and the relevant linguistic features are italicized in the excerpt below:

> From my experience, I think that a good teacher *must* plan very interesting lessons so the students will not sleep during that lessons. Also she *must* love her job because that will let her to enjoy her job and she will do it in the best way she can. In addition, a good teacher *needs to* have lots of knowledge not only about English but about other subjects or issues. Also she *needs to* build a very strong relationship with her students and she *needs to* be the teacher, friend and mother … Moreover, a good teacher *needs to* be very flexible and be able to solve any problem she faces. She *needs to* study the problem and find out the most suitable solutions for it. Also she *needs to* do many action researches which will help her to find more about problems that students face in their learning or about problems she faces in her teaching.

In some ways the pedagogical sights are set lower here than we have seen elsewhere, with the need for interesting lessons couched in terms of keeping students awake rather than in terms of promoting learning, and a maternal discourse of care embedded within the educational discourse. Indeed, the first point was picked up on and critiqued by another student teacher in a response posting: 'I disagreed with your point about planning interesting lessons, since the students need to be involved in a variety of strategies … still there is a time when the teacher has to give input sessions … Hope you got what I mean' (*Rukan*).

The parting words of reassurance and the 'wink' indicate a desire to maintain positive interpersonal relations despite the challenge over content. Similarly, in terms of advice for classroom practice, there is more emphasis on interpersonal relationships than on specifically pedagogical practice. Interestingly, in terms of the interpersonal relations within the community, in the final sentence of her posting, Adiva expresses confidence in the other community members, stating that she expects they are '*going to be* good teachers'; but at the same time her expectation places an obligation on them, while her confidence vis-à-vis herself, as reflected in her affinity with this expectation, is hedged: '*hopefully* I will'. This expectation is linked at the very end to the common educational value of making a difference, capitalized for emphasis and locating the posting in the overall discursive construction of the student teachers as bringing about needed (she *needs to,* she *must*) changes in UAE schools. Emphasizing her desire to be part of the 'new' paradigm, Adiva signs herself 'future teacher': 'Hopefully I will work hard to do all these things to be able to consider my self as a 'good teacher' and I expect that all of you are going to be good teachers who will make a DIFFERENCE ... Future Teacher, Adiva'.

The combination of call to arms and rallying cry – almost like a coach giving the team a pep talk before they go out onto the field – that we have seen from Sara and Adiva can also be seen in other students' messages. After listing goals for her teaching career, which included references to 'scaffolding' students in a 'meaningful teaching and learning environment' that challenges students 'with respect to their ZPD' and 'caters for individual differences, learning styles and intelligences' – in other words much of what we have identified as the defining beliefs of the evolving community, one student teacher concluded with a rhetorical question:

> I would like to conclude by saying that if each one of us doesn't look forward in relation to their careers then why have we learned to become teachers and who else is going to make the dynamic and positive changes in the teaching and learning of English in the UAE? (*Areebah What I'm looking forward to in my teaching career, What I'm looking forward ...*)

Again the message is inclusive of all members of the community ('each one of us') and again the assumption is that changes need to be made and the 'mission' of the community (to use Sara's term from the posting cited at the start of Chapter 4) is to make these 'dynamic and positive changes'. Against the background of this overwhelming sense of missionary optimism, it is all the more interesting to explore some tentative steps by a few members to problematize the fundamental underpinnings of the community's discourse.

Tempering the Mission

A minority of students offered reflections which showed them moving beyond a simple opposition between 'new' and 'traditional' education and looking at different classroom approaches in the situated context of wider social practices. In one of the responses to Nashita's posting above about finally making the transition to 'learner-centred' teaching, for example, Adila begins to question the 'learner-centred'/'teacher-centred' dichotomy. 'I think not all lessons can be completely child centred, some times, you need to explain something and be the only one speaking' (*Adila, Insights from the Internship, Re: Yes, I did it ...*), while in the following posting, Karimah describes herself as a 'realistic' teacher and explicitly states that she has tempered her idealism:

> The first thing that helped me shape my teaching characteristic is studying different courses that are related directly and indirectly to teaching ... Secondly, my philosophy about teaching and learning also changed because of my experiences in schools which was the most effective thing in my learning process because it helped me to understand the context in which I will be positioned ... narrowing the gap between the ideal and the real situation in teaching helped me to be more of a realistic teacher than a super teacher. (*Karimah, Beliefs about teaching, I'm a realistic teacher now*)

Karimah uses the discourse of the 'real' (Britzman, 1991), based on experience as the ultimate source of authority, as a counterbalance to the idealism she associates with the courses she has studied. Indeed, she gives priority to experience as the 'most effective thing'. She also mentions in the posting that the readjustment of her sights has been a matter of expediency in so much as it has helped her prepare for life in schools, so that 'I will not be shocked when I work because TP narrowed the gap in my understanding between the ideal model of teaching which I studied and believed in and what is going on in our schools'. This posting did not receive any responses, which would tend to indicate that it did not strike a chord with other community members. In another posting, Asiya reflects on the reasons behind some of the differences between the approaches of the current school teachers and the B.Ed. students, suggesting in a 'but for the grace of God, there go I' sort of way that there is a contingency to the B.Ed. students' development:

> Some teachers believe that they should be in control of everything and that is reflected in the teacher-centred activities they use, their ways of dealing with the students and their beliefs and attitudes. They might not feel secure about displaying the students' work and promoting a child-centred approach in their classrooms ... On the other hand, I want to draw your attention to another issue. We were taught how to create a positive learning environment and we got the chance to see the effectiveness of using child-centred activities through going out to schools and teaching. We were introduced to many educational theories and got the opportunities to put them into practice. Government schools teachers did not get that chance though. If we did not join the B.Ed

programme, do you think we would have had these strong beliefs about teaching? Maybe we would have taught our students the same way we were taught ... (*Asiya, Insights from the Internship, Re: What is an effective learning environment in views of the principal and teachers in the school?!*)

Asiya demonstrates an awareness of the influence of the B.Ed. programme – and the discourses of education that it has advocated – in shaping the community's beliefs in particular ways, which enables her to take a more detached, even critical, stance than we have seen so far in other students' comments. Her reference to the chances for learning that the school teachers have not had reminds us of the ways that the supervising school teachers in the UAE are not trained as mentors and are positioned as representatives of the government school system, rather than as integral partners in the process of professional learning, a factor that no doubt contributes to the othering we have seen. Asiya's sense of the contingency and fragility of the beliefs of the community of practice enables her to question how easy it will be for the B.Ed. students to hold on to their belief in 'student-centred' learning once they begin teaching:

> We can always start with our own classrooms and then try to help other teachers in the school to see our point of view, but what is next? How will we change a procedure that has been followed step by step for so many years? And what if our ideas were completely rejected and we were put under pressure to change our beliefs about teaching when we start working as full time teachers? I am not saying that I will throw what I learned away. I am only thinking ahead and trying to find ways to deal with the challenges that we surely are going to face once we start working as English teachers! (*Asiya, Insights from the Internship, Re: What is an effective learning environment in views of the principal and teachers in the school?!*)

Of course, the reassurance that she is not going to 'throw what I learned away' is there to demonstrate her loyalty to the community and maintain credibility within it. But in contrast to much of the missionary zeal we have seen above, Asiya poses some probing and insightful questions. These mature considerations are indicative of Asiya's sense of the fragility of the B.Ed. students' community of practice and reflect her recognition of the socially situated character of teaching and the complexity of change processes. It is almost as if she is reminding the other community members of their imminent dispersal as they move from being student teachers and begin working as full-time teachers in schools, a move which will see them becoming members of other communities of practice. But that is another story.

Conclusion

In this chapter we have examined the discursive construction of relations on the interpersonal level. Here we have seen how overt bolstering and agreement function as means of consolidating support among community members, thus cementing the community as a coherent and cohesive group mutually engaged in a joint enterprise. But we have also seen how other less direct forms of discourse work to construct the community as a common corps. These methods include the use of inclusive first person pronouns and other inclusive linguistic forms. They also include legitimating strategies of authorization, rationalization, moral evaluation and mythopoesis as ways of working to maintain, sustain and monitor the community and its beliefs and, particularly in the final semester, the strategy of setting common agendas and obligations for the future.

However, the powerful coherence among community members that we have seen fostered through these discursive strategies has been at the expense of an 'otherization' of the community of school teachers. The strength of the common bonds achieved through the use of inclusive forms of address among community members, as well as through the ongoing maintenance and monitoring work of continual legitimation of the community's beliefs, serves to delineate and unite the community, while at the same time defining it against the constitutive outside of the teaching community in the government schools. As we have noted in previous chapters, this often results in the construction of an antagonistic relationship between the students' community of practice and the government school community. This phenomenon is also evident in the agendas for change the students set for their future teaching career, which construct the government schools and teachers as needing reform. Against this trend, we have also seen how some of the students offered counter-considerations to the predominant idealism to temper the overriding sense of reformatory zeal and mission.

But systems of knowledge and belief and interpersonal relations are not the only constitutive effects of discourse. As argued in Chapter 1, discourse is also constitutive at the level of the intrapersonal identities of individual community members. With this in mind, the following chapter explores the discursive construction of the community of practice through the lens of the self-constitution of one of its members.

Chapter 6
The Discursive Construction of Intrapersonal Identity

In this chapter, I look at the development of the evolving community of practice through the lens of intrapersonal identity. This forms the third level of discursive constitution, along with systems of knowledge and belief, and interpersonal relations, discussed in the previous two chapters (Fairclough, 1992, 1993, 2003). By definition, focusing on intrapersonal identity requires a focus on individuals; in order to allow space for in-depth exploration, this chapter will focus on the identity of just one student teacher. Inevitably, the selection of an individual student will seem arbitrary, but the student who forms the basis of this chapter has been selected on very straightforward and pragmatic grounds: she has a lot to say and she says it passionately. However, to the extent that any one student can be described as typical of the group, Manal epitomizes the key themes of this study in particularly graphic ways. She embodies the wider community of practice in her exemplification of learning to teach as the taking on of a new identity, in her enthusiastic embrace of educational discourse, and in her strong identification with the community and its joint enterprise. And although this student only participated in the Web CT discussions, and not the focus groups, she engaged wholeheartedly with the rich potential offered by the Web CT forums for mediated, negotiated and dialogic identity construction. Her intrapersonal identity development thus illustrates the ways in which the online forum was a tool providing opportunities for active and ongoing identity work, rather than being a mere mirror reflecting a pre-given or fixed identity. In this sense the discussion of intrapersonal identity in this chapter echoes the comments of Edwards and Potter in the context of discursive psychology as contrasted with traditional psychological account of individuals:

> the focus has moved from a traditional realist understanding of self discourse, as a more or less adequate description of inner entities, to considering what *activities* particular forms of discourse make possible and how a subject may be *constituted* on any particular occasion in talk or writing. (Edwards & Potter, 1992: 128 emphasis in original)

Moreover, Manal's passion and commitment remind us that discursively constructed identities are not just linguistic descriptions, but also involve our emotions. Identities are 'descriptions of ourselves with which we identify and in which we have emotionally invested' (Barker & Galasinski, 2001: 87). We are thinking *and* feeling beings (Damasio, 1994) and any adequate account of our identities requires recognition of pathos as well as logos (Archer, 2000). By focusing in some depth on the intrapersonal construction of one student teacher's identity, as constituted through the comments that are discursive-performatives of her attitudes, values and beliefs, we are able to get a sense of the meaning of the community and its enterprise, as literally embodied in 'real people'. For learning involves more than knowledge and understanding: 'Learning implies not only a relation to specific activities … it implies becoming a full participant, a member, a kind of person' (Lave & Wenger, 1991: 53). This chapter thus provides a complement to the more thematic focus that emerged when looking at the discursive construction of the community's systems of knowledge and belief. In terms of Miller Marsh's comment, cited in the introductory chapter, about 'the ways in which teacher thought is socially constructed yet individually enacted' (2003: 10), the focus in this chapter is on a single individual's enactment of socially constructed beliefs.

In Chapter 2, I noted that one of the strengths of Fairclough's approach to discourse is that he has elaborated a detailed set of tools for the purposes of textual analysis. In relation to the constitutive level of intrapersonal identity, we can explore identity construction through modality and evaluation, as manifested in an author's/speaker's commitments to – what Fairclough calls in his later work, 'identifications' with – truth, moral values and obligations, and necessity (Fairclough, 2003: 159–190). Although modality and evaluation are complex notions, for the purposes of this study, modality can be defined as referring to a writer's/speaker's degree of commitment to truth, obligation or necessity (see Chapter 2 for a fuller discussion); whereas evaluation involves a writer's/speaker's degree of commitment to what is desirable or undesirable, good or bad, and may be expressed through a range of linguistic structures (including evaluative statements, statements with obligational modalities, statements with affective mental processes and value assumptions). Overall, in linking textual features of modality and evaluation to social identities, we can say 'that what people commit themselves to in texts is an important part of how they identify themselves, the texturing of identities' (Fairclough, 2003: 164).

Thus, in discussing the discursive constitution of one student's identity, this chapter explores what she views as 'true' as opposed to that which she considers mistaken; what she perceives as 'necessary' as opposed to what is merely optional or unnecessary; and what she believes to be desirable as opposed to undesirable, as well as what she considers 'good' and what, by contrast, 'bad'. We begin by exploring truth commitments but bringing other forms of commitment into the discussion insofar as they are interwoven with, or support, a truth commitment.

Commitments to Truth: What I Believe

Commitments to truth entail an expression of epistemic affinity with representations or actions. This can be achieved through modality, or through evaluations. I begin below by looking at some of Manal's commitments to truth as expressed through modality, before going on to examine truth commitments she expresses through evaluation.

Belief and modality

In a Web CT posting, entitled in the form of a rhetorical question, 'Is teaching a lesson to be taught?' (posted during Semester 1 of year 4, in the 'Beliefs about teaching' topic), Manal outlines a number of truth commitments by prefacing a statement with, 'I believe', as part of an overall critique of a model of teaching that is largely focused on getting through a lesson plan. With clear intertextual echoes of Schön (1983, 1987) and Dewey (1933, 1997 [1938]) she states, 'I believe that critical reflection on, in, and for action is a main tool to rethink, improve and plan for our own teaching and learning.' She goes on to outline the value of reflection as part of a cycle of reviewing beliefs in the light of experience, implementing changes on the basis of the reflection, and then reflecting again as part of a continual striving for improved learning in students. 'By taking risks and implementing our beliefs about learning and then reflecting on our experiences, we get more of a sense of the strengths and weaknesses of our teaching'. The influence of discourses of reflective practice and action research (both foci of Year 4 of the programme), with their emphasis on 'reflective' rather than 'routine' teaching, is evident in these statements, as Manal demonstrates the currency of her beliefs and aligns herself with 'progressive' education.

In addition to the value she places on reflection, a significant belief for Manal is the need for collaboration and cooperation among teachers: 'I believe that teachers have to work collaboratively and cooperatively with other teachers in the schools'. This belief is couched in terms of a strong degree of necessity; it is not that teachers should or might work together, they 'have to'. This, she argues, is required 'to make our teaching more effective because we share our thoughts, knowledge and experiences with other teachers.' This belief in the ideal of collaboration extends beyond just English teachers working together: 'As integration between subjects is important, I think we as teachers need to work in collaborative teams and try to integrate between English and other subjects in the UAE.' Prefaced by a justificatory assumption about the value of subject integration (and hence extending beyond Manal's area of teaching experience), this acts as a supporting recommendation to the overarching call to collaboration. Textually, its subordinate status is indicated by the weaker commitments reflected in 'think', rather than 'believe', and 'need to', rather than 'have to'.

Interestingly, the theme of collaboration and cooperation among *teachers* was not one that emerged strongly in the study data overall, although cooperation and group work among students did. This may be because of the strength of the 'us'/'them' division operating between the student teachers and the school teachers, or it may be simply because the focus in the degree on the classroom as a community is more prominent than notions of schools as communities. That Manal should be different in this respect is not surprising, as the existence of common shared beliefs does not entail totally uniform beliefs. As the discourses of a community are appropriated they encounter, and are accommodated within, existing beliefs as part of an ongoing 'internal conversation' (Archer, 2000). Nevertheless, if not a determinant, the discourses operating within the group are an important constraint, since identities are always 'relational', not insular (Miller Marsh, 2003: 9).

Another of Manal's beliefs is that teachers needs to cater for the individual needs of learners, rather than teaching the same lesson to different learners, regardless of their individual requirements, in line with the community's beliefs as outlined in Chapter 4. Thus she argues, 'We have to identify those needs and try to plan and incorporate strategies that help in matching those needs' (*449, Beliefs about teaching, Is teaching a lesson to be taught?*). Following this statement, couched as a commitment to necessity, Manal goes on to make another series of belief statements, about students and the sort of classroom environment they need:

> I have come to believe that students are not empty vessels to be filled with knowledge and facts, the way I learned my English language. I have come to believe that they are tender plants who need the support and scaffolding, either from their peers or teachers, to meet their potentials and zones of proximal development. In my opinion, they have to be actively engaged in a child-centered classroom where they construct their own understandings and interact in social groups ... in my opinion teaching is like an apprenticeship where students and teachers learn

from each other, not as passive bottles. We are preparing active learners to explore, discover and work cooperatively on their learning, not computer programmemers to be fed with basic rote knowledge ... I believe these learners need a supportive positive environment which fosters learning, inquiry and taking risks to make errors and learn from them. For me teaching is still not a lesson to be taught in one day and achieve my short-term objectives. (*449, Beliefs about teaching, Is teaching a lesson to be taught?*)

The cumulative effect here of these personalized belief statements, particularly in the first two sentences beginning with the recurring announcement 'I have come to believe', is of the public recitation of a personal litany. The modality in these statements is uncompromising, evincing strong affinity with truth, as she asserts that 'students *are not* empty vessels', and strong affinity with necessity, as she asserts that 'children *have to be* actively engaged in a child-centered classroom' (emphases added). Interestingly in the passage, all the statements except one begin with a personalization of the truth commitment in the form of 'I believe/ have come to believe', 'in my opinion' or 'for me'. In the single non-'I/me' statement she uses the inclusive 'we' as the subject of a sentence that, like the others in the excerpt, is in declarative mood. This statement thus presupposes consensus at the same time as it asserts truth. And in spite of the slight softening expressed by the tentative bracketing phrases, 'in my opinion' and 'for me' (which are the only concessions to the otherwise high levels of epistemic modality here), the overwhelming force of her commitment comes through in the repeated linguistic structures and phrases. Indeed, it is worth emphasizing again that although the community is partly defined by its shared discourse, the discursive uptake within individual identities will have its own characteristic features. In Manal's case, she is a particularly committed student teacher, and though in instances like the above she tempers her use of language, this does not lessen the sense of passionate commitment to her personal beliefs about education that comes through in her discursive comments.

Interestingly, in her choice of term to contrast with 'empty vessels' – the usual metaphor for the behaviourist view of learners – she uses 'tender plants'. This is not just a chance remark; she uses the same two metaphors in a Web CT posting the following semester, where she recollects her earlier view of learners: 'Students were passive learners like empty vessels to fill with knowledge, not like tender plants to come up with knowledge and ideas for their own learning' (*499, Insights from the internship, Re: Yes I did it*). It is perhaps curious that she chooses the metaphor of 'tender 'plants', rather than the 'apprentice', to contrast with the 'empty vessels', since she is clearly working with a Vygotskian ideal of social learning in mind. Indeed, quite literally mixing her metaphors, she does use the 'apprentice' metaphor later on in the passage.[1] However, beyond these overtly educational discourses, 'apprentices' and 'tender plants' are very different things. The former connotes effort and junior status, while the addition of 'tender' to the latter shifts the metaphor from a primarily biological one to a nurturing one. Meanwhile, 'empty vessels' has a number of other connotations, including religious, biblical associations, as well as more sinister overtones of social manipulation.

This discussion of metaphor raises a number of questions. Among these is the degree to which metaphor use is intentional or incidental. Putting it another way, to what extent is metaphor in the mind of the perceiver? These questions are further complicated when we recall that English is a third language for Manal. (Belush is her first and Arabic her second.) In this context it is worth recalling Lakoff and Johnson's (1984) observation that language per se is thoroughly saturated with metaphor and that we constantly use metaphors in communication without being necessarily aware of the fact. In the final chapter I return to the question of the status we should accord metaphor in conducting textual analysis, as part of the discussion of the implications of the study.

The main excerpt above, along with the other excerpts from the same posting cited so far in this section, is also remarkable in the way so many key educational discourses of the past half-century are referenced. These are reflected by the use of a number of key lexical items: learners being *plants* (rather than *empty vessels*); *critical reflection; collaboration; scaffolding; zones of proximal development; child-centered classrooms; construct; apprenticeship; explore; discover; inquiry; risk taking*. That she employs so many key words from modern-day 'education-speak' reflects how thoroughly she, like the other members of this evolving community of practice, has internalized contemporary educational discourses.

Referencing yet more key terms and tenets of 20th century 'education-speak' (italicized below), Manal goes on in the same posting to put forward another series of personalized truth statements:

> I believe that my classroom environment should *support the students' mother tongue and culture* even if we are learning a foreign language because I think we have to *start with learners' prior knowledge and experiences* that they bring from their cultures and homes and try to build on them to *make learning more related to their interests* ... For me teaching is not a blackboard, chair, table or book, it is a *lifelong learning* process.

Through the opening personalized statement of belief ('I belief') and the inclusive statement of necessity that follows the causal conjunction ('we have to') Manal again aligns herself with key tenets of 'progressive' education. The implicit contrast with 'traditional' approaches becomes explicit in the last statement, beginning with 'For me ... ', where the accoutrements of an industrial model of schooling are set up against one of the key themes of late 20th century education and knowledge management that is also common currency in business and government discourse.

The implicit contrast with government school teachers is again made explicit later in the posting when Manal concedes, 'I can't blame the teachers who are teaching in the government schools because all of the beliefs that I mentioned above might not be taught to them.' Thus the 'new' teacher represented by the B.Ed. students and the theoretical knowledge gained in their degree is opposed to the 'traditional' government school teachers within the 'us' and 'them' framework we have seen in previous chapters; though it is worth noting that while Manal concedes that the beliefs she has referred to *might* not have been taught to them, her choice of modality gives the impression of a rather dubious expression of doubt that does little to weaken the basic opposition that is being constructed. Within this discursively constructed framework, the identities of the 'new' teachers of the B.Ed. cohort are defined via emphatic statements of truth, for example, that 'we have to start with learners' prior experience', in contrast to the practices operating in government schools, where teaching is seen in terms of 'blackboard(s), chair(s), table(s) or book(s)'.

In addition, the notion in Manal's posting that the B.Ed. degree has been teaching 'beliefs', conflates knowledge and beliefs. This blurring of categories is also evident in other student teachers' oral comments and postings. Her emphasis on beliefs is a reminder of the religious metaphor we discussed in the previous chapter in relation to the student teachers as converts to 'student-centred' teaching and 'new' methods. Indeed, so powerful is the hegemonic sway of the discursive system that, like any true believers, the students are for the large part unaware of the fundamental conflation of knowledge and belief operating within the community.

Thus far we have focused on the textual expression of belief through modality. In the section below, we continue our examination of Manal's expressions of belief, but turn our focus to the ways in which she achieves this through evaluations.

Belief and evaluation

In the second semester of Year 4, as part of a supportive response to Nashita's posting, (*499, Insights from the internship, Yes, I did it ...*), which we encountered in the previous chapter and in which Nashita is celebrating her achievement of finally implementing a 'learner-centred' approach in her classroom, Manal is reminded of her own development, 'So I reflected on my teaching and I would like to share them with all'. In another of the public testimonies we saw in the previous chapter she proceeds to outline 'my teaching styles then and now'. After noting how she began teaching 'using a more traditional approach' she goes on to describe the personalized educational philosophy that now guides her:

> I came up with my own philosophy in education which starts with a classroom ethos which helps in developing the child as a whole in physical, emotional, social, linguistic and cognitive ways ... My philosophy in teaching is rooted in combinations of communicative and social theories. Also it includes one aspect of behaviorism theory, which is the reinforcement. I started to develop different activities that allow for communication or informal interactions between peers in the classroom like interviews, surveys.

> Also new input or knowledge is simplified through context, props and body language and varied discourse using stories, role-plays and authentic reading materials like folk tales in free-time reading. I have established a print-rich and literacy-rich environment and the students have opportunities for easy access to them. I thought about skills that the students lack like sharing and cooperative skill work in pairs. My classroom ethos improves these weaknesses by fostering group work and establishing rules that suit all learners to have a good learning time in my class. I started to look at students as individuals who learn in different ways and have different learning styles ... I plan activities for individuals if their needs require it, and I also give instructions for individuals rather than the whole class. EFL learners need to learn language in a meaningful context to help them comprehend it. Now I looked for more strategies or ways to introduce new vocabulary or content in different contexts like songs, stories or games to let the students observe the use of authentic language. I also look for fluency first to make the students feel confident in using English then I focus on errors they make because most of my students do not talk or communicate in English. Increasing my own knowledge and having different teaching experiences and taking a risk and implementing new strategies and then reflecting on the effectiveness of these strategies helps in building

my own teaching style. (*499, Insights from the internship, Re: Yes, I did it ...*)

Manal uses the negative term 'weaknesses' to describe the characteristics of her students. These characteristics are ones associated with the 'traditional' model of education. By introducing and implementing 'new' strategies she is able to 'improve' on these weaknesses and provide her learners with a 'good learning time in *my* class'. Indeed, the personal is foregrounded in this posting, as she engages in this process of creating '*my* classroom ethos', she is guided by '*my own* teaching style' and '*my own* philosophy in education'. Such personalized expressions reflect a key theme in this study, i.e. the ways in which the student teachers embody the notion of learning to teach as taking on of a new identity.

The philosophy that she has gone on to develop is perhaps an eclectic one, mixing elements from behaviourism, constructivism and sociocultural theory, but as we saw in the excerpt from 'Is teaching a lesson to be taught?' above, it is also remarkable in the way it reflects so many key educational discourses of the past 50 or so years. These are referenced by a number of key lexical items: *the child as a whole; different learning styles group work; communicative, social and behaviourism; authentic reading materials, print-rich and literacy-rich environments; meaningful context and authentic language; reflecting*. Manal also shows evidence of engagement in reflective practice, stating that she has thought about 'the skills that students lack' and created a classroom ethos 'that improves these weaknesses.' Overall, Manal describes how she has incorporated many of these key features of the community's defining beliefs within her own teaching as part of the process of developing her own philosophy of education and her own teaching style. Whatever else we might say about the desirability of these values, the presence of so many of them together is a statement in its own right about the potential power of teacher education to shape the belief system and identity of the student teacher.

In another Web CT posting (from Semester 2 of Year 4, in the broad topic of 'Insights from the internship') entitled '*What is an effective learning environment in the view of principals and teachers in our schools?!*', Manal critiques the unrealistic show that is presented to visitors from the Ministry of Education at the school where she is placed, in tones that echo Sabah's mythopoetical – and satirical – posting encountered in the previous chapter: 'I saw that all the teachers decorated their classrooms with commercial displays. I was not able to see one empty wall; bookshelves were full of stories ... what funny things are happening in our school?' Her negative evaluation of the mere display put on for visitors, that she felt constituted an effective learning environment in the view of the principal and teachers, led her to pose the question of what was an effective learning environment for her. Again, she offers a picture that is aligned with the key tenets of the community's beliefs but with her own emphasis on community and interpersonal relations in the classroom. She uses a sequence of present tense descriptions, expressed almost entirely in the positive, to create a vivid picture of her ideal:

> For me a positive and effective learning environment means respect and good relationships between the teacher and her students and the students to each other. There are different types of interaction going on between the teacher and the students. In this environment the students are given responsibilities to share things and their ideas are expected. There are certain norms and rules which the students follow in the classroom. Their behaviour is discussed and they are praised for positive behaviour. Their work is displayed to increase their self-esteem. Their learning is supported and they are looked upon as individuals who have different learning styles and who learn differently in different rates of their development. They work cooperatively in groups and take turns and help each other. They feel relaxed and motivated to learn in this environment because they belong to it and are considered effective members. They are not named as 'donkeys' or 'stupid' if they take risks and make mistakes. This is really an effective learning environment for me.

The by now familiar themes of interactive, cooperative learning in a warm and secure classroom environment that caters to different learning styles and respects difference comes through clearly here. Of course, within this positive picture lies the implicit negative evaluation of the current educational practices that she has observed. Manal makes this explicit at the end of her posting, which concludes with two rhetorical questions that utilize repetition and punctuation effectively to create the cumulative effect:

> For me, the types of interaction that the students have in a classroom are a part of an effective learning environment. However, in all classes the students are seated in rows where they are not allowed to interact with their peers. Is this an effective learning environment, which creates a competitive learning environment for young learners? Is this an effective learning environment?!

The repetition in the last two sentences is indicative of the significance of an issue for her, i.e. the lack in government schools of what she believes constitutes an effective learning environment that has assumed great significance for Manal. Her evaluative stance on this issue is one strategy that she uses to define herself as distinct from, and in opposition to, much of what she sees in the schools. In the following section, I look in more detail at some ways that similar discursive ends of self-definition are achieved through statements of necessity.

Commitments to Necessity: What Has to Be Done

We have noted a number of statements of necessity in Manal's posting above (*Is teaching a lesson to be taught?*). We have seen that 'teachers *have to* work collaboratively and cooperatively' and how in relation to learners' needs 'we *have to* identity those needs' while 'learners *have to* be actively engaged in a child-centered classroom' (emphases added). Although the focus of the discussion is learning and teaching, these statements are not couched as epistemic claims about how children learn or how teachers can be most effective, but rather, as demands for action. Moreover, they are demands carrying a strong degree of obligation. We can see this by comparing the statements with alternatives, such as 'teachers are *supposed* to work collaboratively', 'we *should* identify those needs' or 'learners *ought* to be actively engaged'. The sense of urgency Manal conveys in the strong modality choices she makes are consonant with what we have seen already of the urgency and passion of her educational beliefs. These strongly held beliefs stand out all the more by being so frequently constructed in contrast to the beliefs operating in government schools. We see this strategy used in two messages (both from Semester 1 of Year 4 in the topic, 'Beliefs about teaching') discussed below, where the strength of conviction is achieved through statements of necessity, linked to an ideal world of teaching and learning. At the same time, the identity constructed in these statements is defined all the more distinctly by being juxtaposed with a contrasting statement regarding the inadequate realities of the practices of government school teachers.

In the first posting, this time in response to a posting about the need for utilization of 'real life' experiences in the classroom (*449, Beliefs about teaching, Teaching + real life = learning!*), Manal begins by assuring her correspondent that 'I agree with you that teaching has to be linked to what the students know (prior knowledge) and expand on that to make learning more enjoyable and comprehensible.' Again, we have the statement couched as a commitment to necessity through the choice of 'has to'. And, again, the contrast with the government school teachers is established with the observation, 'This is not seen in the schools because some teachers only want to finish lessons quickly' (*449, Beliefs about teaching, Re: Teaching + real life = learning!*). In what becomes a familiar rhetorical pattern which we will see again later in this chapter, the statement of the necessary ideal of the first sentence is dampened by the resigned realism of the sequel sentence. The opening up of future possibility, implicit in the statement of necessity, is negated by present actuality.

This pattern of juxtaposing statements of necessity with statements of reality occurs again in Manal's next posting, a response to another student's message about different learning styles. Manal takes this opportunity to reiterate one of her beliefs, which we encountered earlier: 'I agree with you strongly that every teacher has to cater for different learning styles and multiple intelligences. As we know every child learns differently. We have to prepare materials which suit each individual's learning style'. (*449, Beliefs about teaching, Re: Different learning styles*). Strengthened by a shift in voice from the individual 'I' to the 'we' that speaks for the whole community, Manal's statement of necessity is justified by understanding gained in the programme that 'every child learns differently', which she assumes to be common knowledge among her peer audience – what Edwards and Potter refer to as a 'category entitlement' (Edwards & Potter, 1992: 161; Potter, 1996: 132–142). This justification is reflected in the rhetorical structure where the two statements of necessity, i.e. what teachers have to do, are linked by her epistemological assertion about learners. This discursive-rhetorical organization reflects Potter's point that epistemological and action orientations are often combined within statements: 'epistemological orientation is not an abstract concern with truth; it is a practical, situated concern with making a description credible' (Potter, 1996: 121). In Manal's case, *knowledge* about the nature and needs of learners provides a basis for outlining what is required in terms of teaching *practices*.

However, having established the necessity for 'every teacher' to cater for different learners, Manal goes on to observe the deficiencies of the government school teachers again: 'In fact I did not see any teachers in the government schools who know about each individual's learning style and multiple intelligences because they use the same materials with all learners'. The rhetorical structure we have seen employed twice above is again used to remind her audience of the dismal realities she perceives to be predominating in government schools and classrooms. The overall effect achieved in both these instances, by the strategy of juxtaposing statements of necessity relating to the ideal world of Manal's educational beliefs and philosophy with a reminder of the very different realities of teaching as practised in government schools is to both heighten the contrast, and at the same time, in effect, to chastise the schools for the breach between the ideal and the real. Here, we see the familiar ongoing process of identity construction in opposition to the 'inadequate' practices that characterize the government schools and the teachers working in them.

Besides identification with statements of truth and statements of necessity, another means of defining and constituting ourselves is through identification with 'right' and 'wrong', 'good' and bad', 'desirable' and 'undesirable', which are the focus of the next section.

Moral Commitments: What Is Right

Our moral values and judgements are a key means of establishing who we are and what we stand for and against. In developing her teaching identity, Manal derives considerable impetus from the incongruence she perceives between her own developing values and those she witnesses in schools. This is something Danielewicz calls an 'oppositional affiliation', noting, 'some identities will be created through dissimilarity and difference, in opposition to persons and positions' (Danielewicz, 2001: 120). In the following discussion I look first at Manal's oppositional affiliation in terms of the micro-level of classroom practice, before moving on to examine her critique of aspects of the wider UAE educational system.

'Rights' and 'wrongs' in the classroom

Not surprisingly, a significant number of evaluative moral statements appear in postings under the broad topic of 'Moral issues' (from Semester 1 of Year 4). I noted earlier how Manal builds the force of her argument through a pattern of repeated sentence structures. Here, this strategy, often involving repeated rhetorical questions, becomes overwhelming as Manal underlines the strength of her convictions. We see this in a posting entitled 'Some of my moral concerns about education and teaching in the UAE's schools', where Manal begins by noting that 'corporal punishment is used with both genders'. She then builds support for her argument by assuming consensus from her audience, arguing that 'As we know classroom management is an emotional and a psychological part of teaching'. This is followed by the uncompromisingly categorical assertion of moral values by which Manal defines herself in contradistinction to the prevalent classroom practice in the UAE (though her oppositional stance is countered by the use of the inclusive 'we'): 'If we think that corporal punishment is an appropriate strategy to make students behave well, we are wrong'. After listing some of the deleterious effects of corporal punishment, Manal proceeds to outline further her negative evaluation of corporal punishment as a series of rhetorical questions:

Why don't we as educators examine our own classroom structures, rules or techniques for behaviour management rather than the students physically? Why don't we look for reasons that lead the students to misbehave? Why don't we look for alternative strategies or positive reinforcement rather than using negative reinforcement wrongly?

In relation to the punishment of children with special educational needs she asks: 'Why don't we search and look for ways or ask for help from specialists to deal with these children rather than punishing them or ignoring their cases?' And in relation to the practice of punishing children in public forums like whole school assemblies she asks: 'Why don't we see the assembly as a place to gather all the children and share with them positive things? Does punishment improve the students' behaviour? She then offers an evaluation as a statement, 'In my opinion, schools should be considered as social organizations that complete the home's role' before launching into another series of rhetorical questions:

What about the children who have tough home lives and their parents beat them, do we repeat this role at school? Where will these children find security to build their self-esteem and confidence? Are our roles to teach these children positive morals which increase their self-esteem and moral self worth ... or are we as teachers preparing criminals to be well prepared for their world of crime? Why don't we let the students learn from their mistakes among good role models like their peers? Why don't the UAE's school system and democracy go hand in hand? Why don't we consider classrooms as a 'miniature democracy for the purpose of study and inquiry into social and interpersonal problems' (Dewey in Arends, 2000: 317) rather than punishing the students and not asking them why do they misbehave?

The rhetorical questions here, referencing many of the community's key beliefs, function as evaluative moral statements. The cumulative rhetorical effect of this relentless questioning is a powerful identification of Manal and what she stands for in stark opposition to the predominant practice in schools as constructed here. In a related posting (*449, Moral issues, Re: Verbal attack*), Manal responds sympathetically to another student's posting lamenting the practice of criticizing students publicly in the classroom for 'poor' performance in classroom tasks. We have already encountered the students' concept of 'verbal attack' in our earlier discussion of students' motivation and self-esteem. Here, Manal states what she sees as the ultimate futility of such practices in that 'By using abusive verbal attacks with young children we won't make the students learn better or answer the questions.' Her frustration with the current classroom regime then pours forth in another series of rhetorical questions:

> Why don't we consider the classroom as a positive learning environment, which allows children to feel secure and take risks to participate? Why don't we help the students to build their self-esteem in the school? Instead of letting the students feel down, why don't we look for alternative ways to help children who need more scaffolding instead of labeling them as weak or stupid? Why don't we consider schools as working environments that help in developing the students socially, emotionally, linguistically cognitively, physically and academically? (449, Moral issues, Re: Verbal attack)

As before, we have the series of rhetorical questions that function as an evaluative moral critique of current school practices. Thus, through her oppositional stance to those practices and the teachers who perpetuate them, Manal identifies herself as an opponent of the status quo. Even in the midst of this critique, Manal utilizes many of the key lexical items that we saw are part of the community's repertoire of discursive self-constitution: 'positive learning environment'; 'self-esteem'; 'scaffolding'; and the different domains of development that make up the students' concept of the child. This pattern of protest is repeated in other of Manal's postings, challenging such practices as giving children extra work as punishment in schools, where, after introducing her observations, a series of rhetorical questions serve to embody her negative evaluations of the current system.

In another posting on the shortcomings of UAE schools and classrooms (499, Insights from the internship, Re: Model schools!?), that begins with the rhetorical question, 'Aren't the government students victims in this system?', Manal goes on to outline characteristics, across a range of areas of educational practice in the UAE, that fall far short of her ideals. The shortcomings reference many of the themes we have already encountered in the wider community's discursive construction, such as 'traditional' teaching approaches that ignore students' needs and interests, are based on memorization and passive learning and enforced by verbal and physical punishment; an inflexible, lock-step curriculum dominated by the course book and final assessments; and the lack of adequate teaching resources. As a rhetorical strategy, the repetition of 'Not' and 'No' in the posting builds a momentum of discontented protest, indicative of her anger and frustration:

> Not enough time is given to practice English and connect it more to their real life experiences ... No risk taking is fostered and encouraged

as a means for learning from language errors. No opportunity is given to many aspects of their learning. Assessments mainly aim to prepare the learners to use English for the final testing. No cooperative learning and group work is encouraged as a way to learn from each other. All of these aspects related to learning. As for teaching: No flexibility is given to the teachers. No time is provided to expand on things. No cooperative and teamwork is fostered as a means for sharing ideas and learning from each other as professionals. No resources are provided for the schools. (*499, Insights from the internship, Re: Model schools!?*)

Eight of the sentences here begin with 'Not' or 'No' as Manal spells out the various ways in which educational practice in the UAE fails to embody the ideals for teaching and learning in which, as we have seen, she along with other members of the community of practice have made such a deep investment. The community's ideals are referenced through the strategies we have seen advocated previously, such as *risk taking, cooperative learning, group work* and *teamwork*. Manal uses the by now familiar pattern of repetition to convey her sense of frustration and moral indignation. As in previous examples that employed repeated interrogatives as a rhetorical strategy, here the repeated negatives express both disapproval of current practices and a clear sense of purpose that is tantamount to a manifesto for change. As argued above in the discussion of the systems of knowledge and belief that the community is discursively constructing in order to define itself, Manal's predominant strategy of self-constitution here is one of drawing a clear dividing line between the discourses of education that she embraces and identifies with and the practices of education she sees in schools.

So far the evaluative statements we have looked at have been focused on issues relating to the management of student behaviour and performance focused mainly at the micro-level of the classroom. However, Manal's moral critique does not stop there and the last sentence in the passage above, like the question we saw earlier in this section, 'Why don't the UAE's school system and democracy go hand in hand?,' is a broader indictment of the wider school system. This is explored in the following section.

'Rights' and 'wrongs' in the school system

In another posting (again under the topic of Moral issues), entitled 'Discrimination between teachers or students', Manal critiques the practice of 'discrimination between national and non-national teachers by giving them special places to sit separately' which leads 'some teachers to feel insecure or rejected by national teachers.' After the negative evaluation of this practice implicit in her observation, Manal's critique is extended by a personalized assertion: 'I think teachers are professionals and they have to work together, share ideas, resources and experiences.' The emphasis on the need for more cooperation and less competition is a theme we have already noted in Manal's identifications. Indeed, she would no doubt empathize with the following comment from a Vygotskian teacher educator: 'Teachers often see themselves as rugged individuals in a profession that breeds more competitiveness than collaboration' (Samaras, 2003: 127). Later in the posting, Manal's negative evaluation is extended from the schools she has observed discrimination in, to the UAE education system as a whole. After describing her ideal educational environment in which 'teachers can create cooperative learning environments where they can work as professionals' she proceeds by noting, 'We lack these things in teaching in the UAE.' In contrast to the more optimistic rhetorical structure of moving from the given to the possible, here, after the aspirational statement of possibilities comes the rueful statement of reality.

In a posting entitled 'Is there racism in our schools?' under the broad topic of 'Insights from the internship' (Semester 2 of Year 4) she returned to the differential treatment of national and non-national teachers in UAE schools. She was taken aback by a principal inviting her and another student teacher to sit in the national teachers' room.

> This principal's attitude really surprised me especially if we consider that the principals are leaders in the school who are supposed to facilitate and support collaboration between teachers, to work professionally in a cooperative learning environment, which aims to support students' learning and lead to success for all members in the school. I really don't blame non-national teachers who feel threatened and insecure working in this type of environment where they are not accepted. Why do we blame these teachers that they are not dedicated and motivated in their teaching, even though they teach the same amount as national teachers do, but they [national teachers] take higher salaries? Where is the fairness? (*499, Insights from the internship, Is there racism in our schools?*)

Echoing the community's preference that we noted in the preceding section for equality over hierarchy, Manal identifies herself here more closely with the 'threatened' and 'insecure' non-national teachers than with the school principal (or indeed with other national teachers, who are 'othered' in the text through being positioned as 'they', despite the fact that Manal herself is a 'national teacher') whose attitude is promoting non-acceptance rather than 'cooperation', 'collaboration' or 'fairness'. This practice is linked to the overall detriment of student learning. Thus, although her identification is still oppositional, her opposition has become more nuanced and politically informed than some of the attitudes we have observed elsewhere in her and her peers' discussion. Returning to the theme of prizing cooperation over competition, she goes on to note that 'This way we are trying to create a competitive environment for teachers, not a collaborative and cooperative environment.'

The second semester of Year 4 was one in which the student teachers were being formally evaluated for the first time by the Ministry of Education's 'zone supervisors' who fulfil the role of school inspectors for UAE schools. The students had seen and spoken to the supervisors in previous semesters. But not surprisingly, this closer working contact with representatives of an institution – the Ministry of Education – that the students defined themselves in overall contrast to, led to further negative evaluations of educational practices in the UAE as a strategy of self-definition. A peer of Manal's posted a message under the topic, 'Dealing with challenging behaviour', entitled 'Oh my God ...', in which she castigated a zone supervisor for wanting to observe and evaluate her without prior notice. In Manal's supportive response the theme of community is inserted as a positive value again, defined in opposition to a judicial metaphor:

> I don't see the effective point in coming to school without telling us and I really don't understand if we are working in a social system, a school, where we work effectively in a community, where we share the same values, or a court where there is a judge and we as teachers are being judged if we are doing our jobs effectively by teaching the course book page by page ... (499, *Dealing with challenging behaviour, Re: Oh my God*)

The judicial metaphor used here is reminiscent of the criminal metaphor we saw earlier in Chapter 4's discussion of motivation and self-esteem. In both cases, drawing on the notions of discipline and punishment evoked by the legal reference, Manal constructs a contrast between an impersonal, uncaring, oppressive educational system, with hapless individuals as its victims, and an ideal system where educators cooperate and collaborate, rather than evaluate and compete with each other and where teachers seek to support and understand, rather than punish, their students. In the above discussion, taking the need for change as given, she goes on to exonerate some of the practices of teachers by laying the blame at another level in the educational hierarchy:

I really don't blame teachers in our government schools when they plan a model lesson for a supervisor because they are afraid of being judged or they might lose their jobs ... As we know change is a slow process but having these types of people who think in this way, in my personal view, they are the main factors that hinder the change process in any educational system in the world. (*499, Dealing with challenging behaviour, Re: Oh my God*)

Manal's assumption is that change is both necessary and desirable, again identifying herself in opposition to the status quo in the UAE school system; since the supervisors are perceived as hindering change, they are clearly a negative force. Her low opinion of the supervisors is evident in her characterization of them as 'these types of people who think in this way', even though the sharpness of the critique is softened by the generalization to 'any educational system in the world.'

In a later posting (from Semester 2 of Year 4 in the broad topic, 'Insights from the internship', actually the second message she posted within the thread, *'What is an effective learning environment in the views of the principal and teachers in the school?!'*), she broadens her critique to the inherently bureaucratic features of the wider education system. She does this in a pattern of problem, exoneration and moderation which enables us to track her deliberations as she works through the complexities of the issue, thinking aloud as she moves between attitudes and balances different pressures and considerations:

The problem is that change in our system is bureaucratic and its procedures are taken step by step and all decisions are taken through a top down approach and teachers don't have a voice. Then who am I (as a student teacher) to blame teachers, principals or zone supervisors? The wrong thing in the system overall is bureaucracy; there isn't any democracy in education or allowing choice related to making decisions about how to teach. (*499, Insights from the internship, 'What is an effective learning environment in the views of the principal and teachers in the school?!'*)

We can see the interplay of *figurative* (as she envisions herself within 'our system'), *positional* (as she places herself in relation to teachers, principals and supervisors) and *authored* identities (as she constitutes herself as an advocate of democracy in education) in this passage. The process of ongoing negotiation of beliefs, values, ideas and emotions that comprise identity continues as she writes and thinks aloud. Despite exonerating the teachers above, she goes on to criticize them implicitly as she identifies herself with a rebellious stance, recommending defying the supervisors and subverting the status quo in order to be true to prized educational beliefs:

> My point is that if I have certain beliefs about teaching and learning, I will take risks and try to implement these beliefs or put my own philosophy of education (beliefs) into practice, not fully, but trying to adapt things if they don't work and not trying to say that the supervisors don't allow me to implement them or use modern methodology. (*499, Insights from the internship, 'What is an effective learning environment in the views of the principal and teachers in the school?!'*)

This is a highly personalized statement – first person pronouns are used five times within this single sentence – which clearly valorizes the individual educational conscience over the requirements of the system. The use of 'modern' at the end also places it clearly within the overall 'us' and 'them' opposition between the 'new' and the 'traditional' that we have seen Manal and other students repeatedly constructing. Later in this long posting – which runs to over a thousand words – Manal offers a more conciliatory message again, generalizing responsibility for the inadequacies she sees in government schools:

> My final thought is that there was rapid development and change in the UAE's education system during the last thirty years. There wasn't enough attention given to evaluating and reflecting on decisions. Therefore, many things were done without everybody knowing why they are done. (*499, Insights from the internship, 'What is an effective learning environment in the views of the principal and teachers in the school?!'*)

Each sentence here is agent-less, emphasizing the generalization of responsibility and blame. I should emphasize that these shifts of position, between placing the main criticism on the teachers, the principals, the supervisors, the bureaucratic system and finally the phenomenon of rapid change, should not be devalued as signs of 'inconsistency'; as I have argued in earlier chapters, 'identities on the individual level resist closure and reveal complicated, shifting, multiple facets' (Kondo, 1990: 307, cited in Miller Marsh, 2003: 8).

I should also note that not all of Manal's 'rhetorical assertions' are criticisms of current school practices. In the postings in the following section she often outlines her positive vision as she reflects on many of the practices she has implemented in schools. Even here though, she often follows this with rhetorical questions asking why the elements of her ideals are not part of current educational practice in the UAE, further entrenching the pattern we have seen of the construction of 'us' in opposition to 'them'.

Summing Up and Looking Ahead

Britzman reminds us that 'learning to teach is a time when desires are rehearsed, refashioned and refused' (1991: 220). Similar to a number of students, Manal took the opportunity in a number of postings under the broad topic, 'What I'm looking forward to in my teaching career', to offer a summation of her educational philosophy and to look forward to anticipated challenges. This prompted a further process of rehearsal, refashioning and refusal as she re-outlined her commitments to educational beliefs, values and requirements and her aspirations for teaching.

In response to a posting 'Making a difference' in which another student emphasized the key role teachers can play in the lives of generations and communities, Manal voiced her agreement and went on to describe the key role that her college teachers have played in her own life:

> I agree that there are always some people who have an important role in making a difference in our lives in certain ways. I can say this because I really think that our college teachers have supported and guided us gradually throughout four years and they have made a difference in our lives by teaching us different beliefs about teaching and learning that we then shape into our own beliefs about education. By doing this, I really can transfer this to my own students' lives. (499, *What I'm looking forward to in my teaching career, Re: Making a difference*)

The comment that 'they made a difference in our lives' is an acknowledgement of the pivotal role that her college teachers have played in the development of her beliefs. This acknowledgement of the 'difference' made in her life by her teacher educators offers some insight into why she has been so passionate in her educational beliefs. However, echoing Tharp *et al.*'s (2000: 48) comment that 'more is learned than is taught, and more is developed than is intentionally developed', she has not just adopted her teacher educators' beliefs but shaped them 'into our own beliefs about education.' This she sees as enabling her to go on and make a similar difference 'to my own students' lives'.

Manal concludes this posting with another series of rhetorical questions, which we can see are framed in 'oppositional affiliation' against current government school educational practices:

> I also always asked myself questions: Is education only a page to be taught in a book? Does education mean using a stick to deal with inappropriate behaviour? Does education mean to show our power as teachers over students? ... What values are fostered in teaching and

learning for young learners? (*499, What I'm looking forward to in my teaching career, Re: Making a difference*)

Manal's concern with power in the micro-world of the classroom is something she shares with educators such as Hooks (1994), Canagarajah (1999) and Norton (2000). In the final posting that she initiated, Manal looks ahead and outlines her positive aspirations for teaching. She reflects on the positive experience of collaborating with a peer during her internship in creating a 'print-rich and literacy-rich environment' and hints at possible obstacles that may lie ahead, as she notes that 'I am looking forward to creating and establishing a similar type of environment, if I will have the same opportunity'. Summing up much of what she has developed in terms of her educational philosophy, implicitly contrasted against much of what she has described as current practice in schools, she goes on to outline her ideals:

> I am also looking forward to implementing different strategies that promote cooperation between students [as well as], reciprocal learning and active engagement with meaningful and authentic activities that will support their learning and help guide them to learn and acquire their second language in a meaningful context. I am also looking forward to creating an effective learning environment which will build a good rapport between me and my students. It will cater for individual differences. It will support and enhance learners' whole development, physically, socially, emotionally, cognitively, linguistically and academically. [It will be] an environment where the learners will feel relaxed and it will be away from pressure, from labeling learners and attacking them ... an environment which maintains positive and desirable behaviours. Also in this supportive environment, the learners will develop a positive attitude towards learning their second language because their work is valued and they have their own identity as effective members in this classroom. (*499, What I'm looking forward to in my teaching career, Theories into practice*)

Among the mixture of aspirations and predictions here, values and evaluations are clearly fundamental. Key among these values are many that we have noted as characteristic of the community's discursive construction, such as active learning, equality, sensitivity, motivation and self-esteem, while the positive value she places on meaningful and authentic activities as well as membership and identity in the classroom community is reminiscent of Norton's (2000: 142) emphasis on the need for the language teacher to 'make the lived identities and experiences of the language learner an integral part of classroom practice'. As Norton notes this is not common in so-called 'communicative language' classrooms (Norton, 2000: 138–140), let alone the world of UAE government schools. We get a hint of the ways this need might be addressed in the posting's concluding emphasis on 'practice related to the community in order to support learning and teaching.'

> I am looking forward to working collaboratively and professionally with different people in the larger community of the school including parents, staff members, colleagues and students in order to support learning and teaching. I am looking forward to seeing changes in the UAE's system and I hope that we make a difference in our students' lives by implementing what we have learned (philosophy of education), supporting each other and trying to work and deal professionally with different obstacles we will face in our career. (*499, What I'm looking forward to in my teaching career, Theories into practice*)

Alongside the emphasis on teamwork and collaboration is the identification with the need for changes in UAE education. The juxtaposition of this with the hope to make a difference 'by implementing what we have learned' is an acknowledgment of 'oppositional affiliation' vis-à-vis the status quo as is the reference to the 'obstacles we will face'. Manal's – and the community's – identities are being constituted through contrast to the current practice of teaching in UAE schools to the very end.

I noted at the beginning of this chapter examining Manal's self-constitution that she had been particularly active in using the online discussion board as a medium and sharing her thoughts and ideas with her peers. This has fostered both affirmation and exploration, for, as Danielewicz argues, 'it is not experience itself that makes us who we are; rather it is the act of naming as well as the ways we talk about and represent that experience that constructs identities' (2001: 113). We might say, paraphrasing Piaget, that through the act of naming herself and her beliefs and values on the discussion boards, Manal has been actively engaged in her own identity development. Or in Zhu's (1998) model, her 'zone of engagement', linked to her 'zone of development', has been particularly productive of new knowledge, new perspectives, new understanding and new insights. Certainly, given the interrelatedness of learning, meaning, community, practice and identity (Wenger, 1998), Manal's proactive participation in the practice of sharing the meanings she has discovered and the learning she has created – that is her investment in belonging to her community as reflected in her 'rhetorical assertions' – has given life to a vivid and dynamic identity development within the community. As Wenger notes,

Engagement in practice is a double source of identification: we invest ourselves in what we do and at the same time we invest ourselves in our relations with other people. As we build communities of practice through the process, we work out our relations with each other and with the world, and we gained a lived sense of who we are. (Wenger, 1998: 192)

The point is that although we have focused in this chapter on the identity development of one individual, the implications are also valid for the development of the community. In the terms used in this chapter, our identifications, in terms of our commitments to truth, necessity and morality, are inextricably intertwined with our representations of the world and our relations to each other. Critically for this book, the meaning of each is constructed in discourse. That is, intrapersonal identity is co-constructed with systems of knowledge and belief and with interpersonal relations.

Conclusion

In this chapter we have examined the discursive self-constitution on the intrapersonal level of one of the student teachers as a member of the evolving community of practice. This was achieved by focusing on Manal's commitments to truth, her commitments to necessity and her moral commitments, as represented in her Web CT postings across a year. We saw, unsurprisingly, that many of the key themes that defined the community's beliefs such as an emphasis on 'student-centred' teaching and sensitivity in the classroom were also prominent in Manal's self-constitution. But in line with the active and dialogic notion of the construction of identities outlined in this book, involving far more than just a simple faxing process from the social to the individual (Holland et al., 1998), Manal has particular priorities and preoccupations that were less significant features of the wider community such as collaboration and teamwork, rather than competition, as a desirable professional value among practising teachers.

We also saw that, as was the case with the construction of the community's system of knowledge and beliefs, to a large extent Manal's self-constitution is through what I have termed, following Danielewicz (2001), an 'oppositional affiliation'. Indeed, as expressed by Manal's characteristic discursive strategy of building cumulative force through repetition, as well as her strategy of juxtaposing the possibilities of the ideal next to the grim realities of the given, this oppositional affiliation often comes through as an expression of outright hostility and antagonism towards the government schools and their teachers. In many ways this oppositional affiliation is the flipside of the incredible strength of purpose and commitment that characterizes Manal as a member of the community. Indeed, as we have already noted, the ideational and the interpersonal go hand in hand in constructing language teacher identities; the beliefs that define a community are also the bonds that unify and unite it. In the next and final chapter we will draw together the findings from the study and consider some of the implications in terms of teacher education in the local and regional context as well as outlining some possibilities for further research.

Note

1 In the educational discourse the students are introduced to in Year 1, 'empty vessels/blank slates' represents behaviourist learners; 'plants' represent Piagetian, cognitive-developmental learners; and the 'apprentice' represents Vygotskian, sociocultural learners. However, in another model (Freeman and Freeman, 2001) that the students encounter in Year 3, 'plant' is the choice of metaphor for the behaviourist learner, with the 'builder' representing the cognitive-developmental learner, and the 'explorer' representing the sociocultural learner.

Chapter 7

Summary of Findings and Future Directions[1]

This book is about the power of discourse and community in shaping language teacher identities. In this final chapter I discuss the findings of the UAE study, relate them to other regional studies, and consider their implications for language teacher education and teacher education more widely. As emphasized in Chapter 2 and consistent with the premises of discourse theory, the findings presented here are an attempt to identify the operations of the 'taken for granted' within the student teachers' discourse; but rather than revealing the true picture behind the filter, all these findings can do is replace one filter with another that perhaps reveals different angles and perspectives and hence new shades of meaning, as part of what Phillips and Jorgensen (2002) describe as a positioned opening for discussion. This final chapter also considers possible ways forward in relation to the immediate context of the study and finally in terms of potential directions for future research.

Revisiting the Research Issues

The interrelated factors that I observed in working with the student teachers, including the students' embodiment of learning to teach as the taking on of a new identity, the strength of their sense of community and the enthusiasm with which they embraced particular educational discourses, prompted the research issues underlying the UAE study, concerning the ways in which the social and educational discourses that have shaped the contemporary UAE context and the HCT's teacher education programme are taken up by the students as they construct their identities as teachers and a community of practice. Below, some of the more obvious connections between these discourses and the student teachers' identities and community are discussed, before exploring the situation in a more complex light.

In considering the ways the students' construction of their identities and their community reflects the wider social discourses operating in the contemporary UAE, there are some clear connections that have been identified in earlier chapters. The students' embrace of educational change and modern pedagogy, as well as their largely positive views with respect to the teaching and learning of English as an additional language, resonates with the progressive discourse of positioning the UAE advantageously in the new global economy. However, this is not just a matter of their being colonized by discourses of globalization and associated discourses of global English. Consonant with the notion of 'glocalization' (Robertson, 1995; Urry, 2003; see Chapter 2), the students are keen to creatively use global English for local purposes. On the other hand, the concern we saw expressed by a number of students with regard to the cultural appropriateness of the textbook series used in government schools, and the underlying concern for cultural preservation in the face of the forces of Westernization represented by English, are expressions of a more conservative discourse, which seeks to safeguard the Arab and Islamic cultural heritage of the UAE against perceived threats. The comments made by a number of the student teachers making reference to the suitability of teaching as a career for women in the eyes of their families also showed the students taking note of, if not advocating, this conservative social discourse.

Likewise, in thinking about the particular strength of the student teachers' community of practice, social discourses of the contemporary UAE are also relevant to our understanding. Discourses of Emiratization and national development may be part of the explanation for the students' sense of community, though also relevant here is no doubt the minority status of Emiratis in the UAE where they comprise only 20% of the population. However, we should recall Findlow's (2000: 43) argument that it is the positive influences of nation building and the development of social infrastructure that is the predominant factor in the development of UAE national identity, rather than any sense of exclusivity as a negative response to the presence of a large expatriate population. Further impetus to group cohesion among the community members may derive from the additional minority status of the student teachers as degree students in a system mainly offering diplomas and higher diplomas and as education students in a college system specializing in technical vocational education. But again, the positive dimension of embracing educational discourses and seeing themselves as teachers, and thus contributing to the UAE's development seems more significant. These are fairly obvious and straightforward connections that can be drawn.

But by now it should be clear that the three factors initially noted as the impetus for the study, the students' embodiment of learning to teach as the taking on of a new identity, the strength of their community and the strength of their beliefs, are integrally related. At a theoretical level this reflects the three constitutive effects of discourse in terms of individual identities, interpersonal relations and systems of knowledge and beliefs. Although these effects are separated out for analytical purposes, they are co-effects of discursive construction that are *effected* simultaneously through meaning making within the practices of the community. In Hallidayan terms the ideational, interpersonal and textual meta-functions of meaning are always constructed concurrently. Thus the strength of the students' beliefs has necessarily been accompanied by a corresponding strength of community along with the wholehearted embrace of a new teaching identity.

We can see this interrelatedness in thinking about how the student teachers embodied the notion of learning to teach in terms of the formation of an identity as a teacher, as well as in terms of the students' work of belonging to the evolving community of practice through the modes of engagement, imagination and alignment. The aspects of *figurative identities*, in terms of the students' wholehearted *engagement* in scripting themselves into the social role of teaching, in identifying with the required competence and in taking on the signification of ('new' or 'progressive') 'teacher', are all related to the aspects of *authored identities*, in terms of how the student teachers have seen and created fresh links across time and space, drawn on past recollections (of 'traditional' and 'progressive' teachers), and *imagined* future selves as part of a process of re/invention, re/fashioning and realization of authored identities. And these aspects of figurative and authored identities are reflected in and reaffirmed by aspects of the student teachers' *positional identities*, such as the predominance of an 'us' and 'them' division – what I have referred to previously as an 'oppositional affiliation' or mis*alignment* – between the ('progressive') student teachers and the ('traditional') government school teachers.

A similar pattern presents itself in thinking about the students' enthusiastic embrace of educational discourses and the corresponding strength of their teaching beliefs. In many ways the predominant theme that has emerged in analysing the data during the study, indeed one that has been repeatedly touched on within each of the last four chapters, is this incredible commitment of the student teachers to a set of educational beliefs. But as emphasized above, this wholehearted and passionate enthusiasm with which the student teachers have embraced the discourses of 'new' or 'progressive' education that they have encountered during their degree, cannot be separated from the strength of the interpersonal relations among members of the community, nor can the strength of these shared beliefs and the bond between the community's members be separated from the vivid forcefulness of many of the students' individual teaching identities.

In many ways from my perspective as a teacher educator, the strength of the students' educational beliefs and the intensity of their personal and professional commitment at the individual and the community level are very pleasing to see. Furthermore, their determination to be agents of change is both unsurprising, given the dissatisfaction of most of the student teachers with their own schooling, and welcome, given the UAE's avowed ambitions in terms of school reform. Indeed, the students' degree of focus, dedication and seriousness of purpose are in many ways exemplary. But, as has been highlighted on a number of occasions in the preceding chapters and is further explained below, this strength of commitment and belief has been built through a discursive strategy of constructing an oppositional affiliation with regard to the government schools and teachers, which at times spills over into hostility and antagonism. We can gain further insights into the dynamic at work here from discourse theory.

Discourse and Differentiation

Discourse and the discursive construction of community and identity have been fundamental to this study. We have discussed discourse as a particular pattern of signifying practices that structure meaning from the 'riot of inchoate potential messages' (Holquist, 1990: 47) that otherwise comprises 'reality'. That is, discourse involves taking a partial and contingent 'cut' or 'take' on 'reality' from the myriad of other possible 'cuts'. In a similar fashion, discursive processes of identity and community construction involve a 'closure' of meaning, in that individual and community are constructed in particular contingent and temporary ways. This contingent and temporary fixing of meaning necessarily 'closes off' and excludes other possible meanings that might be available within the realm of possible meanings. Thus, dividing the world of teachers and teaching into the 'traditional' and 'new' paradigms tends to foreclose possible alternatives, such as the 'eclectic' or 'pragmatic' teacher – Karimah's claim to be a 'realistic' teacher was very much the expression of a lone voice. We can best understand the essential dynamic operating here in the discursive construction of the students' identities and community by considering Laclau and Mouffe's logics of equivalence and difference.

Within discourse theory, meaning focuses around 'logics of equivalences' and 'logics of differences'; however, these are not given or fixed (Andersen, 2003; Howarth, 2000; Laclau & Mouffe, 1985; Torfing, 1999). We may see a 'Mercedes' and a 'BMW' car as different or we may see them as equivalent in their difference from a 'Ford'; which logic prevails depends on context and purpose, and is the very stuff of politics. It also reflects the power of hegemonic discourses and discursive practices, which, rather than *re*presenting pre-given interests, actively constitute them as Laclau and Mouffe argue: 'Indeed, politico-hegemonic articulations retroactively create the interests they claim to represent' (2001: xi). In a similar fashion, an Emirati student teacher may see herself as equivalent to an Egyptian teacher insofar as they are both non-Western, Arabic speakers and fellow professionals in the field of education; or she may focus on her UAE nationality as a source of distinction and difference. The logic of equivalence will strive to delimit and dissolve difference by creating 'chains of equivalence'; yet because meaning and identity are necessarily differential, the operation of a logic of equivalence is always operationalized through the construction of a purely negative opposite. An extreme example of this is the Jacobin discourse in the French Revolution which simplified differences by dividing society into the 'people' and the 'ancien régime' (Torfing, 1999: 97). By contrast, the 'logic of difference' will strive to break chains of equivalence, thereby weakening oppositions and downplaying division. Howarth (2000: 107) offers the apartheid regime with its ideology of separate development, organized around expanding differentiations among social groups, yet at the same time resistant to the construction of chains of equivalence between various anti-apartheid forces, as the classic example of the logic of difference in operation.

As we have seen, for the student teachers' community, meaning revolves around a constructed opposition between 'traditional' and 'new' or 'progressive' teaching. Although necessarily temporary and contingent, these particular constructions have achieved a degree of naturalization, becoming hegemonic among the community members. The individual and community identities involved are built up through 'chains of equivalence' between elements of 'new' or 'progressive' teaching. These elements include teacher as 'facilitator', practising 'student-centred' teaching within a 'complex' classroom environment that values 'high motivation' and 'active learning' and prizes 'sensitivity' towards learners, who are recognized as having varied 'learning needs' and individual 'learning styles'. The meaning of these elements is dependent upon their opposites ('transmitter', 'teacher-centred', etc.) which also form a chain of equivalence. This opposite chain serves to distinguish the students from the government school teachers, as we saw in Chapter 4, by comprising the 'constitutive outside' that offers the condition of possibility for construction of the identities in question (Torfing, 1999: 124). That is, the meanings that make up the student teachers' identities are established relationally, or differentially, by being equated with some, and contrasted with other, key signifiers.

Within this discursive construction of hegemonic meaning and identities, the two chains of equivalence (lining up with 'new versus 'traditional' teaching), are mutually exclusive, in that it is impossible to be a 'new' and a 'traditional' teacher at the same time, or for the classroom to be a site of both 'new' and 'traditional' teaching. This is reflected in thread titles that set the concerns of the government school teachers in opposition to those of the student teachers' community, such as 'Discipline versus learning'. A consequence of this pattern – and we can see this in thread titles such as 'My SST is the problem' – is that the 'traditional' teachers are constructed as – and resented for – 'blocking' the full fruition of the student teachers' identities as 'new' teachers (Howarth, 2000: 106–107). As Connolly reminds us, 'Identity requires difference in order to be, and it converts difference into otherness in order to secure its own self-certainty' (2002: 64).

In addition to this antagonism, another possible consequence of the hegemonic status of the discourse of 'new' teaching is likely to be a degree of blindness towards elements of the excluded 'traditional' discourse that may be present in their practice, since logically this is *im*possible within the possibilities for meaning defined by the chain of equivalence. Thus, given the persistence of this theme, it is important to ask what might be possible reasons for, as well as implications of, its predominance, both for the subjects of the study and for possible future research. These issues are addressed below.

Interpreting the Research Findings

Overall, it is not surprising to see a degree of commitment along with agreement and consensus among the students. Establishing a community of practice involves establishing and maintaining the belief systems that define the community. As Miller Marsh notes

> In order to attain membership in a given group, an individual must appropriate one or more of the discourses that flows in and through the community ... As individuals become immersed in social communities, they appropriate the ways of thinking, speaking, and interacting that provide them access to group membership. (Miller Marsh, 2003: 7)

Gee (1996, 2004; see also Lankshear & Knobel, 2006) makes the same point, arguing that discourses tend to be totalizing and resistant to any internal criticism, since this would undermine the very coherence and persuasiveness upon which their existence depends.

Still the question remains as to why the students have been so powerfully receptive to discourses of progressive education, which are so at odds with the 'traditional' schooling they themselves experienced in the past. Given their strong protective feelings towards their own culture, in addition to the gap between progressive educational theory and current practice in local schools, a reasonably anticipated reaction might have been of skepticism and even rejection. One obvious factor in the students' positive embrace of what we have described as 'new' approaches to education, is their immersion in them as part of a teacher education programme that models this progressive pedagogy. This is a reason that came through time and time again in student comments as they contrasted the approaches they experienced at college with those they recollected from school. It may also be that the 'missionistic' rhetoric that underpins progressive approaches, maps readily onto the mission and rhetoric of nation building that is part of the Emiratization project. Youthful naivety may have a role to play too, as may issues of gender, insofar as learning to teach has provided the student teachers with opportunities for heightened agency in a context characterized by multiple constraints on women's lives.

But another possible insight into what the processes at work here might be is offered by the findings of a recent study with Jewish and Arab teacher education students in Israel. In this study, Eilam relates the powerful uptake of theory on the part of the Arab students and speculates on the reasons underlying their strong confidence in the ability to relate theory to practice: 'The Arab educational milieu, which traditionally involves firm discipline and grants teachers high status and respect, may have encouraged Muslim Arab students to believe more in their ability to successfully apply what they had learned' (2003: 180). The UAE student teachers' eager and wholehearted acceptance of progressive theory coupled with, indeed intensified by, criticism of their own schooling resonates with findings in Eilam's earlier study: 'The difficulties the Arabs had experienced in learning made them invest much more energy into making sense of and trying to apply the new knowledge' (Eilam, 2002: 1695). Harold *et al.* (2002: 7) reported a similar 'impact of academic course content' on teacher education students at Zayed University in the UAE.

Thus, in line with both these studies, it can be argued that the students are now so critical of their schooling because pedagogically it was at odds with the approaches to education they have encountered in the HCT's B. Ed. degree. But ironically, it may also be that the students' backgrounds in a 'teacher-centred' milieu, contribute to their ready acceptance of 'student-centred' approaches. Eilam goes on to suggest that 'causing students to deeply contrast other cultures with their own constitutes an effective training method' (2002: 1695). This may well be so in terms of prompting a sort of Piagetian cognitive dissonance, which forces the learner to rethink their prior assumptions.

But assuming for the sake of argument that the 'progressive' educational discourses are in the interests of UAE education, three issues immediately suggest themselves in relation to the future. The first relates to the practical difficulties the students are likely to face in trying to bridge the gulf between the practices that characterize their beliefs and the practices currently predominating in government schools. The second relates to the potential struggle to maintain their current beliefs that the students are likely to face as they take up roles within an environment and a set of practices predicated upon a different and contrary set of educational beliefs. And the third relates to the challenges they are likely to encounter in working alongside the teachers in those schools, given the construction of antagonistic relations in the predominant discourse of the student teachers' community of practice that we have observed. These topics are discussed briefly below but all warrant further research.

In discussing the sense of deep conviction and commitment that came though in the data, I have often used a religious metaphor to convey the intensity of the students' beliefs. I described the student teachers in Chapter 4 as 'converts' to progressive education, offering 'testimonies' as 'affirmations' of their 'beliefs'. I described the student in Chapter 5 who 'confessed' to her struggle to live up to the 'creed' of student-centred teaching as a 'repentant sinner' who was welcomed back into the fold by the somewhat patronizing 'pastor'. The use of a religious metaphor is very deliberate as it points to a significant aspect of the student teachers' discourse. It also reflects the extent to which all language use is deeply rooted in imagination and metaphor (Lakoff & Johnson, 1984), as well as the extent to which any analysis is inevitably a matter of interpretation, for as Rorty reminds us, 'The world does not speak. Only we do' (1989: 6). As Rorty and others have gone on to point out, the basis for our judgements must be based on a mixture of moral and practical criteria (Smith & Deemer, 2000). Indeed, it can be argued that 'we are obliged to look for processes that might increase the coherence of narrative and analytic practice' (Mello, 2002: 235). Similarly, Koro-Ljunberg stresses the productive, functional aspect of metaphorical analysis and argues that from a poststructuralist perspective 'the meanings of the metaphors are viewed as partial, textual and shaped by discursive understanding' and thus 'the utility of the metaphor is expanded and utilized according to the researcher's purposes' (Koro-Ljunberg, 2004: 343 and 355).

Thus from a research perspective, the value of the religious metaphor was to capture the strength, passion, conviction and commitment that resonate in the students' descriptions of their wholehearted embrace of 'new' educational approaches, which indeed has something of the all encompassing enthusiasm of a religious conversion. We have seen numerous examples of this, but perhaps a particularly representative one is Nashita's statement in Chapter 4 'MY WHOLE LIFE HAS CHANGED'. There is also a tangible sense of relief that the discovery of 'new' pedagogical approaches has saved them from becoming like their former teachers, captured succinctly by Nabila's comment, introduced in Chapter 4 and noted again in Chapter 5 because of its explicit religious discourse, 'We thought that we would be as our teachers but thanks, no. Thanks to God we are not like them.' The religious metaphor as an interpretive tool is also useful since it also alludes to the Manichean division into good and bad teaching that we have seen evolving as part of the community's belief system.

The use of religious metaphors is just one example of the pervasive presence of metaphor as a linguistic and cognitive device and my discussion of it should not be read as an attempt at a totalizing explanation; other examples of metaphors employed by the student teachers are of education as a journey (e.g. the discussion thread title 'My beliefs have changed in stages') or as a battle ('Up hill battle'; 'Standing on my ground'). The students' explicit and implicit use of metaphorical discourse is a topic that would be of potential interest for further research as a source of insight into the way they are constructing teaching, learning and education.

In addition, we should recall that a religious or any other *metaphor* remains just that: a device that relates different phenomena by analogy in order to gain deeper insights, rather than a literal linking of the phenomena in question. But at the same time we need to appreciate the generative, as opposed to purely descriptive, potential of metaphors which, by recontextualizing one thing in terms of another, can offer surprising insights and suggest new lines of inquiry (Pryke *et al.*, 2003; Rorty, 1989). Thus, in addition to capturing the passion and intensity of many of the student teachers' educational beliefs, the religious metaphor helps us in perceiving and framing potential future risks and dangers that can accompany intensely held beliefs, and alerts us to the need to be vigilant in promoting tolerance and understanding. On this note, Zizek cautions against striving too zealously for our ideals lest we become intolerant ideologues; rather, we need to accept a degree of imperfection and incompleteness as the constitutive condition for the presence and existence of what we value, for to seek its totalization often leads towards oppression. As Zizek (2003: 37) comments with regard to the religious and political forms of zealotry, how many fanatical defenders of religion started up by ferociously attacking contemporary secular culture and ended up by forsaking religion itself ... And is it not a fact that, in a strictly analogous way, liberal warriors are so eager to fight antidemocratic fundamentalism that they will end up flinging away freedom and democracy themselves, if only they can fight terror?

Indeed, hostility towards differences of belief can be a sign of insecurity with respect to the beliefs in question, which perhaps accompanies any attempt to elevate a belief or set of beliefs to the status of universal truth. At the same time our hostility towards 'other' beliefs can unwittingly be a sign of our attributing to them the very reality and actuality we wish to deny them (Weedon, 2004). As Zizek (2003: 26) comments in relation to religious monotheism, 'For that reason true monotheists are tolerant: for them, others are not objects of hatred, but simply people who, although they are not enlightened by the true belief, should nonetheless be respected because they are not inherently evil'. In a similar way, extreme political – or educational – correctness and the belief in the possibility of a purified, non-discriminatory language or a totally just educational practice – and this is not to advocate the use of discriminatory language or bias in education – is liable to have unintended totalitarian effects through its misrecognition of the essentially partial, contextualized and impure nature of even our most cherished values (Torfing, 1999: 286). In this context, Fettes argues for the appropriation of a broad range of cultural tools as the true goal of education:

> Different cultural tools – for instance those associated with the oral language of a community, with popular literacy, or with disciplinary thinking – engender somewhat distinct ways of understanding the world, which are not always easily reconciled. Yet the greater range of tools we have at our disposal, the more flexible and powerful our thinking is likely to be; therefore the proper goal of education is to attempt a reconciliation, to cultivate the best of each kind of understanding and avoid a reliance on any single way of relating to the world. (Fettes, 2005: 6–7)

While not wishing to suggest that the student teachers' views can be equated to those of political or religious fanatics, it is nevertheless possible to suggest that their (at times) exclusionary adherence to the discourse of 'new' pedagogy, and their concomitant tendency to demonize 'traditional' teachers and teaching through the establishment and maintenance of binary oppositions, would benefit by being tempered with insights into the contingency, partiality and fragility of all beliefs. Continuing the religious metaphor, we might say that the proper goal of teacher education is to discourage discursive orthodoxy or pedagogic fundamentalism but rather to foster a latitudinarian openness to contingency and heterogeneity, a temperate tolerance for uncertainty and ambiguity and an imaginative and empathetic engagement with diversity and difference. We should be wary, however, of reading their penchant for dichotomous schema as unique to this context. In their work with teacher education students in North America, Hinchman and Oyler noted a rejection of ambiguity and a 'desire not only for stability but also for what we called Utopian harmony' (2000: 503). The authors acknowledge the function of dichotomies in reducing the tensions inherent in uncertainty, but argue that teacher educators

> must also help students to understand that the importance of the issue is not necessarily diminished by the fact that disagreements are not readily resolved ... that the same data generates multiple interpretations ... that there are not many universal prescriptions for teaching. (Hinchman & Oyler, 2000: 506–507)

Drawing on Rorty's notion of the liberal ironist (1989), Hinchman and Oyler urge teacher educators to cultivate an appreciation of contingencies, contradictions and ironies in student teachers, so as to guard against susceptibility to overly coherent constructions of pedagogical 'reality'. The spirit of advocacy needs to be balanced at all times by a spirit of enquiry (Mitchell and Sackney, 2000). Such an approach would view educational theory ideas not so much as a source of truth, but rather from a perspective whereby 'theory effectively becomes a tool kit that offers different ways of analyzing and theorizing social and cultural phenomena and practices' (Weedon, 2004: 9). In the following section I consider some conceptual frameworks which might assist future cohorts of student teachers in moving in this direction.

Looking to the Future

In a *Gulf News* article (25 November 2004) soon after the student teachers graduated, it was reported that (former) Minister of Education, 'Sheikh Nahayan demanded that schools be institutions that encourage students to innovate.' According to the report, he went on to outline the following demands:

> We want students to think creatively and not just memorize to pass exams. We want to develop their skills and we want students to be

active partners in the educational process. I am very keen on revolutionizing the educational system and teachers have a huge role in achieving this process. They have to encourage students to learn and make them love the subjects they are teaching. We want to test students differently based on a system that evaluates their skills and not what they have memorized. (Al Nowais, 2004)

This statement could have been written by one of the student teachers and they would certainly take heart from the minister's words, which echo so many of the sentiments we have seen expressed throughout this study. Nevertheless, despite the implications of this message for the likely diminishment of dissonance between the given and the possible, the real and the ideal, for future cohorts of HCT teacher education students, it is worth considering the potential lessons and implications of one of the key findings of this study: the predominance of a discourse that constructs relations of antagonism between the student teachers and their espoused beliefs, and the perceived practices of the schools. We do so by revisiting the discourse theory that has provided the conceptual framework for this book.

Discursive hegemony and antagonism

We have seen how discourse is fundamental to the creation of a community – and vice versa. The very possibilities of seeing, thinking, understanding and acting depend on a certain carving up of the inchoate riot of 'reality', through the structuring into meaningfulness that discourse provides through processes of articulation, or fixation of meaning, though this can only ever be partial because of 'the constant overflowing of every discourse by the infinitude of the field of discursivity' (Laclau & Mouffe, 1985: 113). Thus, as we have seen, this structuring involves a temporary closure of other possibilities for meaningfulness. As a particular discourse is articulated and rearticulated over time it achieves hegemonic status. As Mitchell and Sackney (2000: 133) comment in relation to the predominance of traditional, 'mechanistic' discourses of education and schools, its assumptions and claims become 'so deeply embedded in cognition and practice that they are not seen as assumptions at all but as reality itself'. As part of this process of semiotic domination, a given discourse discredits and destroys the meaningfulness of other possibilities for understanding the field in question, represented by other discourses. Thus in Chapter 5, in the section on 'embracing a struggling soul', we discussed the impossibility of a student teacher proclaiming their willing adherence to the values and beliefs of 'traditional' teaching.

Implicit here is the restriction of possibilities for identities as the hegemonic discourse relegates certain identities to the realm of the constitutive outside, in the way that we have seen how 'progressive' teaching is constituted by its differences from 'traditional' teaching. However, as we have seen in the discourse of the student teachers' community of practice, the outsider identities will not just be constructed as different, but as oppositional. As Torfing (1999: 120–121) notes,

> The hegemonic force which is responsible for the negation of individual or collective identity, will tend to construct the excluded identity as one of a series of threatening obstacles to the full realization of the chosen meanings and options ... the negation of identity always gives rise to social antagonism.

Certainly this reflects and provides a means of interpreting the majority discourse that I have examined in this study. Over time it is quite possible that this antagonism will be naturally reduced as the school system moves towards the new Minister of Education's vision, which as we have noted is closely aligned to the beliefs and values of the community; and as the student teachers move on to become teachers, populating the field with more, to them, congenial educational discourses and practices. The overall effect of these developments will probably be to reduce the 'frontier effect' which to some degree will cease 'to be grounded upon an evident and given separation' between the given and the possible (Laclau & Mouffe, 1985: 134). Nevertheless, these changes will take time and there is likely to be a considerable 'transition shock' for the cohort of student teachers in this study as they take up positions in schools, as is the case for new teachers elsewhere (Rogers & Babinski, 2002). Thus, in terms of identity formation of future cohorts of HCT student teachers, it is important to consider other ways in which the students can be assisted in the performance of authoring identities that move beyond the oppositional affiliation I have noted, so that this antagonism can be mitigated and reduced. I briefly consider some of these possibilities in the final sections below.

From antagonism to agonism

A situation of hostility between student teachers and government school teachers is unlikely to be in the interests of either party. It also runs the risk of fusing with other constructed differences such as that between Emirati nationals and expatriate Arabs, leading to situations of mutual resentment, thereby entrenching oppositional stances and obstructing possibilities for cooperation and collaboration. In addition, it is worth noting that a sustained pattern of negative, antagonistic expression towards government schools and teachers is not a healthy state of affairs for the student teachers themselves; as Mitchell and Sackney (2000: 139) note, 'when we direct negativity towards another person, we are injecting it into our own lives, and when we respect others, respect shall return to us.' One way to surmount the latent and sometimes explicit antagonism that we have seen in the discourse of the student teachers' community of practice is to promote what Laclau and Mouffe describe as an *agonistic* approach, which 'acknowledges the real nature of its frontiers and the forms of exclusion they entail, instead of trying to disguise them under the veil of rationality or morality' (Mouffe, 2000: 105). Yet while antagonism entails an us/them relation in which those we disagree with are our 'enemies', agonism sees them transformed into 'adversaries' whose legitimacy is accepted (Mouffe, 2005: 20). This would entail moving beyond characterizations of teaching as good and bad, but rather, seeing education and schools, teachers and students, teaching and learning, within a wider socio-discursive perspective. We saw a few of the students moving towards such a position as they tentatively challenged the frontiers established by the community's predominant discourse. An example of this was the following comment from Asiya, cited in Chapter 5:

> On the other hand, I want to draw your attention to another issue. We were taught how to create a positive learning environment and we got the chance to see the effectiveness of using child-centred activities through going out to schools and teaching. We were introduced to many educational theories and got the opportunities to put them into practice. Government schools teachers did not get that chance though.

Here Asiya recognizes the fragility and contingency of the community and its discourse, which allows her to evince empathy with the government teachers rather than constructing them in adversarial terms. This, in turn, considerably widens the scope for a more genuine and constructive engagement with the 'other', as well as creating possibilities for self-transformation:

> Critique, I believe, is most powerful when it leaves open the possibility that we might also be remade in the process of engaging another's worldview, that we might come to learn things that we did not already know before we undertook the engagement. This requires that we occasionally turn the critical gaze upon ourselves, to leave open the possibility that we may be remade through an encounter with the other. (Mahmood, 2005: 36–37)

This insight is related to an aspect of agonism, in the form of *nomadization*, which 'refers to the attempt to undercut the allegiance of a specific identity to a certain place or a certain property, and thereby to show that all identities are constructed in and through hegemonic power struggles' (Torfing, 1999: 255). This emphasis on developing awareness of the discursive construction of all identities resonates with Gee's recent urging of the need for language teachers to become 'masters' of the 'political geography of discourses' (Gee, 2004: 30). And on a similar note, Britzman (1994: 72) urges teacher educators 'to engage in dialogue with student teachers about each of our ideological processes of becoming' in order to foster 'critical awareness of the constructedness of knowledge and how these images set the terms for and boundaries of identity'.

The implications of this is the need for teacher education programmes in general, and the HCT B.Ed. in particular, to encourage student teachers – and teacher educators – to develop an awareness of the ways in which their own understanding is continuously being constructed in and through discourse and to see in turn the constructed-ness of the government teachers' understandings. In other words, we need 'to affirm the indispensability of identity while contending against the dogmatism of identity; to cultivate care for the agonism of life by disclosing contingent elements in any specific identity; to politicize the ambiguity in human being' (Connolly, 2002: 159). To turn to a religious discourse again, we could say that to understand is to forgive.

Future directions

In terms of practice with future cohorts of student teachers, one possible approach for promoting such an empathetic understanding of the government school teachers would be to implement strategies such as having the students complete a detailed profile of one of their supervising school teachers. This could include documenting issues like why they chose teaching, how and what they studied to become a teacher, their career path to date, their goals for the future and their concerns about teaching and education in the UAE in relation to both their own work and the educational well-being of students. The latter points would position the government school teachers as knowledgeable and concerned professionals who have a vision of how education might be improved. This, in turn, might serve to complicate the student teachers' dominant and somewhat one-dimensional view of the government school teachers as guardians of 'traditional' teaching and obstacles to change. The earlier points might help the student teachers gain insights into the struggles faced by expatriate teachers, on tenuous one-year renewable contracts, paid half the salary of UAE national teachers and with limited options in their 'home' country. This might assist in helping the student teachers' community acknowledge what Mouffe (2000: 105 cited above) refers to as the 'the real nature of its frontiers and the forms of exclusion they entail' in order to move beyond 'the veil of rationality or morality' that constructs the 'problems' of UAE education in purely pedagogical, rather than political, terms.

Simple though it sounds, the very act of questioning the government school teachers in this way might cultivate the spirit of inquiry to complement that of advocacy noted above as it 'signals a willingness to learn something new and affirms the professional capacity of the respondent' (Mitchell & Sackney, 2000: 81). Through fostering a critical engagement with the cultural and political, as well as pedagogical, narratives that construct the government school teachers' world view, such strategies might thus allow for a re-imagination of both the student teachers and the school teachers. In this way such strategies might assist future student teachers in moving beyond the oppositional framework we have seen emerging and to recognize the contingent and fragile nature of all position(ing)s, since they are inevitably constructed within wider social, cultural and political frameworks. Such a strategy could form one part of a broader approach of seeking to establish a common learning community among student teachers, school teachers and college teachers. In order to truly value and support connection rather than separation, such a broad strategy would need to pay attention to the sociocultural conditions of learning on the part of all parties, to structural arrangements for that learning, as well as to the cultivation, development and maintenance of collaborative processes. The development of such a set of strategies could form the basis for further research in this context.

Another element of agonism that offers the potential to move beyond the oppositional impasse is the promotion of an understanding of *hybridity* – of the multiple elements comprising our identities – to enable student teachers to focus upon what they have in common with the school teachers as women, as professionals, as Arabic speakers, rather than only seeing differences. In this way students are encouraged to see that the 'cut' on reality offered through the dominant discourse that constructs them in oppositional terms is only one of many possibilities for identity construction. This entails the *de*construction of the framework the students have constructed around the binary opposition between 'good and 'bad', 'modern' and 'traditional' teaching. There is an ethical component to this call for deconstruction and recognition of hybridity, since by resisting closure it resists the construction of the 'other' as merely the constitutive outside or as the negative side of a binary opposition. As Torfing (1999:

280) notes, 'Deconstruction thus acts ethically against any attempt to instigate a metaphysical closure of self-identity by denying the demanding (non-) presence of the wholly Other.' Recognition of hybridity thus entails continual openness towards an 'other' who, like the 'self', is necessarily heterogeneous.

This notion of ethical deconstruction relates to the later Foucault's notion of ethics as self-formation, achieved through the work of conducting an ongoing historical ontology of ourselves that recognizes the ever-present possibility of being and thinking otherwise (1997a, 1997b). Again, strategies such as the profiling sketched above, along with others directed towards the creation of a learning community embracing student teachers, college teachers and school teachers, might assist the student teachers in resisting the temptation to reduce the government school teachers to the 'other' of 'bad', 'traditional' or 'teacher-centred' teachers but rather to see them in the context of wider social, cultural, economic and political structures and pressures that position them – and all teachers – in particular ways. Such discursive identity work might enable student teachers and teacher educators to recognize the tensions, contradictions, silences and interstices within and between discourses, to acknowledge the consequent contingency and constructedness of their personal and professional identities, and hence to be alert to spaces and possibilities for self-development and self-transformation.

Together these elements of an agonistic politics could potentially encourage students to view existing UAE government school teachers in terms of what unites rather than what divides them and to look from a position of shared empathy for common sources of inspiration for action and collaboration. Implementing, monitoring and evaluating the success of strategies to promote this agonistic approach would be a valuable topic for further research.

Conclusion

This brings us to the end of our exploration of the development of the first cohort of student teachers in a new Bachelor of Education degree to prepare English language teachers for schools in the UAE. But the significance of our journey extends beyond the UAE and beyond language teacher education. In relation to recent theorizations of teacher education as a process of identity formation, the book has offered a way of thinking about teacher formation as a dynamic process of identity development alongside the development of a community of practice. It has also drawn on the insights of discourse theory to recognize the inescapably political nature of meaning and account for the influence of social structures in the development of identity and community, while also suggesting some potential strategies for addressing the antagonistic relations of meaning to which the logic of equivalence may give rise. In addition, this book has afforded insights into the ongoing processes of educational, social and cultural development in a country that is part of an under-researched region of the world, but one that is often subject to stereotyping and caricature, and has suggested some possible directions for future research to provide greater understanding of teacher education in the UAE that may have resonance elsewhere. Such research may offer further insights into the shaping of language teacher identities through the co-construction of discourse and community.

Note
1   Parts of this chapter appeared previously in Clarke, M. (2006) Beyond antagonism? The discursive construction of 'new' teachers in the United Arab Emirates. *Teaching Education* 17 (3), 225–237.

References

Ahsan, M. (2004) Human development in the Muslim world: From theory to practice. *The Muslim World* 94(2), 181–200.
Al Nowais, S. (2004) Education system to get overhaul. *Gulf News* – Online document: http://www.gulfnews.com/News/2004/1125/default.asp
Alsup, J. (2006) *Teacher Identity Discourses: Negotiating Personal and Professional Spaces.* Mahwah, NJ: Lawrence Erlbaum Associates.
Andersen, N.A. (2003) *Discursive Analytical Strategies: Understanding Foucault, Koselleck, Laclau, Luhmann.* Bristol: The Policy Press.
Anderson, B. (1983) *Imagined Communities: Reflections on the Origin and Spread of Nationalism.* London: Verso Books.
Archer, M. (2000) *Being Human: The Problem of Agency.* Cambridge: Cambridge University Press.
Archer, M. (2003) *Structure, Agency and the Internal Conversation.* Cambridge: Cambridge University Press.
Arends, R. and Winitzky, N. (1996) Program structures and learning to teach. In F. B. Murray (ed.) *The Teacher Educator's Handbook* (pp. 526–556). San Francisco, CA: Jossey-Bass.
Barab, S. and Duffy, T. (2000) From practice fields to communities of practice. In D. Jonassen and S. Land (eds) *Theoretical Foundations of Learning Environments* (pp. 22–55). Mahwah, NJ: Lawrence Erlbaum Associates.
Barker, C. and Galasinski, D. (2001) *Cultural Studies and Discourse Analysis: A Dialogue on Language and Identity.* London: Sage Publishing.
Barton, D. and Tusting, K. (2005a) Introduction. In D. Barton and K. Tusting (eds) *Beyond Communities of Practice: Language, Power, and Social Context* (pp. 1–13). Cambridge: Cambridge University Press.
Barton, D. and Tusting, K. (eds) (2005b) *Beyond Communities of Practice: Language, Power, and Social Context.* Cambridge: Cambridge University Press.
Beattie, M. (1997) Fostering reflective practice in teacher education: Inquiry as a framework for the construction of a professional knowledge. *Asia-Pacific Journal of Teacher Education* 25(2), 111–128.
Benwell, B. and Stokoe, E. (2006) *Discourse and Identity.* Edinburgh: Edinburgh University Press.
Black, P. (1998) *Testing: Friend or Foe? The Theory and Practice of Assessment and Testing.* London: Falmer Press.
Block, D. (2002) 'McCommunication': A problem in the frame for SLA. In D. Block and D. Cameron (eds) *Globalization and Language Teaching* (pp. 117–133). London: Routledge.
Blommaert, J. (2005) *Discourse.* Cambridge: Cambridge University Press.
Bloomfield, D. (2000) Voices on the web: Student teachers negotiating identity. *Asia-Pacific Journal of Teacher Education* 28(3), 199–213.
Bonk, C. and King, K. (1998) *Electronic Collaborators: Learner Centered Technologies for Literacy, Apprenticeship, and Discourse.* Mahwah, NJ: Lawrence Erlbaum Associates.

References

Borg, S. (2003) Teacher cognition in language teaching: A review of research on what language teachers think, know, believe and do. *Language Teaching* 36(2), 81–109.

Boud, D. and Middleton, H. (2003) Learning from others at work: Communities of practice and informal learning. *Journal of Workplace Learning* 15(5), 194–203.

Bove, P. (1995) Discourse. In F. Lentricchia and T. McLaughlin (eds) *Critical terms for literary study* (pp. 50–65). Chicago: The University of Chicago Press.

Braine, G. (ed.) (1999) *Non-native Educators in English Language Teaching*. Mahwah, NJ: Lawrence Erlbaum Associates.

Britzman, D. (1991) *Practice Makes Practice: A Critical Study of Learning to Teach*. Albany, NY: State University of New York Press.

Britzman, D. (1992) The terrible problem of knowing thyself: Towards a poststructural account of teacher identity. *Journal of Curriculum Theorizing* 9(3), 23–46.

Britzman, D. (1994) Is there a problem with knowing thyself? Towards a poststructuralist view of teacher identity. In T. Shanahan (ed.) *Teachers Thinking, Teachers Knowing: Reflections on Literacy and Language Education* (pp. 53–75). Urbana, IL: National Council of Teachers of English Press.

Britzman, D. (1998) *Lost Subjects, Contested Objects: Towards a Psychoanalytic Inquiry of Learning*. Albany, NY: State University of New York Press.

Brown, T. and McNamara, O. (2005) *New Teacher Identity and Regulative Government: The Discursive Formation of Primary Mathematics*. New York: Springer.

Bruner, J. (1996) *The Culture of Education*. Cambridge, MA: Harvard University Press.

Buchman, M. and Floden, R. (1993) *Detachment and Concern: Conversations in the Philosophy of Teaching and Teacher Education*. New York: Cassel.

Burns, A. (1999) *Collaborative Action Research for English Language Teachers*. Cambridge: Cambridge University Press.

Burr, V. (1995) *An introduction to Social Constructionism*. London: Routledge.

Butler, J. (1997) *Excitable Speech: A Politics of the Performative*. New York: Routledge.

Butler, J. (2005) *Giving an Account of Oneself*. New York: Fordham University Press.

Buysse, V., Sparkman, K. and Wesley, P. (2003) Communities of practice: Connecting what we know with what we do. *Exceptional Children* 69(3), 263–278.

Calderhead, J. and Shorrock, S. (1997) *Understanding Teacher Education: Case Studies in the Professional Development of Beginning Teachers*. London: Falmer Press.

Canagarajah, A. S. (1999) *Resisting Linguistic Imperialism in English Language Teaching*. New York: Routledge.

Carter, D. (1999) Extending 'supervisory reach': Using new information management technology in the teacher education practicum. *Journal of Information Technology for Teacher Education* 8(3), 321–333.

Chong, S.-M. (1998) Models of asynchronous computer conferencing for collaborative learning in large college classes. In K. Bonk and K. King (eds) *Electronic Collaborators: Learner Centered Technologies for Literacy, Apprenticeship, and Discourse* (pp. 157–182). Mahwah, NJ: Lawrence Erlbaum Associates.

Chouliaraki, L. and Fairclough, N. (1999) *Discourse in Late Modernity: Rethinking Critical Discourse Analysis*. Edinburgh: Edinburgh University Press.

Clark, K. and Holquist, M. (1984) *Mikhail Bakhtin*. Cambridge, MA: Bellknap Harvard.

Clarke, M., Hamston, J. and Love, K. (2007) New teachers on the job: Investigating trajectories of HCT B.Ed. graduates. In L. Stephenson and P. Davidson (eds) *Teacher Education and Continuing Professional Development: Insights from the Arabian Gulf* (pp. 95–106). Dubai: TESOL Arabia.

Cochran-Smith, M. (2000) The future of teacher education: Framing the questions that matter. *Teaching Education* 11(1), 13–24.

Coldron, J. and Smith, R. (1995) *Teaching as an amalgam of discourses and the consequent need for appropriate modes of reflection*. Paper presented at the Annual Meeting of the American Educational Research Association, San Francisco, CA, April 18–22.

Connelly, F. M. and Clandinin, D. J. (1989) *Teachers as Curriculum Planners: Narratives of Experience*. New York: Teachers College Press.

Connolly, W. (2002) *Identity/Difference: Democratic Negotiations of Political Paradox* (expanded edn.). Minneapolis: University of Minnesota Press.

Corson, D. (2001) *Language, Diversity and Education*. Mahwah, NJ: Lawrence Erlbaum Associates.

Crandall, J. (2000) Language teacher education. *Annual Review of Applied Linguistics* 20, 34–55.

Creese, A. (2005) Mediating allegations of racism in a multiethnic London school: What speech communities and communities of practice can tell us about discourse and power. In D. Barton and M. Hamilton (eds) *Beyond Communities of Practice: Language, Power, and Social Context* (pp. 55–76). Cambridge: Cambridge University Press.

Cummins, J., Bismilla, V., Chow, P., Giampapa, F., Cohen, S., Leoni, L. and Sastri, P. (2005) Affirming identity in multilingual classrooms. *Educational Leadership* 63(1), 38–43.

Damasio, A. (1994) *Descartes' Error: Emotion, Reason and the Human Brain*. New York: Putnam Publishing.

Danielewicz, J. (2001) *Teaching Selves: Identity, Pedagogy and Teacher Education*. Albany, NY: State University of New York Press.

Davidson, C. (2005) *The United Arab Emirates: A Study in Survival*. Boulder, CO: Lynne Rennier Publishers.

Day, C. (1999) *Developing Teachers: The Challenges of Lifelong Learning*. London: Falmer Press.

Day, C., Kington, A., Stobart, G. and Sammons, P. (2006) The personal and professional selves of Teachers: stable and unstable identities. *British Educational Research Journal* 32(4), 601–616.

De Fina, A., Schiffrin, D. and Bamber, M. (eds) (2006) *Discourse and Identity*. Cambridge: Cambridge University Press.

Dewey, J. (1933) *How We Think: A Restatement of the Relation of Reflective Thinking to the Educative Process*. Chicago, IL: Henry Regnery.

Dewey, J. (1963 [1916]) *Democracy and Education*. New York: Macmillan.

Dewey, J. (1997 [1938]) *Experience and Education*. New York: Collier Books.

Dimitriadis, G. and Kamberelis, G. (2006) *Theory for Education*. New York: Routledge.

du Gay, P., Evans, J. and Redman, P. (eds) (2000) *Identity: A Reader*. London: Sage Publications.

Eagleton, T. (1991) *Ideology: An Introduction*. London: Verso.
Eagleton, T. (2000) *The Idea of Culture*. Oxford: Blackwell.
Edwards, D. and Potter, J. (1992) *Discursive Psychology*. London: Sage.
Eggington, W. and Kelly Hall, J. (eds) (2000) *The Sociopolitics of English Language Teaching*. Clevedon: Multilingual Matters.
Eilam, B. (2002) 'Passing through' a Western Democratic Teacher Education: The Case of Israeli Arab Teachers. *Teachers' College Record* 104(8), 1658–1701.
Eilam, B. (2003) Jewish and Arab Teacher Trainees' Orientations toward Teaching-Learning Processes. *Teaching Education* 14(2), 169–186.
Eraut, M. (1994) The acquisition and use of theory by beginning teachers. In G. Harvard and P. Hodgkinson (eds) *Action and Reflection in Teacher Education* (pp. 69–88). Norwood, NJ: Ablex Publishing.
Evans, K. (2002) *Negotiating the Self: Identity, Sexuality, and Emotions in Learning to Teach*. New York: Routledge.
Fairclough, N. (1992) *Discourse and Social Change*. Cambridge: Polity Press.
Fairclough, N. (1993) Critical discourse analysis and the marketization of public discourse: The universities. *Discourse and Society* 4(2), 133–168.
Fairclough, N. (2003) *Analyzing Discourse: Textual Analysis for Social Research*. London: Routledge.
Fetterman, D. (2002) Empowerment evaluation: Building communities of practice and a culture of learning. *American Journal of Community Psychology* 30(1), 89–103.
Fettes, M. (2005) Imaginative transformation in teacher education. *Teaching Education* 16(1), 3–12.
Findlow, S. (2000) *The United Arab Emirates: Nationalism and Arab-Islamic Identity*. Abu Dhabi: Emirates Center for Strategic Studies and Research.
Findlow, S. (2005) International networking in the United Arab Emirates higher education system: Global–local tensions. *Compare* 35(3), 285–302.
Findlow, S. (2006) Higher education and linguistic dualism in the Arab Gulf. *British Journal of Sociology of Education* 27(1), 19–36.
Forman, E. and McCormick, D. (1995) Discourse analysis: A sociocultural perspective. *Remedial and Special Education* 16(3), 150–158.
Foucault, M. (1972) *The Archaeology of Knowledge and the Discourse on Language* (A. M. S. Smith, trans.). London: Tavistock.
Foucault, M. (1978) *The History of Sexuality. Vol 1: An Introduction* (R. Hurley, Trans.). New York: Pantheon Books.
Foucault, M. (1980) Truth and power. In C. Gordon (ed.) *Power/Knowledge: Selected Interviews and Other Writings 1972–1977* (pp. 109–133). New York: Pantheon.
Foucault, M. (1997a) The ethics of the concern for self as a practice of freedom. In P. Rabinow (ed.) *Ethics, Subjectivity and Truth: The Essential Foucault 1954–1984* (Vol. 1). New York: The New Press.
Foucault, M. (1997b) What is enlightenment? In P. Rabinow (ed.) *Ethics, Subjectivity and Truth: The Essential Foucault 1954–1984* (Vol. 1). New York: The New Press.
Freebody, P. (2003) *Qualitative Research in Education: Interaction and Practice*. Thousand Oaks, CA: Sage.
Freeman, D. (1996) 'To take them at their word': Language data in the study of teachers' knowledge. *Harvard Educational Review* 66(4), 732–761.

Freeman, D. E. and Freeman, Y. S. (2001) *Between Worlds: Access to Second Language Acquisition*. Portsmouth, NH: Heinemann and Heinemann.
Fullan, M. (2001) *The New Meaning of Educational Change* (3rd edn). Columbia University, NY: Teachers' College Press.
Furlong, J. and Maynard, T. (1995) *Mentoring Student Teachers: The Development of Professional Knowledge*. London: Routledge.
Furlong, J., Barton, L., Miles, S., Whiting, C. and Whitty, G. (2000) *Teacher Education in Transition: Re-forming Professionalism?* Buckingham: Open University Press.
Gaad, E., Arif, M. and Scott, F. (2006) Systems analysis of the UAE education system. *International Journal of Educational Management* 20(4), 291–303.
Gandhi, L. (1998) *Postcolonial Theory: A Critical Introduction*. Sydney: Allen and Unwin.
Gardner, H. (1983) *Frames of Mind: The Theory of Multiple Intelligences*. New York: Basic Books.
Gardner, W. (1995) Developing a quality teaching force for the United Arab Emirates: Mission improbable. *Journal of Education for Teaching* 21(3), 289–301.
Gee, J. P. (1996) *Social Linguistics and Literacies: Ideology in Discourses* (2nd edn). London: Taylor and Francis.
Gee, J. P. (2000) Identity as an analytic lens for research in education. *Review of Research in Education*, 25, 99–125.
Gee, J. P. (2004) Learning languages as a matter of learning social languages within discourses. In M. Hawkins (ed.) *Language Learning and Teacher Education: A Sociocultural Approach* (pp. 13–31). Clevedon: Multilingual Matters.
Gee, J. P. (2005) Semiotic social spaces and affinity spaces: From the age of mythology to today's schools. In D. Barton and K. Tusting (eds) *Beyond Communities of Practice: Language, Power, and Social Context* (pp. 214–232). Cambridge: Cambridge University Press.
Gee, J. P., Hull, G. and Lankshear, C. (1996) *The New Work Order*. St Leonards, NSW: Allen and Unwin.
Geer, R. and Au, W. (1998) Electronic mail and student learning: Where is IT&T at? ACEC 98 Refereed Conference Proceedings. CEGSA, Adelaide.
Goodson, I. and Sikes, P. (2001) *Life History Research in Educational Settings*. Buckingham: Open University Press.
Graham, W., Osgood, D. and Karren, J. (1998) A real-life community of practice. *Training and Development* 52(5), 34–39.
Gray, J. (1997) *False Dawn: The Delusions of Global Capitalism*. London: Granta.
Hall, S. and du Gay, P. (eds) (1997) *Questions of Cultural Identity*. London: Sage.
Halliday, F. (2003) *Islam and the Myth of Confrontation: Religion and Politics in the Middle East*. London: I.B. Taurus Publishing.
Harold, B., McNally, P. and McAskill, T. (2002) 'Everything will be different for us' Emirati student teachers as 'agents of change' in classrooms. Paper presented at the New Zealand Association for Research in Education Annual Conference, Palmerston North, December 5–8.
Harris, S. R. and Shelswell, N. (2005) Moving beyond communities of practice in adult basic education. In D. Barton and K. Tusting (eds) *Beyond Communities of Practice: Language, Power, and Social Context* (pp. 158–179). Cambridge: Cambridge University Press.

Hinchman, K. and Oyler, C. (2000) Us and them: Finding irony in our teaching methods. *Journal of Curriculum Studies* 32(4), 495–508.
Hobsbawm, E. and Ranger, T. (eds) (1992) *The Invention of Tradition*. Cambridge: Cambridge University Press.
Holland, D., Skinner, D., Lachicotte, W. and Cain, C. (1998) *Identity and Agency in Cultural Worlds*. Cambridge MA: Harvard University Press.
Holliday, A. (1997) Evaluating the discourse: The role of applied linguistics in the management of evaluation and innovation. In P. Rea-Dickins and K. P. Germaine (eds) *Managing Evaluation and Innovation in Language Teaching* (pp. 195–219). Harlow: Longman.
Holliday, A. (2002) *Doing and Writing Qualitative Research*. London: Sage Publications.
Holquist, M. (1990) *Dialogism: Bakhtin and His World*. New York: Routledge.
Hooks, B. (1994) *Teaching to Transgress: Education as the Practice of Freedom*. New York: Routledge.
Howarth, D. (2000) *Discourse*. Buckingham: Open University Press.
Hung, D. and Nichani, M. R. (2002) Bringing communities of practice into schools: Implications for instructional technologies from Vygotskian perspectives. *International Journal of Instructional Media*, 29(2), 171–184.
Janks, H. (1997) Critical discourse analysis as a research tool. *Discourse* 18(3), 329–341.
Jenkins, R. (1996) *Social Identity*. London: Routledge.
Johnson, K. E. (1999) *Understanding Language Teaching: Reasoning in Action*. Toronto: Heinle and Heinle.
John-Steiner, V. (1997) *Notebooks of the Mind: Explorations of Thinking*. New York: Oxford University Press.
Jonassen, D. (1996) *Computers in the Classroom: Mindtools for Critical Thinking*. Columbus, OH: Merrill/Prentice-Hall.
Kamberelis, G. and Dimitriadis, G. (2005) *On Qualitative Inquiry: Approaches to Language and Literacy Research*. New York: Teachers College Press.
Karmani, S. (2005a) English, 'terror', and Islam. *Applied Linguistics* 26(2), 262–267.
Karmani, S. (2005b) Petro-linguistics: The emerging nexus between oil, English, and Islam. *Journal of Language, Identity and Education* 4(2), 87–102.
Kazim, A. (2000) *The United Arab Emirates A.D. 600 to the Present: A Sociodiscursive Transformation in the Arabian Gulf*. Dubai: Gulf Book Center.
Kemmis, S. and McTaggart, R. (1988) *The Action Research Planner* (3rd edn). Geelong: Deakin University Press.
Kemmis, S. and McTaggart, R. (2000) Participatory action research. In N. K. Denzin and Y. S. Lincoln (eds) *The Handbook of Qualitative Research*. Thousand Oaks, CA: Sage.
Khalaf, S. (2000) Poetics and politics of newly invented traditions in the Gulf: Camel racing in the United Arab Emirates. *Ethnology* 39(3), 243–262.
Kornerup, I. (2001) Constructions of pre-school teacher identity. Paper presented at the Roskilde University and the Danish Research Agency Third Summer School in Lifelong Learning.
Koro-Ljunberg, M. (2004) Displacing metaphorical analysis: Reading with and against metaphors. *Qualitative Research* 4(3), 339–360.
Korthagen, F. (2001) *Linking theory and Practice: The Pedagogy of Realistic Teacher Education*. Mahwah, NJ: Lawrence Earlbaum Associates.

Kramsch, C. and Lam, W. S. E. (1999) Textual identities: The importance of being non-native. In G. Braine (ed.) *Non-native Educators in English Language Teaching* (pp. 57–75). Mahwah, NJ: Lawrence Earlbaum Associates.

Krieger, S. (1991) *Social Science and the Self: Personal Essays on an Art Form*. New Brunswick, NJ: Rutgers University Press.

Kumaravadivelu, B. (1999) Theorising practice: Practising theory: The role of critical classroom observation. In H. Trappes-Lomax and I. McGrath (eds) *Theory in Language Teacher Education* (pp. 33–45). Harlow: Longman.

Kureishi, H. (2003) *The Body*. London: Faber and Faber.

Kuzmic, J. (2002) Research as a way of knowing and seeing: Advocacy for the other. In J. Loughran and T. Russell (eds) *Improving Teacher Education Practices Through Self-Study* (pp. 222–235). London: Routledge-Falmer.

Kvale, S. (1996) *Interviews: An Introduction to Qualitative Research Interviewing*. Thousand Oaks, CA: Sage Publishing.

Laclau, E. and Mouffe, C. (1985) *Hegemony and Socialist Strategy: Towards a Radical Democratic Politics*. London: Verso.

Laclau, E. and Mouffe, C. (2001) Preface to the second edition. In *Hegemony and Socialist Strategy* (2nd edn). London: Verso.

Lakoff, G. and Johnson, M. (1984) *Metaphors We Live By*. Chicago, IL: University of Chicago Press.

Lankshear, C. and Knobel, M. (2006) *New Literacies: Everyday Practices and Classroom Learning* (2nd Edn). Maidenhead: Open University Press and McGraw-Hill

Lantolf, J. (1999) Second culture acquisition: Cognitive considerations. In E. Hinkel (ed.) *Culture in Second Language Teaching and Learning* (pp. 28–46). Cambridge: Cambridge University Press.

Lather, P. (1993) Fertile obsession: Validity after poststructuralism. *Sociological Quarterly* 34, 673–693.

Lave, J. and Wenger, E. (1991) *Situated Learning, Legitimate Peripheral Participation*. Cambridge: Cambridge University Press.

Le Cornu, R. and White, B. (2000) Email supervision in the practicum. Paper presented at the The British Educational Research Annual Conference, Cardiff, September 7–10.

Lee, J. and Valdarrama, K. (2003) Building successful communities of practice. *Information Outlook* 7(5), 28–32.

Lefrere, P. (2007) Competing higher education futures in a globalising world. *European Journal of Education* 42(2), 201–212.

Lemke, J. (1995) *Textual Politics*. London: Taylor Francis.

Lim, C. (1991) 'English for technology—Yes! English for culture—No!' A writer's views on a continuing Southeast Asian dilemma. Paper presented at the International Conference on Language Education: Interaction and Development, Ho Chi Mihn City, Vietnam.

Lortie, D. (1975) *Schoolteacher: A Sociological Study*. Chicago, IL: University of Chicago Press.

Loughran, J. and Russell, T. (eds) (1997) *Teaching about Teaching: Purpose, Passion and Pedagogy in Teacher Education*. London: Routledge-Falmer.

Loughran, J. and Russell, T. (eds) (2002) *Improving Teacher Education Practices Through Self-Study*. London: Routledge-Falmer.

Loughrey, B., Hughes, A., Bax, S., Magness, C. and Aziz, H. (1999) *English Language Teaching in the UAE: Evaluation Report*. Roehampton: University of Surrey.

Luke, A. (1996) Text and discourse in education: An introduction to critical discourse analysis. In M. W. Apple (ed.) *Review of Research in Education* (Vol. 21) (pp. 3–48). Washington, DC: American Research Association.
Luke, A. and Luke, C. (2001) A situated perspective on cultural globalisation. In N. Burbules and C. Torres (eds) *Globalization and Education: Critical Perspectives* (pp. 275–298). London: Routledge.
MacLure, M. (1993) Arguing for your self: Identity as an organising principle in teachers' jobs and lives. *British Educational Research Journal* 19(4), 311–322.
MacLure, M. (2003) *Discourse in Educational and Social Research*. Buckingham: Open University.
Mahmood, S. (2005) *Politics of Piety: The Islamic Revival and the Feminist Subject*. Princeton, NJ: Princeton University Press.
Mansfield, N. (2000) *Subjectivity: Theories of the Self from Freud to Haraway*. St Leonards, NSW: Allen and Unwin.
Marginson, S. (1997) *Markets in Education*. St Leonards, NSW: Allen and Unwin.
Maxwell, E. (2004) Online mentoring in English for young learners (EYL) teacher education. Unpublished Master's thesis, University of Melbourne.
Mayer, D. (1999) Building teaching identities: Implications for preservice teacher education. Paper presented at the Australian Association for Research in Education and New Zealand Association for Research in Education Conference – Online document: http://www.aare.edu.au/99pap/may99385.htm.
McConaghy, C. (2000) *Rethinking Indigenous Education: Culture, Colonialism and the Politics of Knowing*. Flaxton, Queensland: Post Pressed.
Mello, R. (2002) Collocation analysis: A method for conceptualizing and understanding narrative data. *Qualitative Research* 2(2), 231–243.
Mercer, N. (2000) *Words and Minds: How We Use Language to Think Together*. London: Routledge.
Miller Marsh, M. (2003) *The Social Fashioning of Teacher Identities*. New York: Peter Lang Publishing.
Mills, S. (2004) *Discourse* (2nd edn). London: Routledge.
Mitchell, C. and Sackney, L. (2000) *Profound Improvement: Building Capacity for a Learning Community*. Lisse, The Netherlands: Swets and Zeitlinger.
Mitchell, C. and Weber, S. (1999) *Reinventing Ourselves as Teachers: Beyond Nostalgia*. London: Falmer Press.
Mograby, A. (1999) Human development in the United Arab Emirates. In *Education and the Arab World* (pp. 279–308). Abu Dhabi: Emirates Center for Strategic Studies and Research.
Mohd-Asraf, R. (2005) English and Islam: A clash of civilizations? *Journal of Language Identity and Education* 4(2), 103–118.
Moreno, A. (2001) Enhancing knowledge exchange through communities of practice at the inter-American development bank. *Aslib Proceedings: New Information Perspectives* 53(8), 296–308.
Morgan, D. (1997) *Focus Groups as Qualitative Research* (2nd edn). Thousand Oaks, CA: Sage.
Mouffe, C. (2000) *The Democratic Paradox*. London: Verso Books.
Mouffe, C. (2005) *On the Political*. Abingdon: Routledge.
Muysken, J. and Nour, S. (2006) Deficiencies in education and poor prospects for economic growth in the Gulf countries: The case of the UAE. *The Journal of Development Studies* 42(6), 957–980.

Norton, B. (2000) *Identity and Language Learning: Gender, Ethnicity and Educational Change*. Singapore: Pearson Education.

Ormrod, J. (1995) *Educational Psychology: Principles and Applications*. Englewood Cliffs, NJ: Prentice-Hall.

Pavlenko, A. and Blackledge, A. (2004a) Introduction: New theoretical approaches to the study of negotiation of identities in multilingual contexts. In A. Pavlenko and A. Blackledge (eds) *Negotiation of Identities in Multilingual Contexts* (pp. 1–33). Clevedon, Avon: Multilingual Matters.

Pavlenko, A. and Blackledge, A. (eds) (2004b) *Negotiation of Identities in Multilingual Contexts*. Clevedon: Multilingual Matters.

Pennycook, A. (1989) Incommensurable discourses? *Applied Linguistics* 15(2), 115–138.

Pennycook, A. (1994) *The Cultural Politics of English as an International Language*. Harlow: Longman.

Pennycook, A. (1998) *English and the Discourses of Colonialism*. London: Routledge.

Pennycook, A. (2000) The social politics and cultural politics of language classrooms. In J. Kelly Hall and W. Eggington (eds) *The Sociopolitics of English Language Teaching* (pp. 89–103). Clevedon: Multilingual Matters.

Phillips, D. K. (2002) Female preservice teachers' talk: Illustrations of subjectivity, visions of 'nomadic' space. *Teachers and Teaching: Theory and Practice* 8(1), 9–27.

Phillips, L. and Jorgensen, M. (2002) *Discourse Analysis as Theory and Method*. Thousand Oaks, CA: Sage.

Phillipson, R. (1992) *Linguistic Imperialism*. Oxford: Oxford University Press.

Pirandello, L. (1964 [1904]) *The Late Mattia Pascal* (W. Weaver, trans.). New York: Doubleday.

Porter, M. (2003) Fostering L.I.N.C.S. among educators: The role of international service-learning in fostering a community of practice. *Teacher Education Quarterly* 30(4), 51–62.

Potter, J. (1996) *Representing Reality: Discourse, Rhetoric and Social Construction*. London: Sage.

Poynton, C. and Lee, A. (2000) Culture and text: An introduction. In A. Lee and C. Poynton (eds) *Culture and Text; Discourse and Methodology in Social Research and Cultural Studies* (pp. 1–18). St Leonards, NSW: Allen and Unwin.

Pryke, M., Rose, G. and Whatmore, S. (eds) (2003) *Using Social Theory: Thinking Through Research*. London: Sage Publishing.

Ramanthan, V. (2005) Ambiguities about English: Ideologies and critical practice in vernacular-medium college classrooms in Gujarat, India. *Journal of Language, Identity and Education* 4(1), 45–65.

Reid, J. A. and Santoro, N. (2006) Cinders in snow? Indigenous teacher identities in formation. *Asia-Pacific Journal of Teacher Education* 34(2), 143–160.

Richards, J. and Lockhart, C. (1996) *Reflective Teaching in Second Language Classrooms*. Cambridge: Cambridge University Press.

Richards, K. (1999) Theory in practice: Design and argument. In H. Trappes-Lomax and I. McGrath (eds) *Theory in Language Teacher Education* (pp. 21–32). Harlow: Longman.

Richards, K. (2003) *Qualitative Inquiry in TESOL*. New York: Palgrave.

Richardson, P. (2004) Possible influences of Arabic-Islamic culture on the reflective practices proposed for an education degree at the Higher Colleges of

Technology in the United Arab Emirates. *International Journal of Educational Development* 24, 429–436.

Ritzer, G. (1995) *The McDonalidization of Society: An Investigation into the Changing Character of Contemporary Social Life*. London: Sage.

Roberts, J. (1998) *Language Teacher Education*. London: Arnold.

Robertson, R. (1995) Glocalization: Time-space and homogeneity-heterogeneity. In M. Featherstone, S. Lash and R. Robertson (eds) *Global Modernities* (pp. 25–44). London: Sage Publications.

Rogers, D. and Babinski, L. (2002) *From Isolation to Conversation: Supporting New Teachers' Development*. New York: State University of New York Press.

Rorty, R. (1989) *Contingency, Irony, and Solidarity*. Cambridge: Cambridge University Press.

Rose, N. (1996) *Inventing Ourselves: Psychology, Power, and Personhood*. Cambridge: Cambridge University Press.

Rover, D. (2003) A sense of community: Learning about versus learning to be/ What is a community of practice? *Journal of Engineering Education* 92(1), 3–5.

Sachs, J. (1999) *Teacher professional identity: Competing discourses, competing outcomes*. Paper presented at the Australian Association for Research in Education – Online document: http://www.aare.edu.au/99pap/sac99611.htm.

Safi, O. (2003) *Progressive Muslims*. Oxford: One World Press.

Salama, S. (2004) Restructuring of cabinet sees first woman minister. *Gulf News*, 03/11/2004 – Online document: http://www.gulfnews.com/News/2004/1103/default.asp.

Salloum, H. (2003) Women in the United Arab Emirates [Electronic Version]. *Contemporary Review*, 8/1/2003 – Online document: http://www.highbeam.com/library/.

Samaras, A. (2003) *Self-study for Teacher Educators: Crafting a Pedagogy for Educational Change*. New York: Peter Lang Publishers.

Santoro, N. (1997) The construction of teacher identity: An analysis of school practicum discourse. *Asia-Pacific Journal of Teacher Education* 25(1), 91–99.

Schlagel, B., Trathen, W. and Blanton, W. (1996) Structuring telecommunications to create instructional conversations about student teaching. *Journal of Teacher Education* 47(3), 175–183.

Schön, D. A. (1983) *The Reflective Practitioner: How Professionals Think in Action*. New York: Basic Books.

Schön, D. A. (1987) *Educating the Reflective Practitioner*. London: Jossey-Bass.

Seel, R. (2000) Culture and complexity: New insights on organizational change. *Culture and Complexity-Organizations and People* 7(2), 2–9.

Seidlhofer, B. (1999) Double standards: Teacher education in the expanding circle. *World Englishes* 18(2), 233–245.

Shi-xu. (2005) *A Cultural Approach to Discourse*. New York: Palgrave Macmillan.

Shi-xu (ed.) (2007) *Discourse as Cultural Struggle*. Hong Kong: University of Hong Kong Press.

Sim, S. (1998) *The Icon Critical Dictionary of Postmodern Thought*. St Leonards, NSW: Icon.

Smith, J. K. and Deemer, D. K. (2000) The problem of criteria in the age of relativism. In N. K. Denzin and Y. S. Lincoln (eds) *The Handbook of Qualitative Research* (2nd edn) (pp. 877–896). Thousand Oaks, CA: Sage.

Søreide, G. E. (2006) Narrative construction of teacher identity: Positioning and negotiation. *Teachers and Teaching: Theory and Practice* 12(5), 527–547.
Taha-Thomure, H. (2003) 'Need to revamp Arab schools' [Electronic Version]. *Gulf News*, 29.10.2003 – Online document: http://www.gulfnews.com/News/2003/2910/default.asp.
Taylor, C. (1989) Interpretation and the sciences of man. In P. Rabinow and M. W. Sullivan (eds) *Interpretive Social Science: A Second Look* (pp. 33–81). Berkeley, CA: University of California Press.
Taylor, S. (2001) Locating and conducting discourse analytic research. In M. Wetherell, S. Taylor and S. J. Yates (eds) *Discourse as Data: A Guide for Analysis* (pp. 5–48). Milton Keynes: Open University Press and Sage.
Thanasoulas, D. (2000) Language and culture: A thesis – Online document: http://www.developingteachers.com/articles_tchtraining/culture2_dimitrios.htm.
Tharp, R., Estrada:, Dalton, S. and Yamauchi, L. (2000) *Teaching Transformed: Achieving Excellence, Fairness, Inclusion and Harmony*. Boulder, CO: Westview Press.
Tharp, R. and Gallimore, R. (1988) *Rousing Minds to Life: Teaching, Learning and Schooling in Social Context*. Cambridge, MA: Cambridge University Press.
Tharp, R. and Gallimore, R. (1990) Teaching mind in society: Teaching, schooling and literate discourse. In L. Moll (ed.) *Vygotsky and Education: Instructional Implications and Applications of Sociohistorical Psychology* (pp. 175–205). Cambridge: Cambridge University Press.
Threadgold, T. (2000) Poststructuralism and discourse analysis. In A. Lee and C. Poynton (eds) *Culture and Text: Discourse and Methodology in Social Research and Cultural Studies* (pp. 40–58). St Leonards, NSW: Allen and Unwin.
Tollefson, J. (ed.) (1995) *Power and Inequality in Language Education*. Cambridge: Cambridge University Press.
Torfing, J. (1999) *New Theories of Discourse: Laclau, Mouffe and Zizek*. Oxford: Blackwell.
Tusting, K. (2005) Language and power in communities of practice. In *Beyond Communities of Practice: Language, Power, and Social Context* (pp. 36–54). Cambridge: Cambridge University Press.
Urry, J. (2003) *Global Complexity*. Cambridge: Polity Press.
Varghese, M., Morgan, B., Johnston, B. and Johnson, K. A. (2005) Theorizing language teacher identity: Three perspectives and beyond. *Journal of Language Identity and Education* 4(1), 21–44.
Volosinov, V. N. (1973 [1929]) *Marxism and the Philosophy of Language* (L. Matejka and I. R. Titunik, trans.). Cambridge, MA: Harvard University Press.
Vygotsky, L. (1978) *Mind in Society: The Development of Higher Psychological Processes*. Cambridge, MA: Harvard University Press.
Walker, R. (2003) Teacher development through communities of learning. In D. McInterney and S. V. Etten (eds) *Sociocultural Influences and Teacher Education Programs* (pp. 223–246). Greenwich, CT: Information Age Publishing.
Weedon, C. (1987) *Feminist Practice and Poststructuralist Theory*. London: Blackwell.
Weedon, C. (2004) *Identity and Culture: Narratives of Difference and Belonging*. Maidenhead Open University Press.
Wells, G. (1999) *Dialogic Inquiry: Towards a Sociocultural Practice and Theory of Education*. Cambridge: Cambridge University Press.

Wenger, E. (1998) *Communities of Practice: Learning, Meaning and Identity*. Cambridge: Cambridge University Press.
Wesley, P. and Buysse, V. (2001) Communities of practice: Expanding professional roles to promote reflection and shared inquiry. *Topics in Early Childhood Special Education* 21(2), 114–124.
Whitcomb, J. (2003) Practice matters: Reflections on the importance of teacher educator's practice. In D. McInterney and S. V. Etten (eds) *Sociocultural Influences and Teacher Education Programs* (pp. 15–33). Greenwich, CT: Information Age Publishing.
Widdowson, H. (1998) The theory and practice of critical discourse analysis. *Applied Linguistics* 19(1), 136–151.
Widdowson, H. (2004) *Text, Context, Pretext: Critical Issues in Discourse Analysis*. Oxford: Blackwell Publishing.
Williams, M. (1999) Learning teaching: A social constructivist approach – theory and practice or theory with practice? In H. Trappes-Lomax and I. McGrath (eds) *Theory in Language Teacher Education* (pp. 11–20). Harlow: Longman.
Williams, R. (1983) *Keywords*. London: Fontana Press.
Willinsky, J. (1998) *Learning to Divide the World: Education at Empire's End*. Minneapolis, MN: University of Minnesota Press.
Woodward, K. (2002) *Understanding Identity*. London: Arnold.
Wortham, S. (2003) *Learning Identity: The Joint Emergence of Social Identification and Academic Learning*. New York: Cambridge University Press.
Zeichner, K. and Liston, D. (1996) *Reflective Teaching: An Introduction*. Mahwah, NJ: Lawrence Erlbaum.
Zembylas, M. (2003a) Emotions and teacher identity: A poststructural perspective. *Teachers and Teaching: Theory and Practice* 9(3), 213–238.
Zembylas, M. (2003b) Interrogating 'teacher identity': Emotion, resistance, and self-formation. *Educational Theory* 53(1), 107–127.
Zhu, E. (1998) Learning and Mentoring: Electronic discussion in a distance learning course. In C. Bonk and K. King (eds) *Electronic Collaborators: Learner Centered Technologies* (pp. 233–259). Mahwah, NJ: Lawrence Erlbaum Associates.
Zizek, S. (1989) *The Sublime Object of Ideology*. London: Verso
Zizek, S. (2003) *The Puppet and the Dwarf: The Perverse Core of Christianity*. London: Verso Books.

Index

agency 20, 21, 26-29, 36, 40, 103, 188
agonism 13, 194-197
antagonism 13, 104, 127, 134, 136, 180, 185, 187, 192-195
Arab-Islamic 13, 21, 46, 50, 63
assisted performance 57-58

Bakhtin, M. 24, 27, 29, 38, 40, 57, 59
beliefs, teacher 8, 53, 58-60, 63, 95, 104-135, 140-146, 149-156, 159-167, 169, 170, 172, 175-181, 183-185, 189-194
binaries, binary oppositions (*see also* dichotomies, dichotomous frameworks) 12, 67-68,106-107, 111, 113, 126-127, 133-134, 191, 197
Britzman, D. 8, 9, 19, 51, 59, 64, 95, 97, 98, 154, 177, 196

cohesion 17, 70-2, 136, 143, 183
communication 1, 13, 24, 71, 90-1, 99-100, 102, 136, 162, 164
– online 56-57, 64
communities of practice 1, 9-14, 15, 20, 29-40, 54, 60, 75-104, 106-107, 110, 116-117, 122, 127, 133-135, 138-144, 146-147, 149-158, 160-163, 165-166, 168, 170-173, 178-181, 182-184, 187, 189, 194, 198
– dimensions of 30-33
    mutual engagement 30-33, 85-88
    joint enterprise 30-33, 88-89
    shared discourse repertoire 30-33, 90-92
– modes of belonging to 9, 30, 35-37, 85-103
    belonging and engagement 85-92
    belonging and alignment 92-98
    belonging and imagination 98-103
– locality 32-35, 92-97
    boundaries and boundary practices 34-35, 94-97
community xi, 9-14, 16, 19, 47, 53, 56, 64, 71-72, 88, 91, 123,136, 138, 160, 174, 177, 179, 181, 187, 193-195, 197-199
Connolly, W. 26, 66, 134, 187, 196
conservative (*see* discourse)

critical discourse analysis (*see also* discourse analysis) 18, 67
culture, cultural 1, 2, 4, 9, 11-13, 15-16, 19-29, 35, 38, 40, 46-47, 49, 50-51, 61, 63-65, 68, 78-79, 86, 93, 127-135, 162, 183, 188, 191, 197-198
culturalism 20-22, 25, 29, 40, 46, 82
curriculum 11, 13, 44, 54-55, 58, 86, 91, 93, 114, 127-128, 134, 151, 171

Danielewicz, J. 8-9, 14, 51, 53, 63, 81-82, 98, 169, 179-180
Davidson, C. 11, 46-47
Dewey, J. 1, 13, 57, 59, 136, 159, 170
dialogic, dialogism 6, 22, 24, 27-28, 37-39, 59-60, 157, 180
dichotomies, dichotomous frameworks (*see also* binaries, binary oppositions) 6, 7, 11-12, 14, 22, 29, 42, 61, 65, 68-69, 112, 133, 152, 173, 192
discourse, discourse theory 9, 14-20, 26, 38-39, 65-72, 185-198
– and community 10, 11, 37-40
– and culture 22-23, 127-131
– and education 9, 10, 61, 89-91, 94
    conservative-'traditional' 11-13, 18-19, 54, 84, 105-27, 134, 136-138, 143-144, 146-148, 150, 153, 163-165, 171, 176, 184-188, 191, 193-194, 196-198
    progressive-'new' 11-13, 18-19, 54, 65, 84, 99, 105-127, 133-135, 139-140, 142, 144, 147, 153, 159, 163, 165, 183-192, 194, 196-198
– and English 83-84, 127-131
– and gender 51 -53, 78-90, 131-133
– and identity 9-11, 23-25, 30, 37-40
– and pedagogy 105-127
– and shared repertoire 30-32, 40, 75, 85, 90-92, 104, 147
– and teaching 11, 41, 97
– and UAE socio-history 41-48
    conservative discourse 13, 45, 76, 78-79, 134, 165, 183
    progressive discourse 45, 49
    moderate discourse 45

Index

discourse analysis 17-18, 32, 40, 62, 66-73, 134
discursive construction 12-13, 19, 37, 72, 77, 97, 105, 107, 127, 133-135, 153, 156, 158, 171, 178, 180, 184-185, 187, 196, 199
discursive practice 18-19, 24-26, 28, 40, 65-66, 186
discursive strategies 85, 106-108, 110, 127, 139, 140, 146, 156, 180, 185
discussion forums
– focus groups 11, 62-64, 68, 72-73, 79
– online forums 11, 56, 59, 60, 62-64, 68, 72, 86, 114, 117, 127, 157, 179

Emiratization 2, 47, 135, 183, 188
empathy 85, 87, 109, 147, 194, 197
engagement (*see* communities of practice)
enterprise (*see* communities of practice)
epistemic affinity (*see also* modality) 159, 161, 167
epistemology 15, 61-62, 72, 73
ethics, ethical 59, 73 n3, 101, 197-198
expatriate teachers 2, 3, 14, 33, 49-50, 194, 196

Fairclough, N. 16, 18-19, 38, 62, 67-70, 72-73, 127, 141-142, 149, 157-158
focus group interviews (*see* discussion forums)
Foucault, M. 16. 18, 32, 40 n2, 42, 92, 101, 105, 198

Gee, J. P. 6, 9, 31-32, 187, 196
gender xi-xii, 18, 45-46, 51-52, 72, 78-80, 103, 131-133, 169, 188
globalization 1-2, 41, 45, 47, 50-51, 56, 72, 131, 183

Halliday, M.A.K. 38, 46, 57, 105, 140, 198
Holland, D., Skinner, D., Lachicotte, W. & Cain, C. 19, 25, 27-29, 78, 18
Holliday, A. 15, 21-22, 51, 61, 135
Howarth, D. 10, 185-187

identity, identities 20-29, 35-40, 72, 75, 79, 81, 84, 88, 98, 101, 134-135
– authored 26-28, 98-103
– figurative 25-26, 77, 85, 94
– positional 23-25, 92, 94
– teacher xi-xiii, 1, 8-14, 56-57, 60-62, 64, 92, 98, 100-101, 157-181, 182-187, 194, 199
– UAE 44-48
ideology 15, 40 n1, 127, 130, 140, 186
imagination (*see* communities of practice)

intertextual, intertextualilty 39, 66, 69, 159
Islam (*see also* Arab-Islamic) 41-44, 46, 52, 63, 79, 183

joint enterprise (*see* communities of practice)

Kazim, A. 11, 42, 45, 47-48, 50, 132

Laclau, E. & Mouffe, C. 10, 14, 17, 26, 40 n2, 65, 67, 70, 185-186, 193-195
Lave, J. & Wenger, E. 7, 29, 158
learning to teach 1-11, 20, 28-31, 33-34, 53-60, 64, 72, 76, 94, 99, 100, 103, 113, 157, 165, 177, 182-183
legitimation 69, 141-146, 156
– authorization 141-142
– moral evaluation 143-144, 158, 163-166, 169-171, 173-174, 178
– mythopoesis 144-146
– rationalization 142-143
literacy 48, 52, 164, 165, 178, 191

metaphor 53, 80, 111, 114, 116, 161, 162, 163, 174, 181 n1, 189-190, 192
Miller Marsh, M. 9-10, 16, 23, 28, 151, 158, 160, 176, 187
modality 70-71, 149, 158-159, 161, 163, 167
Mouffe, C. (*see also* Laclau & Mouffe) 195, 197
multiperspectival (approach to discourse) 17, 40
mutual engagement (*see* communities of practice)

nationalism 16, 37, 44, 45, 50-51, 69, 72, 135, 186
Norton, B. 10, 51, 64, 178-179

online forums (*see* discussion forums)
oppositional
– affiliation 14, 169, 174, 177, 179, 180, 184-5, 194
– framework 82, 95, 114, 117, 127, 197
– identities 11, 174, 194
– stances 169, 171, 194
othering, otherization 61, 133, 155-156

pedagogy 4, 11, 13, 53-55, 134, 182, 188, 191
Phillips, L. & Jorgensen, M. 11, 14-18, 61-62, 73, 182
post-structuralism 4, 17, 22-23, 67, 73 n3
power, power relations 9-10, 15, 18-19, 21, 25, 31, 36-38, 40, 68, 92, 94, 127, 147, 177-178, 182, 186, 196

progressive (*see* discourse)

reflection, reflective practice 7, 21, 27, 39, 51, 56-57, 59, 75, 99, 100-101, 104, 146-147, 153, 159, 162, 164-165

scaffolding 52, 91, 153, 160, 162, 171
school system, UAE 2-3, 12-14, 34, 49-51, 82, 86-87, 101, 111, 114-116, 119, 121, 126-127, 133, 143, 153, 155-156, 163, 166-169, 170-172, 174-176, 179-180, 183, 185, 189, 194-195
shared narrative 91, 144
shared repertoire (*see* communities of practice)
sociocultural, sociocultural theory 7-8, 24, 26, 29, 64, 165, 181 n1, 197
socio-discursive 8, 11, 41, 42-45, 195

teacher education (*see also* learning to teach and beliefs) 1-11, 19, 28, 35, 49, 51, 53-60, 81, 98, 134, 165, 181-182, 188, 192-193, 196, 198-199
teacher formation (*see also* learning to teach and beliefs) 1, 15, 36, 126, 198

teaching practice, teaching practicums 2, 4, 54-56, 60, 63, 96, 110, 116, 119, 125, 140, 146
textual meaning 62, 66-72
Torfing, J. 10, 16-17, 26, 67, 70, 185-186, 191, 194, 196-198
traditional (*see* discourse)
trajectories 37, 39, 98, 100, 102
transformation xi, xiii, 8, 18, 35, 97, 102, 195, 198

UAE nationals 2, 47, 60
UAE education (*see also* discourse) 48-53
UAE schools (*see also* school system, UAE) 48-53
United Arab Emirates 1, 3, 21, 41-53

Volosinov, V. N. 1, 40 n2, 140
Vygotsky, L. S. 25-29, 38-39, 40 n2, 57-58, 141

Web CT (*see* discussion forums)
Wenger, E. 7, 9, 12, 29-33, 35-37, 40 n2, 98, 179-180

Zizek, S. 14, 70, 190-191

For Product Safety Concerns and Information please contact our EU Authorised Representative:

Easy Access System Europe

Mustamäe tee 50

10621 Tallinn

Estonia

gpsr.requests@easproject.com

www.ingramcontent.com/pod-product-compliance
Ingram Content Group UK Ltd.
Pitfield, Milton Keynes, MK11 3LW, UK
UKHW022217250326
4937IPUK00005B/34